Designing Brand Identity

fifth edition

☐ **I am not a robot.**

one eye sees

the other feels

—PAUL KLEE

Who are you?

Who needs to know?

How will they find out?

Why should they care?

Library of Congress Cataloging-in-Publication Data:

Wheeler, Alina, author.
  Designing brand identity: an essential guide for the entire branding team / Alina Wheeler.

  Fifth edition. | Hoboken, New Jersey : John Wiley & Sons, Inc.,
  [2017] | Includes bibliographical references and index.

  LCCN 2017022067 (print) | LCCN 2017030982 (ebook) |
  ISBN 9781119375418 (pdf) | ISBN 9781118980828 (cloth)

  LCSH: Brand name products. | Branding (Marketing) |
  Trademarks—Design. | Advertising—Brand name products.
  Classification: LCC HD69.B7 (ebook) | LCC HD69.B7 W44 2017 (print) |
  DDC 658.8/27—dc23

  LC record available at https://lccn.loc.gov/2017022067

V10010507_052819

Alina Wheeler

Designing Brand Identity

fifth edition

an essential guide for the entire branding team

WILEY

No one does it alone.

Books, like brands, are built over time. This book is not my book. It is our book. It is the result of an extensive collaboration with my colleagues around the world who are branding the future with intelligence, clarity, and boundless creativity. You know who you are. Thank you for sharing your time, your wisdom, and your insights.

My dream team has always risen to the challenge of working on this book. I am eternally grateful for their expertise, their patience, and their sense of humor.

Creating this global resource has been my personal Mount Everest. Love, indeed, does conquer all. My husband Eddy's energy and laughter always make the impossible possible. Tessa and Tearson are our shooting stars. Skylight is my Shangri-La.

This book is dedicated to the memory of Michael Cronan, Wally Olins, Bill Drenttel, and Sylvia Harris.

Perpetual gratitude
All Wheelers
All favorite cousins
Joel Katz
Paula Scher
Richard Cress
Mark Wills
Ange Iannarelli
Heather Norcini
Richard Stanley
Meejoo Kwon
Stephen Shackleford
Tomasz Fryzel
Margie Gorman
Michal Levy
Hilary Jay
Cathy Jooste
Quest sisters
Marie Taylor
Marc Goldberg
Liz Merrill
Chris Grillo
My brother who asked when the film is coming out

Dream Team
Jon Bjornson
cover designer
Lissa Reidel
strategist
Kathy Mueller
senior designer
Robin Goffman
designer + assistant
Gretchen Dykstra
grammarian
Blake Deutsch
avatar

My publishing team at Wiley
Amanda Miller
VP + publisher
Margaret Cummins
executive editor
Justin Mayhew
associate marketing director
Kalli Schultea
editorial assistant
Kerstin Nasdeo
senior production manager

Photo: Ed Wheeler

A. Aiden Morrison
Adam Brodsley
Adam Waugh
Adrian Zecha
Al Ries
Alain Sainson Frank
Alan Becker
Alan Brew
Alan Jacobson
Alan Siegel
Albert Cassorla
Alex Center
Alex Clark
Alexander Haldemann
Alexander Hamilton
Alex Maddalena
Alfredo Muccino
Allie Strauss
Alvin Diec
Alyssa Boente
Amanda Bach
Amanda Duncan
Amanda Liu
Amanda Neville
Amy Grove
Anders Braekken
Andrew Baldus
Andrew Ceccon
Andrew Cutler
Andrew Welsh
Andy Gray
Andy Sernovitz
Angora Chinchilla
Aniko DeLaney
Ann Willoughby
Anna Bentson
Anne Moses
Anthony Romero
Antônio C. D. Sepúlveda
Antonio R. Oliviera
Antony Burgmans
Arnold Miller
Ashis Bhattacharya
Aubrey Balkind
Audrey Liu
Ayse Birsel
Aziz Jindani
Bart Crosby
Bayard Fleitas
Becky O'Mara
Becky Wingate
Beryl Wang
Beth Mallo
Betty Nelson
Blake Howard
Bob Mueller
Bob Warkulwiz
Bobby Shriver
Bonita Albertson
Brad Kear
Brady Vest
Brendan deVallance
Brian Collins
Brian Faherty
Brian Fingeret
Brian Jacobson
Brian Resnik
Brian Tierney
Brian Walker
Bridget Duffy
Bridget Russo

Brie DiGiovine
Bruce Berkowitz
Bruce Duckworth
Bruce Palmer
Bryan Singer
Cale Johnson
Carla Hall
Carla Miller
Carlos Ferrando
Carlos Martinez Onaindia
Carlos Muñoz
Carlos Pagan
Carol Moog
Carol Novello
Caroline Tiger
Cassidy Blackwell
Cassidy Merriam
Cat Bracero
Cathy Feierstein
Charlene O'Grady
Cherise Davis
Charlotte Zhang
Cheryl Qattaq Stine
Chris Ecklund
Chris Grams
Chris Hacker
Chris Marshall
Chris Pullman
Christina Arbini
Christine Sheller
Christine Mau
Clark Malcolm
Clay Timon
Clement Mok
Cliff Goldman
Colin Drummond
Colleen Newquist
Connie Birdsall
Cortney Cannon
Craig Bernhardt
Craig Johnson
Craig Schlanser
Cristian Montegu
Curt Schreiber
Dan Dimmock
Dan Maginn
Dan Marcolina
Dana Arnett
Dani Pumilia
Danny Altman
Darren Lutz
Dave Luck, Mac Daddy
Dave Weinberger
David Airey
David Becker
David Bowie
David Erwin
David Ferrucci
David Kendall
David Korchin
David Milch
David Rose
David Roth
David Turner
Davis Masten
Dayton Henderson
Dean Crutchfield
Debbie Millman
Deborah Perloe
Delphine Hirasuna
Denise Sabet

Dennis Thomas
Dick Ritter
DK Holland
Donald K. Clifford, Jr.
Donna MacFarland
Dr. Barbara Riley
Dr. Delyte Frost
Dr. Dennis Dunn
Dr. Ginny Redish
Dr. Ginny Vanderslice
Dr. Karol Wasylyshyn
Dustin Britt
Ed Wheeler
Ed Williamson
Eddie Opara
Ellen Hoffman
Ellen Shapiro
Ellen Taylor
Emelia Rallapalli
Emily Cohen
Emily Kirkpatrick
Emily Tynes
Erich Sippel
Fo Wilson
Francesco Realmuto
Frank Osbourne
Gabriel Cohen
Gael Towey
Gail Lozoff
Gavin Cooper
Gayle Christiansen
Geoff Verney
George Graves
Gerry Stankus
Gillian Wallis
Ginnie Gehshan
Greg Farrington, PhD
Greg Shea
Gustavo Koniszczer
Harry Laverty
Hans-U. Allemann
Heather Guidice
Heather Stern
Heidi Caldwell
Heidi Cody
Helen Keyes
Hilly Charrington
Howard Fish
Howard Schultz
Ian Stephens
Ilise Benum
Ioanna Papaioannou
Isabella Falco
Ivan Cayabyab
Ivan Chermayeff
J. T. Miller
Jacey Lucas
Jack Cassidy
Jack Summerford
Jaeho Ko
Jaime Schwartz
Jamie Koval
Jane Randel
Jane Wentworth
Janette Krauss
Janice Fudyma
Jason Orne
Jay Coen Gilbert
Jay Ehret
Jaya Ibrahim
Jaye Peterson

Jayoung Jaylee
Jean-Francois Goyette
Jean Pierre Jordan
Jean-Michel Gathy
Jeffrey Fields
Jeffrey Gorder
Jeffrey R. Immelt
Jen Jagielski
Jen Knecht
Jenie De'Ath
Jenn Bacon
Jennifer Francis
Jennifer Knecht
Jennifer L. Freeman
Jenny Profy
Jerome Cloud
Jeremy Dooley
Jeremy Hawking
Jerry Greenberg
Jerry Selber
Jessica Berwind
Jessica Robles Worch
Jessica Rogers
Jim Barton
Jim Bittetto
Jinal Shah
Joan Carlson
Joanna Ham
Joanne Chan
Jody Friedman
Joe Duffy
Joe Pine
Joe Ray
Joel Grear
Joey Mooring
John Bowles
John Coyne
John Gleason
John Hildenbiddle
John Klotnia
John M. Muldar, PhD
Jon Iwata
Jon Schleuning
Jonah Smith
Jonathan Bolden
Jonathan Mansfield
Jonathan Opp
Joseph Cecere
Josh Goldblum
Joshua Cohen
Joshua Davis
Juan Ramírez
Julia Hoffman
Julia McGreevy
Julia Vinas
Justin Peters
Karin Cronan
Karin Hibma
Kate Dautrich
Kate Fitzgibbon
Kathleen Hatfield
Kathleen Koch
Katie Caldwell
Katie Clark
Katie Wharton
Kazunori Nozawa
Keith Helmetag
Keith Yamashita
Kelly Dunning
Ken Carbone
Ken Pasternak

Kent Hunter
Kevin Lee
Kieren Cooney
Kimberli Antoni
Kim Duffy
Kim Mitchell
Kit Hinrichs
Kurt Koepfle
Kurt Monigle
Larry Keeley
Laura Des Enfants
Laura Scott
Laura Silverman
Laura Zindel
Laurie Ashcraft
Laurie Bohnik
LeRoux Jooste
Leslie Smolan
Linda B. Matthiesen
Linda Wingate
Lisa Kline
Lisa Kovitz
Lori Kapner
Lory Sutton
Louise Fili
Luis Bravo
Lynn Beebe
Malcolm Grear
Marc Mikulich
Marco A. Rezende
Margaret Anderson
Maria D'Errico
Maribel Nix
Marie Morrison
Marilyn Sifford
Marius Ursache
Marjorie Guthrie
Mark Lomeli
Mark McCallum
Mark Selikson
Martha G. Goethals, PhD
Martha Witte
Marty Neumeier
Mary Sauers
Mary Storm-Baranyai
Matt Coffman
Matt Macinnis
Matt Petersen
Matt Salia
Matthew Bartholomew
Max Ritz
Megan Stanger
Megan Stephens
Mehmet Fidanboylu
Melinda Lawson
Melissa Hendricks
Melissa Lapid
Meredith Nierman
Michael Anastasio
Michael Bierut
Michael Cronan
Michael Daly
Michael Deal
Michael Donovan
Michael Flanagan
Michael Graves
Michael Grillo
Michael Hirschhorn
Michael Johnson
Michael O'Neill
Michal Levy

Michele Barker
Michelle Bonterre
Michelle Morrison
Michelle Steinback
Miguel A. Torres
Mike Dargento
Mike Flanagan
Mike Ramsay
Mike Reinhardt
Milton Glaser
Mindy Romero
Moira Cullen
Moira Riddell
Mona Zenkich
Monica Little
Monica Skipper
Nancy Donner
Nancy Tait
Nancye Green
Natalie Nixon
Natalie Silverstein
Nate Eimer
Ned Drew
Niall FitzGerald
Nick Bosch
Nicole Satterwhite
Noah Simon
Noah Syken
Noelle Andrews
Oliver Maltby
P. Fouchard–Filippi
Pamela Thompson
Parag Murudkar
Pat Duci
Patrick Cescau
Paul Pierson
Peggy Calabrese
Per Mollerup
Pete Colhoun
Peter Emery
Peter Wise
Phil Gatto
Philip Dubrow
Philippe Fouchard-Filippi
Q Cassetti
R. Jacobs-Meadway
Rafi Spero
Randy Mintz-Presant
Ranjith Kumaran
riCardo Crespo
Ricardo Salvador
Rich Bacher
Rich Rickaby
Richard C. Breon
Richard de Villiers
Richard Felton
Richard Kauffman
Richard Saul Wurman
Richard Thé
Rick Bacher
Rob Wallace
Robbie de Villiers
Robbin Phillips
Robin Goffman
Rodney Abbot
Rodrigo Bastida
Rodrigo Galindo
Roger Whitehouse
Ronnie Lipton
Rose Linke
Rosemary Ellis

Rosemary Murphy
Roy Pessis
Russ Napolitano
Ruth Abrahams
Ryan Dickerson
Sagi Haviv
Sally Hudson
Samantha Pede
Sandra Donohoe
Sandy Miller
Santa Claus
Sara Rad
Sarah Bond
Sarah Brinkman
Sarah Swaine
Scot Herbst
Sean Adams
Sean Haggerty
Sera Vulaono
Shantini Munthree
Sharon Sulecki
Simon Waldron
Sini Salminen
Sol Sender
Spike Jones
Stefan Liute
Steff Geissbuhler
Stella Gassaway
Stephen A. Roell
Stephen Doyle
Stephen Sapka
Stephen Sumner
Steve Frykholm
Steve Perry
Steve Sandstrom
Steve Storti
Sunny Hong
Susan Avarde
Susan Bird
Susan Schuman
Susan Westerfer
Suzanne Cammarota
Suzanne Tavani
Sven Seger
Ted Sann
Terrence Murray
Terry Yoo
Theresa Fitzgerald
Thor Lauterbach
Tim Lapetino
Tim O'Mara
TJ Scimone
Tom Birk
Tom Geismar
Tom Nozawa
Tom Vanderbauwhede
Tom Watson
Tosh Hall
Tracy Stearns
Travis Barteaux
Trevor Wade
Tricia Davidson
Trish Thompson
Victoria Jones
Vince Voron
Virginia Miller
Wandy Cavalheiro
Wesley Chung
Will Burke
Woody Pirtle
Yves Behar

Contents

Basics

Designing Brand Identity is a quick reference guide. All subject matter is organized by spread for ease of access in the blinding speed of business and life. All that is needed is your desire and passion to be the best.

Process

Part 2 presents a universal process regardless of the project's scope and nature. This section answers the question "Why does it take so long?"

Best Practices

Part 3 showcases best practices. Local and global, public and private, these projects inspire and exemplify original, flexible, lasting solutions.

Foreword by Debbie Millman

Designing Brand Identity reinvents the idea of a marketing textbook, demystifies branding, and illuminates the range of tools and techniques used by experienced practitioners. Since the first edition appeared in 2003, Alina Wheeler's book has become a singular resource providing a common language for the whole branding team.

Designing Brand Identity demonstrates the relationship between strategy and design, and showcases compelling best practice case studies from the public and private sectors, globally.

It's not surprising that the book was an immediate hit, with five updated editions over fourteen years, and translated into seven languages. It strikes a deep chord in culture, and unequivocally proves how the practice of branding engages intelligence, creativity, imagination, and emotion unlike any other business discipline.

Designing Brand Identity has become a trusted resource and road map for designers, brand consultancies, digerati, and their clients. It is rare that one book can be used by both marketing and creative. *Designing Brand Identity*

accomplishes this feat, educating and inspiring the entire branding team, regardless of one's specific role. And its reach extends beyond working professionals: it is a textbook in design and business programs across the globe.

In short, I contend that *Designing Brand Identity* has done more to illuminate the mysteries and significance of branding than any other book of our time.

You are now holding the fifth edition of *Designing Brand Identity*. Each edition has evolved with the massive changes in technology, in behavior, and in our comprehension of the role branding plays in our cognition. Wheeler's contribution to this understanding is unprecedented.

Design is intelligence made visible.

Lou Danziger

Debbie Millman is the cofounder and chair of the Masters in Branding program at SVA, training a new generation of brand leaders. As host of the podcast Design Matters, she has interviewed more than three hundred design luminaries and cultural commentators. She worked with over two hundred brands during her tenure as president of the design division of Sterling Brands from 1995 to 2016.

To mark the occasion of this new edition, I had the opportunity to explore the origins and intention of this effort with the author herself.

Why was this book needed?

I wanted to demystify branding, deconstruct the process, and give teams the tools to build trust and achieve remarkable results. While there were a lot of brilliant brand strategy books, and a lot of inspiring design books, there weren't any about a disciplined process to revitalize a brand. I had met a lot of smart leaders who were eager to understand the fundamentals and benefits of branding, and why good design was a business imperative.

What changes have you seen since the publication of the first edition?

The book underscores how far we have come. In the first edition, there were no apps or social media. Rising above the competitive clamor gets harder each day. Brand expression has exploded across all digital platforms. Content marketing has become a core competency, and armies of algorithms are at work. I've seen a dramatic increase in best practices across organizations big and small, public and private, for profit and nonprofit, driven by a new generation of agile leaders.

You've mapped a disciplined process in *Designing Brand Identity*. How has it evolved over the various editions?

My five-phase process to revitalize a brand is still the bedrock. It works. Readers from around the world share the successes their organizations have had by following the process. Reader feedback has enriched each edition and added important international perspectives.

I find that some CEOs don't know what good design is, and it's shocking. Why do you think they aren't aware of the power of design?

I am not shocked. If I looked under the hood of a Lamborghini, I would not know it's a high performance engine. If no one has ever shared best practices or case studies, how would a CEO know about the power of design? There are voluminous marketing case studies that never even include the "D" word. My aim has always been to spotlight the powerful synergy of strategy and design.

How have *you* changed since the first edition?

I have more empathy for clients. Changing anything takes a great deal of courage. Just because something is the right thing to do doesn't mean it's the easy thing to do.

Why do you think change is so hard to implement?

It's all about people. Getting people on board with change is difficult; there is always resistance. But I am optimistic: employee engagement is being embraced. A key part of my process is taking the time—up front—to build trust and agree on brand strategy, before moving on to design strategy. More participation, less persuasion.

What advice do you have for organizations embarking on revitalizing their brands?

Commit to a disciplined process. Stay customer-centric and trust the process. Engage your employees. Forge emotional connections and life long relationships with your customers. Seize every opportunity to amplify your differentiation. Be innovative, original, and dynamic. Become irreplaceable. Stay calm on the roller coaster of relentless change and keep moving.

What do you hope readers will get from this fifth edition?

The insights, courage, and tools to do the right thing for the right reasons. I want most to give readers the confidence to brand the future.

Understand me.

Make a difference in my life.

Surprise me often.

Give me more than I paid for.

Show me you love me.

Alan Jacobson
President, Ex;it Design
Cofounder, J2 Design

1 Basics

Part 1 illuminates the difference between brand and brand identity, and what it takes to be the best. Don't bypass the fundamentals in the speed of a new project. Establish a shared vocabulary for the entire branding team.

Brand

As competition creates infinite choices, companies look for ways to connect emotionally with customers, become irreplaceable, and create lifelong relationships. A strong brand stands out in a densely crowded marketplace. People fall in love with brands, trust them, and believe in their superiority. How a brand is perceived affects its success—whether it's a start-up, a nonprofit, or a product.

Who are you? Who needs to know?
How will they find out? Why should they care?

Brands now appear regularly on balance sheets in many companies. The intangible value of the brand is often much greater than the corporation's tangible assets.

Wally Olins
The Brand Book

Brands have three primary functions*

Navigation

Brands help consumers choose from a bewildering array of choices.

Reassurance

Brands communicate the intrinsic quality of the product or service and reassure customers that they have made the right choice.

Engagement

Brands use distinctive imagery, language, and associations to encourage customers to identify with the brand.

*David Haigh, CEO, Brand Finance

Brands have become the global currency of success.

Brand Atlas

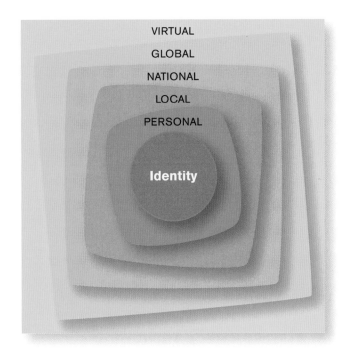

VIRTUAL
GLOBAL
NATIONAL
LOCAL
PERSONAL

Identity

Businesses are now only as strong as their brands, and nothing else offers business leaders so much potential leverage.

Jim Stengel
Grow: How Ideals Power Growth and Profit at the World's Greatest Companies

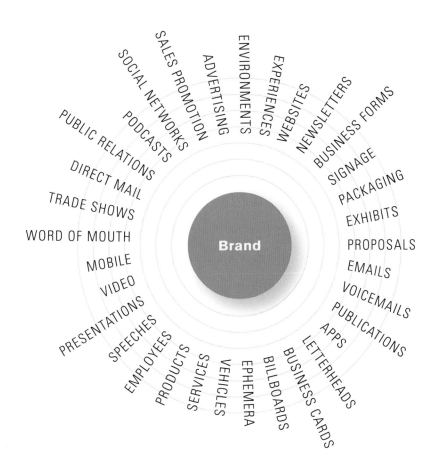

SALES PROMOTION
SOCIAL NETWORKS
ADVERTISING
ENVIRONMENTS
EXPERIENCES
PODCASTS
WEBSITES
NEWSLETTERS
PUBLIC RELATIONS
BUSINESS FORMS
DIRECT MAIL
SIGNAGE
TRADE SHOWS
PACKAGING
WORD OF MOUTH
EXHIBITS
MOBILE
PROPOSALS
VIDEO
EMAILS
PRESENTATIONS
VOICEMAILS
PUBLICATIONS
SPEECHES
APPS
EMPLOYEES
LETTERHEADS
PRODUCTS
BUSINESS CARDS
SERVICES
BILLBOARDS
VEHICLES
EPHEMERA

Brand

Brand touchpoints
Each touchpoint is an opportunity to increase awareness and build customer loyalty.

Brand identity

Brand identity is tangible and appeals to the senses. You can see it, touch it, hold it, hear it, watch it move. Brand identity fuels recognition, amplifies differentiation, and makes big ideas and meaning accessible.

Design differentiates and embodies the intangibles— emotion, context, and essence—that matter most to consumers.

Moira Cullen
VP, Global Beverage Design
PepsiCo

Laura Zindel

Target

Cooper Hewitt

7 Minute Workout on the Apple Watch

Bevel Shave System

McDonald's

vitaminwater

Dale Carnegie

Pitney Bowes

truvia

MALL OF AMERICA.

City of Melbourne

masterpass

Mastercard

5

Branding

Branding is a disciplined process used to build awareness, attract new customers, and extend customer loyalty. Positioning a brand to be irreplaceable requires a daily desire to be the best. To be successful, brand builders need to stick to the basics, stay calm on the roller coaster of relentless change, and seize every opportunity to be the brand of choice.

Branding is deliberate differentiation.

Debbie Millman
Chair and cofounder
Masters Program in Branding
School of Visual Arts

We continue to invest in our core strengths. First, we don't skimp on understanding the consumer. Second is innovation…And third is branding…We're delivering more messages to our consumers.

A. G. Lafley
CEO, P&G
Business Week, 2009

Types of branding

Co-branding
Partnering with another brand to achieve reach

Digital branding
Web, social media, search engine optimization, driving commerce on the web

Personal branding
The way an individual builds a reputation

Cause branding
Aligning a brand with a charitable cause; or corporate social responsibility

Country branding
Efforts to attract tourists and businesses

Emotional branding is a dynamic cocktail of anthropology, imagination, sensory experiences, and visionary approach to change.

Marc Gobé
Emotional Branding

Process

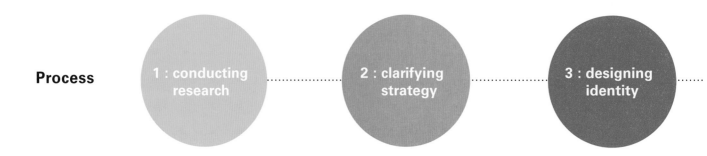

1 : conducting research

2 : clarifying strategy

3 : designing identity

When to start the process

New company, new product

I'm starting a new business. I need a business card and a website.

We've developed a new product and it needs a name and a logo yesterday.

We need to raise millions of dollars. The campaign needs to have its own identity.

We're going public in the fall.

We need to raise venture capital, even though we do not have our first customer.

Name change

Our name no longer fits who we are and the businesses we are in.

We need to change our name because of a trademark conflict.

Our name has negative connotations in our new markets.

Our name misleads customers.

We merged.

We need a new name for the Chinese market.

Revitalize a brand

We want to reposition and refresh the global brand.

We need to communicate more clearly about who we are.

We're going global—we need help to enter new markets.

No one knows who we are.

Our stock is devalued.

We want to appeal to a new and more affluent market.

Revitalize a brand identity

We are innovators. We look behind the times.

We want our customers to have a great mobile experience.

Our identity does not position us shoulder to shoulder with our competitors.

We have 80 divisions and inconsistent nomenclature.

I am embarrassed when I give out my business card.

Everyone in the world recognizes our icon, but admit it—he needs a face-lift.

We love our symbol—it is known by our market. The problem is you cannot read our logotype.

Create an integrated system

We do not present a consistent face to our customers.

We need a new brand architecture to deal with acquisitions.

Our packaging is not distinctive. Our competitors look better than we do, and their sales are going up.

All of our marketing looks like it comes from different companies.

We need to look strong and communicate that we are one global company.

Every division does its own thing when marketing. This is inefficient, frustrating, and not cost-effective. Everyone is reinventing the wheel.

When companies merge

We want to send a clear message to our stakeholders that this is a merger of equals.

We want to communicate that $1 + 1 = 4$.

We want to build on the brand equity of the merging companies.

We need to send a strong signal to the world that we are the new industry leader.

We need a new name.

How do we evaluate our acquisition's brand and fold it into our brand architecture?

Two industry leaders are merging. How do we manage our new identity?

4 : creating touchpoints

5 : managing assets

Brand governance

Brand management requires strategy, planning, and orchestration. It begins with thoughtful leadership, a shared understanding of core purpose and brand fundamentals, and an imperative to grow brand equity. It's finding new ways to delight customers, to engage employees, and to demonstrate your competitive advantage.

A strong brand binds us internally and it differentiates us externally.

Brian Resnick
Director, Global Brand & Communication Services
Deloitte

We're committed to bringing our brand to life each day, and ensuring its continued growth.

Melissa Hendricks
Vice President, Marketing Strategy
Cerner

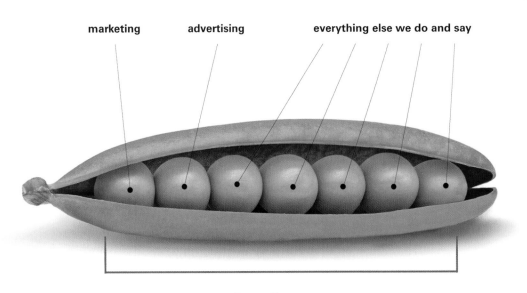

marketing   advertising   everything else we do and say

Branding

Spectrum Health diagram: Crosby Associates

Every Spectrum Health employee, design consultant, agency, and supplier receives a copy of "One System. One Focus. One Brand." It's their "brand bible" and summarizes the organization's vision, attributes, and branding components.

Bart Crosby
President
Crosby Associates

Brand stewardship principles
Developed by Gabriel Cohen, CMO, Monigle

People

Explain why the brand is important instead of telling people what to do.

Think empowerment, not enforcement.

Make it easy for your associates to be on brand.

Educate your internal audiences with workshops, videos, training modules, brand forums, and self-serve content.

Process

Keep the process flexible, agile, and responsive to change. Branding has become digital, social, and experience-based.

Get involved earlier in the creative review process instead of playing a compliance role at the back end.

Showcase best practices regularly and build an inspiration bank.

Not all brand elements have equal importance. Organize them by sacred, interpretive, and customizable.

Tools

Create a brand ambassador program to include key people who will feel a sense of ownership.

Create a user-friendly, online brand center that consolidates brand assets in one place. Streamline requests and capture data.

Tailor guidelines and content for different user groups, both internal and external.

Brand governance is the managed interplay of behavior, communications, design, legal compliance, process and measurement that drive brand performance across an enterprise.

Hampton Bridwell
CEO and Managing Partner
Tenet Partners

How brand governance has evolved

From	To
Centralized command and control	Education, empowerment, and self-service
Review approval at final stage	Strategic partner throughout the process
Rigid	Collaborative and iterative
Static PDF guidelines	Dynamic, evolving applications
General one size fits all approach	Tailored content for different user groups

The difference between branding and marketing
Developed by Matchstic

Branding	Marketing
Branding is why.	Marketing is how.
Branding is long-term.	Marketing is short-term.
Branding is macro.	Marketing is micro.
Branding defines trajectory.	Marketing defines tactics.
Branding is the reason someone buys.	Marketing is the reason someone first buys.
Branding builds loyalty.	Marketing generates response.
Branding is the being.	Marketing is the doing.

Brand strategy

Effective brand strategy provides a central, unifying idea around which all behavior, actions, and communications are aligned. It works across products and services, and is effective over time. The best strategies are so differentiated and powerful that they deflect the competition. They are easy to talk about, whether you are the CEO or an employee.

Brand strategy builds on a vision, is aligned with business strategy, emerges from a company's values and culture, and reflects an in-depth understanding of the customer's needs and perceptions. Brand strategy defines positioning, differentiation, the competitive advantage, and a unique value proposition.

Brand strategy needs to resonate with all stakeholders: external customers, the media, and internal customers (for example, employees, the board, core suppliers). Brand strategy is a road map that guides marketing, makes it easier for the sales force to sell more, and provides clarity, context, and inspiration to employees.

The factors to successfully revitalize a brand: Be inspired by people—your consumers. Take risks—within your strategy. Be bold—to really make a difference.

Mario Bastida
Marketing and Communications Director
Grupo Imagen

Our work as brand strategists is to find a brand's highest, most enduring value.

Shantini Munthree
Managing Partner
The Union Marketing Group

Alignment

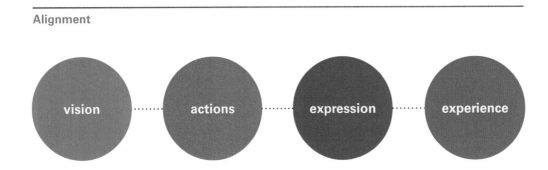

vision ······· actions ······· expression ······· experience

Who develops brand strategy?

It is usually a team of people; no one does it alone. It is a result of an extended dialogue among the leadership team that must stay focused on the customer. Global companies frequently bring in brand strategists: independent thinkers and authorities, strategic marketing firms, and brand consultants. It often takes someone from the outside who is an experienced strategic and creative thinker to help a company articulate what is already there.

Sometimes a brand strategy is born at the inception of a company by a visionary, such as Steve Jobs, Elon Musk, Oprah Winfrey, or Jeff Bezos. Sometimes it takes a visionary team to redefine brand strategy. Companies frequently survive and prosper because they have a clear brand strategy. Companies falter because they do not have one.

At the heart of the strategy is our commitment to delight our guests by consistently delivering the right combination of innovation, design, and value in our merchandising, in our marketing, and in our stores. This is the essence of our "Expect more. Pay less." brand promise.

Bob Ulrich
Chairman and CEO
Target, 1987-2009

Target's brand promise is summed up by its tagline, "Expect more. Pay less." Target has long differentiated itself from other mass discount merchandisers, like Walmart and Costco, through its combination of innovation, design, and value. Its high-profile design partnerships and unconventional advertising have appealed to a younger, hipper demographic. In 2016, Target began to expand a fleet of smaller, urban stores to appeal to city dwellers, office workers, and tourists. Target is also collaborating with the MIT Media Lab and IDEO to explore the future of food to give people better control over their food choices and help them eat healthier.

Why invest

The best identity programs embody and advance the company's brand by supporting desired perceptions. Identity expresses itself in every touchpoint of the brand and becomes intrinsic to a company's culture—a constant symbol of its core values and its relevance.

Brands are powerful assets for creating desire, shaping experience, and shifting demand.

Rick Wise
Chief Executive Officer
Lippincott

You shouldn't think of identity design as a marketing expense. Like other assets a business invests in, well-designed visual assets deliver value long after they are paid for, benefiting a brand for decades with no additional cost. Think of the Amazon logo we designed. Billions of boxes delivered over two decades, and every one of them with a smile in its face. That's an idea that will never grow old. And it works on everything from a packing slip to a fleet of aircraft.

David Turner
Designer and Founder
Turner Duckworth

Impact

When you affect behavior, you can impact performance.

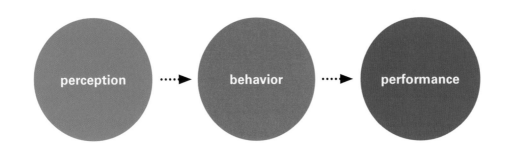

perception ·····▶ behavior ·····▶ performance

The importance of brand strategy and the cost of building brand should be understood at the highest levels of an organization and across functional areas—not just sales and marketing, but in legal, finance, operations, and human resources as well.

Sally Hudson
Marketing Consultant

If you think that good design is expensive, you should look at the cost of bad design.

Dr. Ralf Speth
CEO
Jaguar Land Rover

In any competitive market, what drives margin and growth and separates one business from another— for employees, customers, partners, and investors— is the brand.

Jim Stengel
Grow: How Ideals Power Growth and Profit at the World's Greatest Companies

Make it easy for the customer to buy

Compelling branding presents any company, any size, anywhere with an immediately recognizable, distinctive professional image that positions it for success. An identity helps manage the perception of a company and differentiates it from its competitors. A smart system conveys respect for the customer and makes it easy to understand features and benefits. A new product design or a better environment can delight a customer and create loyalty. An effective identity encompasses such elements as a name that is easy to remember or a distinctive package design for a product.

Make it easy for the sales force to sell

Whether it is the CEO of a global conglomerate communicating a new vision to the board, a first-time entrepreneur pitching to venture capital firms, or a financial advisor creating a need for investment products, everyone is selling. Nonprofits, whether fundraising or soliciting new volunteers, are continually selling. Strategic brand identity works across diverse audiences and cultures to build an awareness and understanding of a company and its strengths. By making intelligence visible, effective identity seeks to communicate a company's unique value proposition. The coherence of communications across various media sends a strong signal to the customer about the laserlike focus of a company.

Make it easy to build brand equity

The goal of all public companies is to increase shareholder value. A brand, or a company's reputation, is considered to be one of the most valuable company assets. Small companies and nonprofits also need to build brand equity. Their future success is dependent on building public awareness, preserving their reputations, and upholding their value. Brand equity is built through increased recognition, awareness, and customer loyalty, which in turn helps make a company more successful. Managers who seize every opportunity to communicate their company's brand value and what the brand stands for sleep better at night. They are building a precious asset.

Branding imperatives

Acknowledge that we live in a branded world.

Seize every opportunity to position your company in your customers' minds.

Communicate a strong brand idea over and over again.

Go beyond declaring a competitive advantage. Demonstrate it!

Understand the customers. Build on their perceptions, preferences, dreams, values, and lifestyles.

Identify touchpoints—places in which customers interface with the product or service.

Create sensory magnets to attract and retain customers.

Stakeholders

Seizing every opportunity to build brand champions requires identifying the constituencies that affect success. Reputation and goodwill extend far beyond a brand's target customers. Employees are now called "internal customers" since their power is far-reaching. Gaining insight into stakeholder characteristics, behavior, needs, and perceptions yields a high return.

Consumers are becoming co-creators. Competitors are becoming collaborators.

Karl Heiselman
CEO
Wolff Olins

Brand is not what you say it is. It's what they say it is.

Marty Neumeier
The Brand Gap

Uncover opinions and biases from a variety of stakeholders to inform positioning and achieve meaningful differentiation.

Ann Willoughby
President and Chief Innovation Officer
Willoughby Design

Willoughby Design designed a deck of cards for their brand workshops. A typical exercise might be, "Find a picture that represents a key stakeholder and tell us what matters most to them." Participants must fully understand the role they are playing.

Persona Cards:
Willoughby Design

Key stakeholders

As the branding process unfolds, research about stakeholders will inform a broad range of solutions, from positioning to the tilt of brand messages, to the launch strategy and plan.

Gen X or Millennial?

Market researchers use the same terms for classifying generation gaps, but don't agree on the dates.

Generation	Born
Seniors	before 1946
Boomers	1946–1965
Gen X	1966–1980
Millennial	1981–1995
Gen Z	1996–now

Gen Z is also diverse. My fifteen-year-old next-door neighbor is a quarter Hispanic, a quarter African-American, a quarter Taiwanese, and a quarter white. That's Gen Z—they are often a mix of ethnicities.

Alexandra Levit
New York Times

Eighty million millennials are the first generation to have grown up in a digital culture. Millennials aspire more to a set of values—freedom, knowledge, and creative self-expression—than to conspicuous consumption.

Patricia Martin
RenGen

Culture

Long-term success is directly influenced by the way employees share in their company's culture—its values, stories, symbols, and heroes. Building the brand from the inside out means inspiring employees to embrace the organization's purpose. A culture that encourages individual difference and free expression is more likely to produce new ideas and products that engage customers.

How strongly people believe in an organization and its basic precepts weighs heavily on success.

Thomas Watson Jr.
President and CEO
IBM, 1952–1971

As a strategic asset, culture must be thoughtfully managed in the same way that other valuable company assets are.

SYPartners

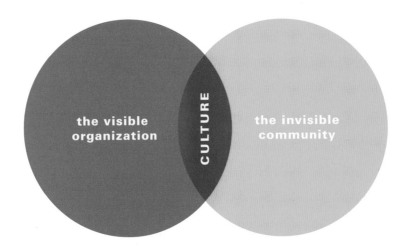

The visible organization	The invisible community
Hierarchy and chain of command	Network of reliable relationships
Official values and vision	Experienced values and vision
Written rules, policies, and procedures	Unwritten rules and social norms
Business contracts (internal and external)	Informal contracts (internal and external)
Business accountabilities	Social accountabilities
Information/communication systems	The back channel and rumor mill

Developed by Hanley Brite, Founder, Authentic Connections

Key benefits of a strong brand culture
Excerpts from *MOO Live your brand from the inside out*

Increased brand awareness

The most successful brands have highly engaged, passionate employees who are their brand's biggest ambassadors when they're out in the world—and who boost awareness more than any advertising campaign ever could.

Attracting (and keeping) the right people

Brands that have a clear vision and well-articulated values attract like-minded people naturally. Your employees should be an authentic embodiment of your brand.

Happier customers

Customers are drawn to brands that share their values. When employees don't represent these ideals, this can lead to dissatisfied customers, internal company challenges, and ultimately, a tarnished image.

Better relationships

Collaboration and working on cross-functional teams is easier when people have things in common, and feel a sense of shared values and that they are part of a bigger story.

Competitive edge

Brand culture is the enormous behind-the-scenes engine that drives your brand every minute of the day. The people you employ can create a clearer differentiation between you and the competition.

Increased productivity

Many studies have found that an engaged, happy workforce is a more productive workforce. Achieving company goals holds intrinsic value.

MOO's core beliefs about how they work

Make it simpler
Always deliver delight
Keep it human
Every detail counts
Imagine it better
Tackle it together

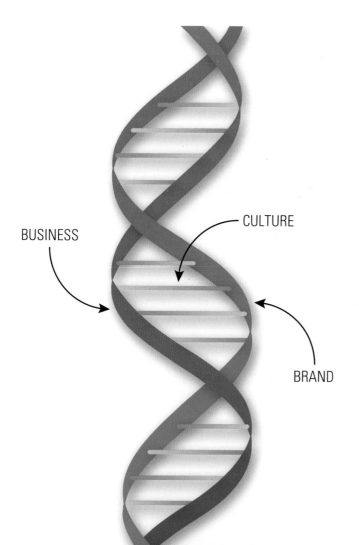

BUSINESS

CULTURE

BRAND

Lincoln said character is like a tree, reputation is like its shadow. Many believe their job is to manipulate the shadow rather than tend to the health of the tree. In this world of transparency and democratized media, it is increasingly difficult for organizations and individuals to lead double lives. The best investment in corporate character is to invest in corporate culture.

Jon Iwata
SVP, Marketing and
Communications
IBM

Diagram adapted courtesy
of SYPartners

Customer experience

Global competition is fierce. Consumers are inundated with choices. Brand builders need to think far beyond the point of sale, and use their strategic imagination and business acumen to deliver one-of-a-kind engaging experiences that no other competitor can replicate. Think barrier to entry.

Compelling experiences attract new customers, extend customer loyalty, and, if they are truly differentiated, command a premium. Every customer interaction must be viewed as an opportunity. A memorable experience generates positive buzz and is fun to share; a bad experience becomes a lost opportunity that can sabotage the brand.

A customer heads to the Genius Bar at the Apple Store for education, American Girl Place for afternoon tea, and Wegmans for dinner and some great live music before he does his marketing. The possibilities are endless.

It is the experience a brand creates and curates, through its products and services, that defines it in the minds of customers.

Nathan Williams
Senior Strategist
Wolff Olins

Stop pretending there's a difference between "online" and "real life." Every aspect of our lives has an online component.

Annalee Newitz
Ars Technica

The art of being a great retailer is to preserve the core while enhancing the experience.

Howard Schultz
Chairman and CEO
Starbucks

Using the Pen, visitors can select wallpapers from the Cooper Hewitt's permanent collection or design their own on large touchscreen tables, and see them projected on the walls from floor to ceiling in the Immersion Room.

Caroline Baumann
Director
Cooper Hewitt, Smithsonian
Design Museum

Photo: Peter Ascoli #immersionroom

Fundamentals of experience

Excerpted from *The Experience Economy*
by B. Joseph Pine II and James H. Gilmore

Work is theater and every business is a stage.

The experience is the marketing.

Even the most mundane transactions can be turned into memorable experiences.

Experiences you create should be treated as distinct economic offerings that engage your customers and create memories within them.

Companies need not limit themselves to the physical realm, but can use virtual experiences as well in a series of related experiences that flow one from another.

Experiences are an opportunity to generate new sources of both revenue and profits in an increasingly commoditized world.

Every element in the experience must have an organizing principle.

Principals of digital experience

Developed by Paul Pierson, Carbone Smolan Agency

Digital is not just a website. Consider all the places your audience uses technology to interact with your brand.

Be human. People often use digital tools as a substitute for human interaction, but the experience shouldn't feel robotic.

Talk to people. Engage in conversation with your audience and listen—it builds trust.

Reach your audience where they are. Brand experiences shouldn't be bound to a destination.

Be authoritative. The .com should be the truest representation of your product or service.

Solve a problem for your users. Consider creating a tool instead of distributing a message.

Brands can amplify engagement and solidify positive impressions by carefully considering the customer's journey, and seeing the interplay between physical sensory experiences and compelling digital experiences.

Paul Pierson
Managing Partner
Carbone Smolan Agency

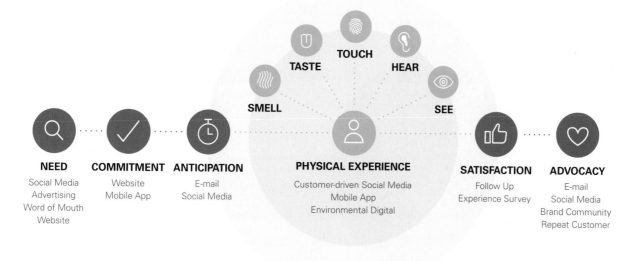

NEED
Social Media
Advertising
Word of Mouth
Website

COMMITMENT
Website
Mobile App

ANTICIPATION
E-mail
Social Media

TASTE · TOUCH · HEAR
SMELL · SEE

PHYSICAL EXPERIENCE
Customer-driven Social Media
Mobile App
Environmental Digital

SATISFACTION
Follow Up
Experience Survey

ADVOCACY
E-mail
Social Media
Brand Community
Repeat Customer

● Personal Space ● Brand Space

Diagram: Carbone Smolan Agency

Cross cultures

While globalization has blurred the distinctions among cultures, the best brands pay attention to cultural differences. In cyberspace, on our desktops, and on our mobiles, geography has become less relevant. Cultural insight is critical to anyone who is building a brand.

Naming, logo design, image development, color, key messages, and retail spaces require the creative team to pay attention to connotation and the complexity of subtle cultural differences. The history of marketing is filled with too many

stories about companies offending the very market that they were trying to impress. Assumptions and stereotypes stand in the way of building brands that understand customers and celebrate their uniqueness.

Understand the different layers of a culture. Show your respect and make it relevant.

Carlos Martinez Onaindia
Global Creative Studio Leader
Deloitte

From local to national, regional, and global, the best brands grow one customer at a time, creating conversations, understanding individual customers' needs, and transcending all geographic boundaries.

Gustavo Koniszczer
Managing Director
FutureBrand Hispanic America

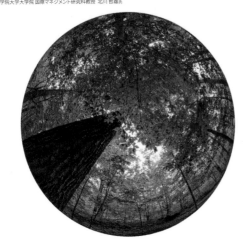

企業リスク Vol.55 2017.04

Enterprise Risk Vol.55 2017.04

特集　ガバナンス・システムの最適化に向けて
経営者、取締役会長、機関投資家、有識者の立場から
中外製薬株式会社 代表取締役会長 最高経営責任者　永山 治氏
アステラス製薬株式会社 代表取締役副社長　御代川 善朗氏
コニカミノルタ株式会社 取締役会議長　松崎 正年氏
一般社団法人スチュワードシップ研究会 代表理事　木村 祐基氏
青山学院大学大学院 国際マネジメント研究科教授　北川 哲雄氏

研究室
企業のリスク・クライシスマネジメント実態調査 2016年版 結果解説
中国サイバーセキュリティ法の概要と日本企業に望まれる対応
M&AにおけるJ-SOX対応
〜短期対応のためには何から手を付けるべきか〜

Deloitte.
デロイト トーマツ

Deloitte is a company that provides professional services through a globally connected network of member firms in more than 150 countries. Binding them, more than anything else, is the brand. This magazine cover from Japan demonstrates how Deloitte makes every effort to express itself consistently while also being respectful of global cultures. The imagery style reflects the Japanese ideals of balance and harmony. White is the dominant color, since black backgrounds, broadly used in other parts of the world, are considered ominous in Japan.

Emoji art supplied by http://emojione.com

Not every culture has a nationality.

HSBC advertisement

Layers of culture
Developed by Carlos Martinez Onaindia, Deloitte

Objective variables

Naming
Language
Writing
Symbols
Color
Sound

Subjective variables

Aspirations
Values
Emotions
Humor
Expectations
Feelings

Cultural variables

Societal
Economic
Spiritual
Religious
Intellectual
Ethical

The Latino market is not monolithic, monochromatic, or one dimensional, and definitely not dull. Do your due diligence, then open your eyes, ears, and minds. Start by being relevant.

Joe Ray
President/Creative Director
Estudio Ray

Fundamental principles
Developed by Ronnie Lipton, *Designing Across Cultures*

Assume cultural complexity. "Hispanic," "Asian," or "Chinese" is not "a" market.

Immerse your team in the cultures of your customers. Explore perceptions, values, behaviors, and trends.

Make sure your team includes trusted native experts. Subtle cultural differences and trends are often invisible to outsiders.

Research and test to avoid stereotypes and other misconceptions.

Test widely to ensure brand connection across diverse cultures within a country or region.

Test often to keep the brand relevant. Plan to keep a team in—or in close touch with—the region.

Brand architecture

Brand architecture is the hierarchy of brands within a single company. The interrelationship of the parent company, subsidiary companies, products, and services should mirror the marketing strategy. Bringing consistency, verbal, and visual order to disparate elements helps a company grow and market more effectively.

As companies merge with others and acquire new companies and products, the branding, nomenclature, and marketing decisions become exceedingly complex. Decision makers examine marketing, cost, time, and legal implications.

The need for brand architecture is not limited to Fortune 100 companies or for-profit companies. Any company or institution that is growing needs to evaluate which brand architecture strategy will support future growth.

This is a very exciting new chapter in the life of Google—the birth of Alphabet.

Larry Page
CEO
Alphabet

Alphabet

Alphabet Subsidiaries

iGoogle	Google Calendar
Google Images	Google Translate
Google Maps	Chrome
Google Translate	Android
Google Play	YouTube
Google Earth	Picasa
Google +	Android
Gmail	DoubleClick
Google Docs	AdMob
Google Alerts	Feedburner

Types of brand architecture

Most large companies that sell products and services have a mixture of strategies.

Monolithic brand architecture

Characterized by a strong, single master brand. Customers make choices based on brand loyalty. Features and benefits matter less to the consumer than the brand promise and persona. Brand extensions use the parent's identity and generic descriptors.

Google + Google Maps
FedEx Express + FedEx Office
GE + GE Healthcare
Virgin + Virgin Mobile
Vanguard + Vanguard ETF

Endorsed brand architecture

Characterized by marketing synergy between the product or division and the parent. The product or division has a clearly defined market presence, and benefits from the association, endorsement, and visibility of the parent.

iPad + Apple
Polo + Ralph Lauren
Oreo + Nabisco
Navy Seals + US Navy

Pluralistic brand architecture

Characterized by a series of well-known consumer brands. The name of the parent may be either invisible or inconsequential to the consumer, and known only to the investment community. Many parent companies develop a system for corporate endorsement that is tertiary.

Tang (Mondelez)
Godiva Chocolatier (Yildiz Holding)
The Ritz-Carlton (Marriott)
Hellmann's Mayonnaise (Unilever)
Bevel (Walker & Company)
Kleenex (Kimberly Clark)
Elmer's (Newell Brands)

Strategic questions

What are the benefits of leveraging the name of the parent company?

Does the positioning of our new entity require that we distance it from the parent?

Will co-branding confuse consumers?

Do we change the name or build on existing equity even though it was owned by a competitor?

Should we ensure that the parent company is always visible in a secondary position?

How do we brand this new acquisition?

Symbols

Brand awareness and recognition are facilitated by a visual identity that is easy to remember and immediately recognizable. Visual identity triggers perceptions and unlocks associations of the brand. Sight, more than any other sense, provides information about the world.

Through repeated exposure, symbols become so recognizable that companies such as Target, Apple, and Nike have actually dropped the logotype from their corporate signatures in national advertising. Color becomes a mnemonic device—when you see a brown truck out of the corner of your eye, you know it is a UPS truck.

Identity designers are in the business of managing perception through the integration of meaning and distinctive visual form.

Understanding the sequence of visual perception and cognition provides valuable insight into what will work best.

Symbols are the fastest form of communication known to humankind.

Blake Deutsch

The sequence of cognition

The science of perception examines how individuals recognize and interpret sensory stimuli. The brain acknowledges and remembers shapes first. Visual images can be remembered and recognized directly, while words must be decoded into meaning.

Shape

Reading is not necessary to identify shapes, but identifying shapes is necessary to read. The brain acknowledges distinctive shapes that make a faster imprint on memory.

Color

Color is second in the sequence. Color can trigger an emotion and evoke a brand association. Distinctive colors need to be chosen carefully, not only to build brand awareness, but also to express differentiation. Companies such as Kodak and Tiffany have trademarked their core brand colors.

Form

The brain takes more time to process language, so content is third in the sequence behind shape and color.

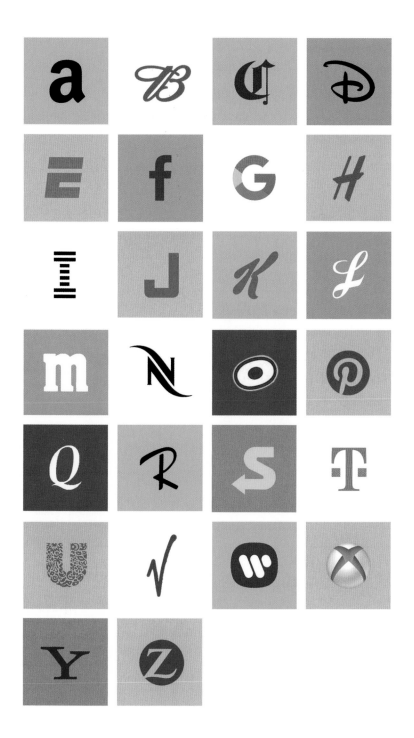

Name that brand

Isn't it amazing how we can recognize a consumer brand by just seeing one letter of a full name? Through frequency, the brand retains and recalls a distinctive shape. This concept was first developed by Heidi Cody, an artist and anthropologist, in her artwork "American Alphabet."

a. Amazon
b. Budweiser
c. Corona
d. Disney
e. ESPN
f. Facebook
g. Google
h. H&M
i. IBM
j. Jell-O
k. Kellogg's
l. Lysol
m. M&M's
n. Nespresso
o. Oreo
p. Pinterest
q. Q-tips
r. Ray-Ban
s. Subway
t. T-Mobile
u. Unilever
v. Virgin Mobile
w. Warner Music Group
x. X-Box
y. Yahoo
z. Zurich Insurance

Names

The right name is timeless, tireless, easy to say and remember; it stands for something, and facilitates brand extensions. Its sound has rhythm. It looks great in the text of an email and in the logo. A well-chosen name is an essential brand asset, as well as a 24/7 workhorse.

A name is transmitted day in and day out, in conversations, emails, voicemails, websites, on the product, on business cards, and in presentations. The wrong name for a company, product, or service can hinder marketing efforts through miscommunication or because people cannot pronounce it or remember it. The wrong name can subject a company to unnecessary legal risks or alienate a market segment. Finding the right name that is legally available is a gargantuan challenge. Naming requires a creative, disciplined, strategic approach.

Tell the story behind your new name and it will be a memorable part of who you are.

Howard Fish
Brand Strategist
Fish Partners

The right name captures the imagination and connects with the people you want to reach.

Danny Altman
Founder and Creative Director
A Hundred Monkeys

Naming myths

Naming a company is easy, like naming a baby

Naming is a rigorous and exhaustive process. Frequently hundreds of names are reviewed prior to finding one that is legally available and works.

I will know it when I hear it

People often indicate that they will be able to make a decision after hearing a name once. In fact, good names are strategies and need to be examined, tested, sold, and proven.

We will just do the search ourselves

Various thoughtful techniques must be utilized to analyze the effectiveness of a name to ensure that its connotations are positive in the markets served.

We cannot afford to test the name

Intellectual property lawyers need to conduct extensive searches to ensure that there are no conflicting names and to make record of similar names. It is too large a risk—names need to last over time.

Just by naming a process, a level of service, or a new service feature, you are creating a valuable asset that can add to the worth of your business.

Jim Bitetto
Partner
Keusey Tutunjian & Bitetto, PC

Qualities of an effective name

Zoom, the PBS show, had a name with long legs.
Zoom brand extensions:
Zoomers
Zoomerang
ZoomNooz
Zoomzones
Zoomphenom
CafeZoom
ZoomNoodle

Birds of a feather flock together:
Twitter
Tweet
Twittersphere
Retweet

Meaningful

It communicates something about the essence of the brand. It supports the image that the company wants to convey.

Distinctive

It is unique, as well as easy to remember, pronounce, and spell. It is differentiated from the competition. It is easy to share on social networks.

Future-oriented

It positions the company for growth, change, and success. It has sustainability and preserves possibilities. It has long legs.

Modular

It enables a company to build brand extensions with ease.

Protectable

It can be owned and trademarked. A domain is available.

Positive

It has positive connotations in the markets served. It has no strong negative connotations.

Visual

It lends itself well to graphic presentation in a logo, in text, and in brand architecture.

Types of names

Founder

Many companies are named after founders: Ford, McDonald's, Christian Louboutin, Ben & Jerry's, Tory Burch. It might be easier to protect. It satisfies an ego. The downside is that it is inextricably tied to a real human being.

Descriptive

These names convey the nature of the business. Good examples are Match.com, Toys "R" Us, Petco, E*TRADE, Evernote, Ancestry.com, and Citibank. The benefit of a descriptive name is that it clearly communicates the intent of the company. The potential disadvantage is that as a company grows and diversifies, the name may become limiting.

Fabricated

A made-up name, like Pinterest, Kodak, or Activia, is distinctive and might be easier to copyright. However, a company must invest a significant amount of capital into educating its market as to the nature of the business, service, or product. Häagen-Dazs is a fabricated foreign name that has been extremely effective in the consumer market.

Metaphor

Things, places, people, animals, processes, mythological names, or foreign words are used to allude to a quality of a company. Good examples are Nike, Patagonia, Monocle, Quartz, Tesla, Kanga, Amazon.com, Hubble, and Hulu.

Acronym

These names are difficult to remember and difficult to copyright. IBM and GE became well-known only after the companies established themselves with the full spelling of their names. Acronyms are difficult to learn and require a substantial investment in advertising. Good examples are USAA, AARP, DKNY, CNN, and MoMA.

Magic spell

Some names alter a word's spelling in order to create a distinctive, protectable name, like Flickr, Tumblr, Netflix, and Google.

Combinations of the above

Some of the best names combine name types. Some good examples are Airbnb, Under Armour, Trader Joe's, Shinola Detroit, and Santa Classics. Customers and investors like names that they can understand.

Taglines

A tagline is a short phrase that captures a company's brand essence, personality, and positioning, and distinguishes the company from its competitors. Deceptively simple, taglines are not arbitrary. They grow out of an intensive strategic and creative process.

Taglines have become shorthand for what a brand stands for and delivers. Originally used in advertising as the centerpiece of a global marketing campaign, taglines historically have had much shorter life spans than logos. The best taglines have a long life, and transcend marketplace and lifestyle changes. They are meaningful and memorable, and require frequent and consistent use. Taglines like Nike's "Just do it" have become part of the popular culture. Target's tagline "Expect more. Pay less" is a brand promise to its consumers.

Brand mantras are poetry. And they are powerful tools, not just for building brands, but for building organizations.

Chris Grams
The Ad-Free Brand

Ashoka Vision

Ashoka envisions an "everyone a changemaker" world: a world that responds quickly and effectively to social challenges, and where each individual has the freedom, confidence, and societal support to address any social problem and drive change.

Essential characteristics

Short

Differentiated from its competitors

Unique

Captures the brand essence and positioning

Easy to say and remember

No negative connotations

Displayed in a small font

Can be protected and trademarked

Evokes an emotional response

Difficult to create

A tagline is a slogan, clarifier, mantra, company statement, or guiding principle that describes, synopsizes, or helps create an interest.

Debra Koontz Traverso
Outsmarting Goliath

The origin of the word "slogan" comes from the Gaelic *slaughgaiirm,* used by Scottish clans to mean "war cry."

A cross-section of taglines

Imperative: Commands action and usually starts with a verb

YouTube	Broadcast yourself
Nike	Just do it
MINI Cooper	Let's motor
Bausch + Lomb	See better. Live better.
Apple	Think different
Toshiba	Don't copy. Lead.
Virgin Mobile	Live without a plan
Unstuck	Live better everyday
Crocs	Feel the love
Coca-Cola	Open happiness

Descriptive: Describes the service, product, or brand promise

TOMS Shoes	One for one
TED	Ideas worth spreading
Ashoka	Everyone a changemaker
Philips	Innovation & You
Target	Expect more. Pay less.
Concentrics	People. Process. Results.
MSNBC	This is who we are
Ernst & Young	Building a better working world
Allstate	You're in good hands
GE	Imagination at work
Nature Conservancy	Protecting nature. Preserving life.

Superlative: Positions the company as best in class

DeBeers	A diamond is forever
BMW	The ultimate driving machine
Lufthansa	Nonstop you
National Guard	Americans at their best
Budweiser	King of beers
Adidas	Impossible is nothing

Provocative: Thought-provoking; frequently a question

Verizon Wireless	Can you hear me now?
Microsoft	Where are you going today?
Mercedes-Benz	What makes a symbol endure?
Dairy Council	Got milk?

Specific: Reveals the business category

The New York Times	All the news that's fit to print
Olay	Love the skin you're in
Volkswagen	Drivers wanted
eBay	Happy hunting
Skittles	Taste the rainbow

Staying on message

Stay on message is the brand mantra. The best brands speak with one distinctive voice. On the web, in a tweet, in a sales pitch, in a speech given by the president, the company needs to project the same unified message. It must be memorable, identifiable, and centered on the customer.

Voice and tone work harmoniously with clarity and personality to engage customers, whether they are listening, scanning, or reading.

Whether it is a call to action or a product description, language must be vital, straightforward, eloquent, and substantive.

Language and communications are intrinsic to all brand expressions. Unified, consistent high-level messages demand buy-in at all levels. Integrated communications require that content and design work together to differentiate the brand.

Vigorous writing is concise. A sentence should contain no unnecessary words, a paragraph no unnecessary sentences, for the same reason that a drawing should have no unnecessary lines and a machine no unnecessary parts.

William Strunk, Jr. and E.B. White
The Elements of Style

Let's give them something to talk about.

Bonnie Raitt

Fewer words can travel further distances.

John Maeda
Global Head
Computational Design and Inclusion
Automatic

Elevator pitch
Developed by Ilise Benun, Marketing-Mentor.com

It may sound like a paradox, but the focus of an elevator pitch should be on your customer, not you. Experiment with three different approaches to see what works best with your ideal customer.

emphasize customer needs

emphasize customer results

emphasize customer pain

Fundamental principles

Developed by Lissa Reidel, Consultant

Use language that resonates with meaning. Readers will complete the message with layers of their own experience.

Aim for clarity, brevity, and precision. A busy executive with only minutes to spare can glean what she needs to know.

Polish and cut as if you were a jeweler. Every sentence will reveal new, intriguing facets to the customer.

Cut through the clutter to produce soundbites that acquire a vibrant identity when they are heard again and again. Consistency is built on repetition.

Edit out modifying phrases, adverbs, and extraneous text. What remains is the distillation, the essence. Eliminate distracting references and the text will have impact. Less is more.

> **We had our client team take each word in the long scientific name, and put it into different parts of speech (verb, adjective, adverb, noun). It was a starting point to exploring meaning, understanding nuance, participating in discovery, and coming together as a team to discuss key messages.**
>
> Margaret Anderson
> Managing Principal
> Stellarvisions

> **Three key messages that are true, aspirational, and hashtag-worthy, will allow others to carry your brand flag.**
>
> Margie Gorman
> Communications Consultant

Powers of three

In brand communications, the unified big idea is ideally supported by three key messages.

Originally developed by Dr. Vincent Covello as a risk communications strategy, message mapping was developed because people at risk can comprehend only three messages. This thinking is helpful in brand communications and press relations.

Each word is an opportunity to be intentional

Nomenclature	Brand essence	Communications	Information	Touchpoints
Company name formal	Mission statements	Voice	Content	Websites + blogs
Company name communicative	Vision statements	Tone	Call to action	News releases
Taglines	Value propositions	Headline style	Phone numbers	FAQs
Descriptors	Key messages	Punctuation	URLs	Press kits
Product names	Guiding principles	Capitalization	Email signatures	Annual reports
Process names	Customer pledges	Emphasis	Voicemail messages	Brochures
Service names	Vocabulary	Accuracy	Abbreviations	Shareholder communications
Division names	History	Clarity	Titles	Call center scripts
	Boilerplate	Consistency	Addresses	Sales scripts
	Elevator speech		Directions	Presentations
	Hashtags			Announcements
				Blast emails
				Advertising campaigns
				Direct mail
				Product directions
				Signage
				Apps

Big idea

A big idea functions as an organizational totem pole around which strategy, behavior, actions, and communications are aligned. The big idea must be simple and transportable, and carry enough ambiguity to allow for future developments that cannot be predicted.

Sometimes the big idea becomes the tagline or the battle cry. The simplicity of the language is deceptive because the process of getting there is difficult. It requires extensive dialogue, patience, and the courage to say less.

A skilled facilitator, experienced in building consensus, is usually needed to ask the right questions and to achieve closure. The result of this work is a critical component in the realization of a compelling brand strategy and a differentiated brand identity.

Marketing without design is lifeless.
Design without marketing is mute.

Von R. Glitschka
Creative Director
Glitschka Studios

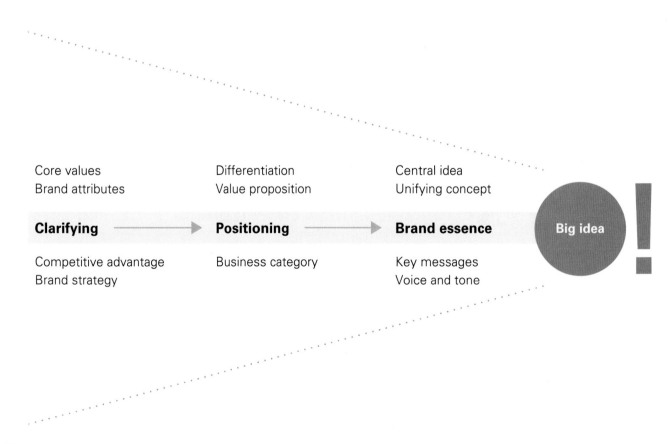

Core values	Differentiation	Central idea	
Brand attributes	Value proposition	Unifying concept	
Clarifying →	**Positioning** →	**Brand essence**	Big idea !
Competitive advantage	Business category	Key messages	
Brand strategy		Voice and tone	

Every profession in every industry in every part of the world is changing, simultaneously, because of data and artificial intelligence. We built IBM Watson for this moment. We believe that man and machine together can deliver outcomes never before possible—outcomes that will make our world healthier, safer, more productive, more creative, fairer.

Jon Iwata

SVP, Marketing and Communications IBM

IBM Smarter Planet

Buildings	Cloud	Food	Education

Cities	Energy	Public Safety	Managing Risk

Healthcare	Rails	Water	Traffic

In 2008, IBM launched the Smarter Planet campaign to explain how a whole new generation of intelligent systems and technologies could have a profound impact on the future.

In 2015, IBM began to promote the concept of cognitive business with IBM Watson at its center, redefining the relationship between man and machine.

IBM Smarter Planet: Ogilvy & Mather Worldwide   IBM Watson: IBM design team

33

Brand ideals

Ideals are essential to a responsible branding process, regardless of the size of a company or the nature of a business. These ideals hold true whether you are launching an entrepreneurial venture, creating a new product or service, repositioning an existing brand, working on a merger, or creating a retail presence.

Functional criteria do not get to the heart of brand identity. There are over one million trademarks registered with the US Patent and Trademark Office. The basic questions are what makes one better than another and why? What are the essential characteristics of the most sustainable solutions? How do we define the best identities? These ideals are not about a certain aesthetic. Design excellence is a given.

The best brands marry intelligence and insight with imagination and craft.

Connie Birdsall
Creative Director
Lippincott

Brand is more than a logo or a tagline; it is a strategic endeavor.

Michelle Bonterre
Chief Brand Officer
Dale Carnegie

Functional criteria

Bold, memorable, and appropriate	Legally protectable
Immediately recognizable	Has enduring value
Provides a consistent image of the company	Works well across media and scale
Clearly communicates the company's persona	Timeless

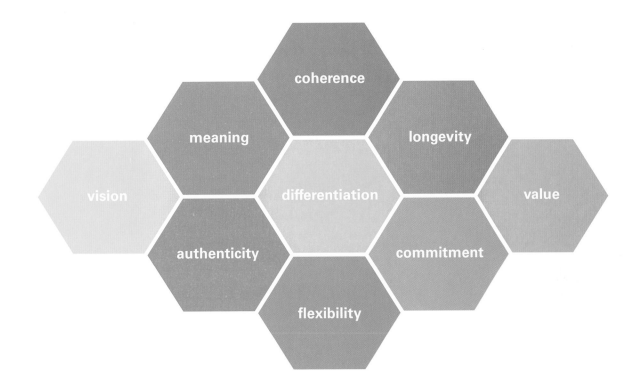

Vision

A compelling vision by an effective, articulate, and passionate leader is the foundation and the inspiration for the best brands.

Meaning

The best brands stand for something— a big idea, a strategic position, a defined set of values, a voice that stands apart.

Authenticity

Authenticity is not possible without an organization having clarity about its market, positioning, value proposition, and competitive difference.

Coherence

Whenever a customer experiences a brand, it must feel familiar and have the desired effect. Consistency does not need to be rigid or limiting in order to feel like one company.

Differentiation

Brands always compete with one another within their business category, and at some level, compete with all brands that want our attention, our loyalty, and our money.

Flexibility

An effective brand positions a company for change and growth in the future. It supports an evolving marketing strategy.

Longevity

Longevity is the ability to stay on course in a world in constant flux, characterized by future permutations that no one can predict.

Commitment

Organizations need to actively manage their assets, including the brand name, trademarks, integrated sales and marketing systems, and standards.

Value

Building awareness, increasing recognition, communicating uniqueness and quality, and expressing a competitive difference create measurable results.

Vision Brand ideal

Vision requires courage. Big ideas, enterprises, products, and services are sustained by organizations who have the ability to imagine what others cannot see and the tenacity to deliver what they believe is possible. Behind every successful brand are passionate leaders who inspire others to see the future in a new way.

Vision is the art of seeing what is invisible to others.

Jonathan Swift

The need for our mission has never been greater. If we can help kids everywhere grow smarter, stronger, and kinder, I believe we can literally help to change the world.

Jeffrey Dunn
President and CEO
Sesame Workshop

Sesame Street

Core purpose

Sesame Street revolutionized children's television and preschool education with a bold, simple idea: to educate kids in an entertaining way. Since 1969, Sesame Street has stretched to more than 150 countries around the globe, featuring a multicultural cast with a powerful and imaginative combination of media and Muppets. Indigenous co-productions reflecting local languages, customs, and educational needs have been produced for millions of children all over the world. Part of popular culture, it has always evolved to be relevant to kids' everyday lives. Its gritty and diverse landscape shows life's imperfections and challenges.

Unifying principles

Our vision is to create a better world for us all.

Our mission is to help kids grow smarter, stronger, and kinder.

Our promise is to educate preschoolers by using our proven recipe for success.

Our impact is grounded in rigorous research and close collaborations.

Our success is reflected in the faces of millions of children around the globe.

The heart of Sesame Street comes from its lovable, huggable Muppets, who connect with the child in each of us.

   SABAI SABAI SESAME **SESAME PARK**

Afghanistan Bangladesh Brazil Cambodia Canada China

  5, RUE SESAME **SESAMSTRASSE** **SZEZÁM UTCA**

Denmark Egypt France Germany Hungary Arab Gulf States

SZEZÁM UTCA **JALAN SESAMA**   **PLAZA SÉSAMO**

Hungary India Indonesia Israel Jordan Latin America

 SESAME SQUARE **SESAME TREE** **SESAM STASJON** **SESAME!**

The Netherlands Nigeria Northern Ireland Norway Palestine The Philippines

 **TAKALANI SESAME** **BARRIO SÉSAMO** **SVENSKA SESAM** **SUSAM SOKAGI**

Poland Russia South Africa Spain Sweden Turkey

It began with a simple but powerful idea. We have taken our proven model across the globe. The heart of Sesame Street comes from its lovable, huggable Muppets, who connect with the child in each of us.

I thought we were creating the quintessential American show. It turned out that they were the most international characters ever created.

What we want to do is see if we can affect the new media the way we affected television. We want to introduce educational value without taking the fun away.

I was really influenced to try to do something good in my life, to try to make a difference. I think when I heard educational television, I thought I could make a difference there.

Joan Ganz Cooney
Founder
Sesame Street

Meaning Brand ideal

The best brands stand for something: a big idea, a strategic position, a defined set of values, a voice that stands apart. Symbols are vessels for meaning. They become more powerful with frequent use and when people understand what they stand for. They are the fastest form of communication known to man. Meaning is rarely immediate and evolves over time.

People don't buy what you do; they buy why you do it. And what you do simply proves what you believe.

Simon Sinek
Start with Why: How Great Leaders Inspire Everyone to Take Action

Stand for something

Meaning drives creativity

Designers distill meaning into unique visual form and expression. It is critical that this meaning is explained so that it can be understood, communicated, and approved. All elements of the brand identity system should have a framework of meaning and logic.

Meaning evolves over time

As companies grow, their businesses may change significantly. Similarly, the meaning assigned to a brandmark will probably evolve from its original intention. The logo is the most visible and frequent reminder of what the brand stands for.

Meaning builds consensus

Meaning is like a campfire: it's a rallying point used to build consensus with a group of decision makers. Agreement on brand essence and attributes builds critical synergy and precedes any presentation of visual solutions, naming conventions, or key messages.

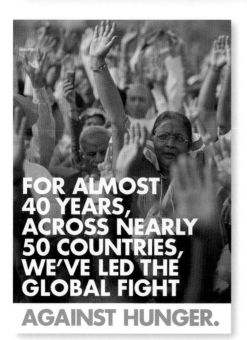

**FOR FOOD.
AGAINST HUNGER
AND MALNUTRITION.**

**FOR CLEAN WATER.
AGAINST KILLER DISEASES.**

**FOR CHILDREN THAT GROW
UP STRONG.
AGAINST LIVES CUT SHORT.**

**FOR CROPS THIS YEAR,
AND NEXT.
AGAINST DROUGHT
AND DISASTER.**

**FOR CHANGING MINDS.
AGAINST IGNORANCE
AND INDIFFERENCE.**

**FOR FREEDOM FROM HUNGER.
FOR EVERYONE. FOR GOOD.**

**FOR ACTION.
AGAINST HUNGER.**

**We were looking for a
rallying cry that could work
in dozens of languages, and
realized that there is a "for"
and "against" in every
language.**

Michael Johnson
Founder
Johnson Banks

Action Against Hunger's new
symbol replaces the ambi-
guity of the old by simply
representing two key ele-
ments of their work—food
and water—while tweaking
and adapting the core colors.
As one employee pointed out,
"If we're driving into a war
zone in Mali and people can't
read our logo, at least they
should be able to recognize
our symbol." The symbol can
also be incorporated into the
typography in certain
applications.

Action Against Hunger: Johnson Banks

Authenticity Brand ideal

In psychology, authenticity refers to self-knowledge. Organizations who know who they are and what they stand for start the identity process from a position of strength. They build brands that are sustainable and genuine. Brand expression must be congruent with the organization's unique mission, target market, culture, values, and personality.

Know thyself.

Plato
First Alcibiades

As reality is qualified, altered, and commercialized, consumers respond to what is engaging, personal, memorable, and above all, what they perceive as authentic.

B. Joseph Pine II
Authenticity

Authenticity, for me, is doing what you promise, not "being who you are."

Seth Godin

logo

look and feel

targeted messages

core messages

we know who we are

We are the only company that is serving the underserved. By focusing on the problem, not the product, we are able to innovate in ways that other people are not.

Tristan Walker
Founder
Walker & Company

Bevel Shave System

Walker & Company's ambitious goal is to make health and beauty simple for people of color. Bevel, its flagship brand, is disrupting the online shaving club market—its target consumers are still very traumatized by a razor, because they have historically been served tools that are not designed for them. They founded their company to challenge the "ethnic aisle," where products geared toward ethnic minorities are marketed.

Coherence Brand ideal

Whether a customer is using a product, talking to a service rep, or making a purchase on her iPhone, the brand should feel familiar. Coherence is the quality that ensures that all the pieces hold together in a way that feels seamless to the customer. It doesn't need to be rigid and limiting—rather, it is a baseline designed to build trust, foster loyalty, and delight the customer.

The most successful brands are completely coherent. Every aspect of what they do and what they are reinforces everything else.

Wally Olins
Brand Strategist

How is coherence achieved?

Unified voice, a dynamic central idea

Every communication uses a consistent voice and evolves from a central dynamic idea.

One company strategy

As companies diversify into new areas of business, consistency jumpstarts awareness and acceptance of new initiatives.

Every touchpoint

Coherence emerges from understanding the needs and preferences of the target customer. Every touchpoint is considered a brand experience.

Look and feel

A brand identity system is unified visually, utilizing a cohesive brand architecture and specially designed colors, typeface families, and formats.

Uniform quality

A high and uniform level of quality imparts a degree of care that is given to each of the company's products and services. Anything less than superior quality reduces the value of the asset.

Clarity and simplicity

Using clear language consistently to communicate about products and services helps the customer navigate choices.

The Mall of America experience is never static; the landmark destination is always new. The identity system is ever changing, and reflects the dynamism of the mall.

Joe Duffy
Chairman & Chief Creative Officer
Duffy & Partners

Mall of America is the largest shopping and entertainment complex in North America. The mall, a top American tourist and vacation destination, is located in Bloomington, Minnesota, and attracts over 30 million visitors a year.

Mall of America: Duffy & Partners

43

Flexibility Brand ideal

Innovation requires brands to be flexible. No one can say with certainty which new products or services a company might offer in five years. Or for that matter, what devices we will all be using and how we will be purchasing our worldly goods. Brands need to be agile to quickly seize new opportunities in the marketplace.

Unify. Simplify. Amplify.

Ken Carbone
Cofounder
Carbone Smolan Agency

Credit Suisse is a global financial services company with over 530 offices in fifty countries. Carbone Smolan Agency used a bold new color palette to create an image bank organized by subjects, ranging from clients and lifestyles, to metaphorical ideas and concepts.

The new Credit Suisse brand added new energy, new quality, and new relevance to our corporate design system.

Ramona Boston
Global Head of Branding & Communications
Credit Suisse

We unified the Credit Suisse brand with a vibrant system to accentuate Credit Suisse's competitive advantage.

Leslie Smolan
Cofounder
Carbone Smolan Agency

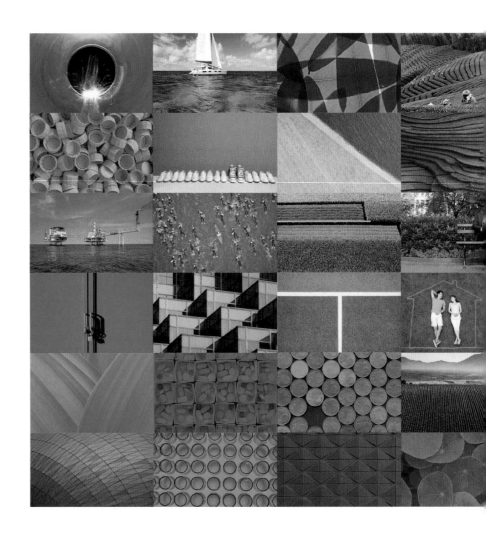

Marketing flexibility

An effective identity positions a company for change and growth in the future. It needs to be a workhorse in a wide range of customer touchpoints, from the website to an invoice to a vehicle or retail environment. A good system embraces the evolution of marketing strategies and methods.

Brand architecture

The marketing of any new product or service is facilitated by a durable brand architecture and an overarching logic to anticipate the future.

Fresh, relevant, and recognizable

A carefully designed balance between control and creativity makes it possible to adhere to the identity standards while achieving specific marketing objectives, keeping the brand immediately recognizable.

Credit Suisse: Carbone Smolan Agency

45

Commitment Brand ideal

A brand is an asset that needs to be protected, preserved, and nurtured. Actively managing the asset requires a top-down mandate and a bottom-up understanding of why it's important. Building, protecting, and enhancing the brand requires desire and a disciplined approach to insure its integrity and relevance.

A decision is made with the brain.
A commitment is made with the heart.

Nido Qubein

True to our Real Beauty Pledge, Dove remains committed to only feature real women, to never digitally alter their appearance, and to help the next generation develop a positive relationship with beauty. And, we are taking our leadership to the next level.

Nick Soukas
VP of Marketing
Dove

Dove has reached 20 million young people with self-esteem education and they are committed to reaching another 20 million by 2020.

#RealBeauty

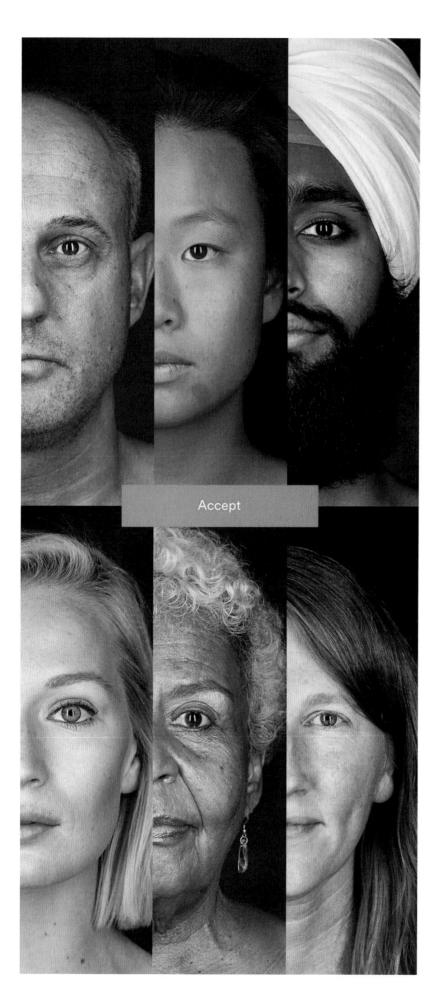

Accept

Airbnb, the world's largest community-driven hospitality company with unique listings in over 190 countries, launched a comprehensive review of its platform in an effort to fight bias and discrimination. In response to the review's findings, it wanted to ensure that everyone who uses Airbnb agrees to a stronger, more detailed nondiscrimination policy. Airbnb began to ask each host and guest to agree to the Airbnb Community Commitment, which says:

I agree to treat everyone in the Airbnb community— regardless of their race, religion, national origin, ethnicity, disability, sex, gender identity, sexual orientation, or age—with respect, and without judgment or bias.

Agreeing to the Community Commitment also means agreeing to adhere to Airbnb's nondiscrimination policy. If anyone chooses to decline, they will not be able to host or book using Airbnb.

#weaccept

Value Brand ideal

Creating value is the indisputable goal of most organizations. The quest for sustainability has expanded the value conversation with consumers. Being socially responsible, environmentally conscious, and profitable is the new business model for all brands. A brand is an intangible asset—brand identity, which includes all tangible expression from packaging to websites, upholds that value.

Business serves more than just shareholders— it has an equal responsibility to the community and to the planet.

Rose Marcario
CEO
Patagonia

Brand identity is an asset

Brand identity is a strategic business tool and an asset that seizes every opportunity to build awareness, increase recognition, communicate uniqueness and quality, and express a competitive difference. Adherence to brand identity, uniform standards, and the relentless pursuit of quality are business priorities.

Value is preserved through legal protection

Trademarks and trade dress are protected in the range of markets that are served, both local and global. Employees and vendors are educated about compliance issues.

Founded in 2000, Method is the pioneer of premium planet-friendly and design-driven home, fabric, and personal care products. The eco-friendly products are made with naturally derived, biodegradable, non-toxic ingredients.

Method was one of the first Cradle to Cradle–endorsed companies, with thirty-seven C2C certified products at launch, among the most of any company in the world. Method, a founding B Corporation, makes social and environmental change a company objective.

Method's iconic teardrop bottle, designed by Karim Rashid, revolutionized the cleaning category with its beauty and style. Method can be found in more than 40,000 retail locations throughout North America, Europe, Australia, and Asia.

Differentiation Brand ideal

Bumper-to-bumper brands clamor for our attention. The world is a noisy place filled with a panoply of choices. Why should consumers choose one brand over others? It is not enough to be different. Brands need to demonstrate their difference and make it easy for customers to understand that difference.

An excessive abundance of choices and options in every aspect of life—from the mundane to the momentous—is causing anxiety, perpetual stress, and actually diminishing our sense of well-being. The best companies of our time help "curate" their offerings.

Paul Laudicina
Chairman Emeritus
A.T. Kearney

In order to be irreplaceable, one must always be different.

Coco Chanel
House of Chanel

When everybody zigs, zag.

Marty Neumeier
Zag

Our approach allowed the packaging and the mango to appear as the hero while allowing us to tell stories and add moments of humor.

Jessica Walsh

Partner
Sagmeister & Walsh

Frooti is one of India's oldest and most loved mango juice brands. For the first time in thirty years, Frooti unveiled a new logo, and asked Sagmeister & Walsh to design a fresh, bold, and playful visual language for a brand launch campaign across print, social, web, games, and a television commercial. Sagmeister & Walsh created a miniature world using tiny-scaled models of vehicles, people, and plant life. Only the Frooti packaging and mangos were kept in real-life scale.

Frooti campaign:
Sagmeister & Walsh
Special Guest
Stoopid Buddy Stoodios

Frooti logo: Pentagram

Brands are messengers of trust. We are all moving at blinding speed and our institutions, technology, science, lifestyles, and vocabulary are in a state of continuous flux. Consumers are reassured by trademarks that are recognizable and familiar. Durability is achieved through a commitment to the equity of a central idea over time, and the capacity to transcend change.

The Morton Salt Girl has lived for over a century. And she doesn't look a day over nine years old.

Morton Salt

1914   1921   1933   1941

Trademarks and their date of origination

Löwenbräu	1383	Morton Salt	1914	Eastman Kodak	1971
Guinness	1862	IBM	1924	Nike	1971
Olympics	1865	Greyhound	1926	Quaker Oats	1972
Mitsubishi	1870	London Underground	1933	United Way	1974
Nestlé	1875	Volkswagen	1938	Dunkin' Donuts	1974
Bass Ale	1875	IKEA	1943	I Love NY	1975
John Deere	1876	CBS	1951	PBS	1976
American Red Cross	1881	NBC	1956	Apple	1977
Johnson & Johnson	1886	Chase Manhattan	1960	AT&T	1984
Coca-Cola	1887	International Paper	1960	Amazon	1994
General Electric	1892	Motorola	1960	Google	1998
Prudential	1896	UPS	1961	Wikipedia	2001
Michelin	1896	McDonald's	1962	LinkedIn	2002
Shell	1900	General Foods	1962	Facebook	2004
Nabisco	1900	Wool Bureau	1964	Airbnb	2008
Ford	1903	Mobil	1965	Uber	2009
Rolls-Royce	1905	Metropolitan Life	1967	Pinterest	2010
Mercedes-Benz	1911	L'eggs	1971	Instagram	2010

In 2014, Morton Salt celebrated its 100th anniversary by refreshing the brand and introducing a new packaging system. Pause for Thought evolved the Umbrella Girl in small and subtle ways, with cleaner linework and a hint of a smile.

1956

1968

2014

Morton Salt: Pause for Thought

Brandmarks

Designed with an almost infinite variety of shapes and personalities, brandmarks can be assigned to a number of general categories. From literal through symbolic, from word-driven to image-driven, the world of brandmarks expands each day.

The boundaries among these categories are pliant, and many marks may combine elements of more than one category. Although there are no hard-and-fast rules to determine the best type of visual identifier for a particular type of company, the designer's process is to examine

a range of solutions based on both aspirational and functional criteria. The designer should determine a design approach that best serves the needs of the client and create a rationale for each distinct approach.

Make every mark count.

Dennis Kuronen

Signature

A signature is the structured relationship between a logotype, brandmark, and tagline. Some programs accommodate split signatures that allow the mark and the logotype to be separated. Other variations may include a vertical or horizontal signature that allows choices based on application need.

Signature

Brandmark Logotype

The original Red Cross mark was designed in 1863 by Henri Dunant.

54

Topology of marks

Wordmarks

A freestanding acronym, company name, or product name that has been designed to convey a brand attribute or positioning

examples: Google, eBay, Tate, Nokia, MoMA, Pinterest, FedEx, Samsung, Etsy, Coca-Cola

Letterforms

A unique design using one or more letterforms that act as a mnemonic device for a company name

examples: Unilever, Univision, Tory Burch, Flipboard, B Corporation, HP, Tesla

Synonyms

Brandmark

Trademark

Symbol mark

Identity

Logo

Pictorial marks

An immediately recognizable literal image that has been simplified and stylized

examples: Apple, NBC, CBS, Polo, Lacoste, Greyhound, Twitter

Abstract/symbolic marks

A symbol that conveys a big idea, and often embodies strategic ambiguity

examples: Chase, Sprint, Nike, HSBC, Merck

Emblems

A mark in which the company name is inextricably connected to a pictorial element or form

examples: KIND, TiVo, OXO, LEED, Elmer's, UNIQLO, IKEA

Wordmarks

A wordmark is a freestanding word or words. It may be a company name or an acronym. The best wordmarks imbue a legible word or words with distinctive font characteristics, and may integrate abstract elements or pictorial elements. The IBM acronym has transcended enormous technological change in its industry.

The new identity helped reposition Sonos from a technology brand beloved by in the know audiophiles to a company of broader appeal, focused on experience and originality.

Bruce Mau Design

Sonos: Bruce Mau Design

IBM: Paul Rand
MoMA: Matthew Carter

Braun: Wolfgang Schmittel
redesign
Sasaki: Bruce Mau Design

Tate: North Design
Barnes: Pentagram

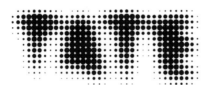 

Pinterest: Michael Deal and
Juan Carlos Pagan
Sonos: Bruce Mau Design

Shinola Detroit: Bedrock
Netflix: Netflix

Letterform marks

The single letter is frequently used by designers as a distinctive graphic focal point for a brandmark. The letter is always a unique and proprietary design that is infused with significant personality and meaning. The letterform acts as a mnemonic device, and is easy to apply to an app icon.

For McDonald's sponsorship of the Green Bay Packers, Moroch Partners created a clever giveaway for fans that looks like McDonald's famous fries. Seven thousand pairs were handed out at Packers' home games. They've been featured on more than 3,000 blogs and have earned upwards of 34 million Twitter impressions.

Pictorial marks

A pictorial mark uses a literal and recognizable image. The image itself may allude to the name of the company or its mission, or it may be symbolic of a brand attribute. The simpler the form, the more difficult it is to draw. The most skillful designers know how to translate and simplify, play with light and shadow, and balance positive and negative space.

OneVoice: Sagmeister & Walsh

The OneVoice Movement is a global initiative that supports grassroots activists in Israel, Palestine, and internationally who are working to build the human infrastructure needed to create the necessary conditions for a just and negotiated resolution to the Israeli-Palestinian conflict.

We tried to avoid traditional peace iconography. Our symbol simply depicts people from different sides working together to create something beautiful.

Stefan Sagmeister
Creative Director/ Partner
Sagmeister + Walsh

Pictorial marks

From left to right:

Dropbox: Dropbox Creative Team

Evernote: Evernote Creative Team

NBC: Chermayeff & Geismar

Starbucks: Starbucks Global Creative Studio with Lippincott

Shell: Raymond Loewy

Twitter: Pepco Studio

Smithsonian: Chermayeff & Geismar

The WILD Center: Fish Partners

Fork in the Road Foods: Studio Hinrichs

MailChimp: Jon Hicks

Paul Frank: Pauk Frank Sunich, Park La Fun

SurveyMonkey: SurveyMonkey

CBS: William Golden

Apple: Rob Janoff

Crocs: Matthew Ebbing

Below:

The Nature Conservancy: In-house Design

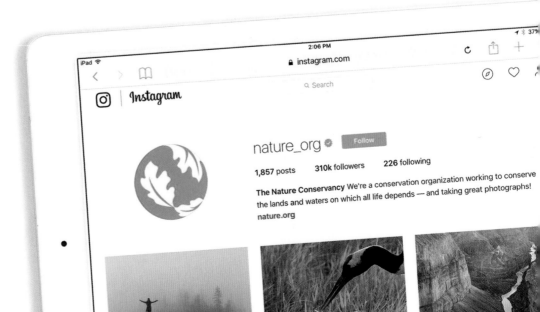

Abstract marks

An abstract mark uses visual form to convey a big idea or a brand attribute. These marks, by their nature, can provide strategic ambiguity, and work effectively for large companies with numerous and unrelated divisions. Abstract marks are especially effective for service-based and technology companies; however, they are extremely difficult to design well.

Grupo Imagen is a new Mexican media conglomerate that unites several major online, print, radio, and television brands under a single banner, with programing in news, entertainment, sports, and lifestyle.

Highlighting the company's central theme of inclusion and diversity, the new symbol brings together two fundamentally different geometric shapes to create a letterform.

Sagi Haviv
Partner
Chermayeff & Geismar & Haviv

Grupo Imagen: Chermayeff & Geismar & Haviv

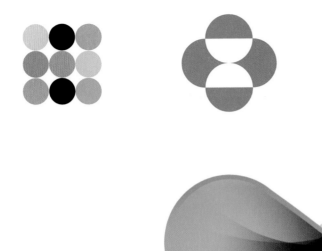

Abstract marks

From left to right:

Hyatt Place: Lippincott

Merck:
Chermayeff & Geismar

NO MORE: Sterling Brands

Novvi: Liquid Agency

MIT Media Labs: TheGreenEyl

Time Warner:
Chermayeff & Geismar

Alina Wheeler: Rev Group

Darien Library: Steff Geissbuhler

Captive Resources:
Crosby Associates

Criativia: Criativia Brand Studio

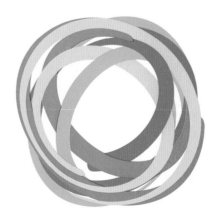

Emblems

Emblems are trademarks featuring a shape inextricably connected to the name of the organization. The elements are never isolated. Emblems look terrific on a package, as a sign, or as an embroidered patch on a uniform. As mobile devices continue to shrink, the emblem presents the biggest legibility challenge when miniaturized.

From the healthy snacks we make to the way we work, live, and give back, our focus is on making the world a little kinder, one snack and act at a time (no arm-twisting here, promise). One simple belief underpins it all: There's more to business than just profit.

Kind Healthy Snacks

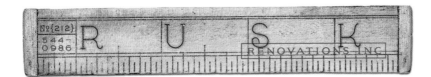

Rusk Renovations:
Louise Fili Ltd.

IKEA: Unknown

Design Within Reach: Pentagram

KIND: Unknown

I Love NY: Milton Glaser

UNIQLO: Kashiwa Sato

TOMS Shoes: Unknown

Ohio & Erie Canalway:
Cloud Gehshan

Brooklyn Brewery: Milton Glaser

Dynamic marks

Creativity always finds a way to challenge convention. Historically brand equity has been achieved in part by the frequency and global reach of a single icon, like Apple's trademark or Nike's swoosh. As life becomes more digital, designers have found new ways to express big ideas. Engineers are beginning to partner with creative teams to craft and program the future.

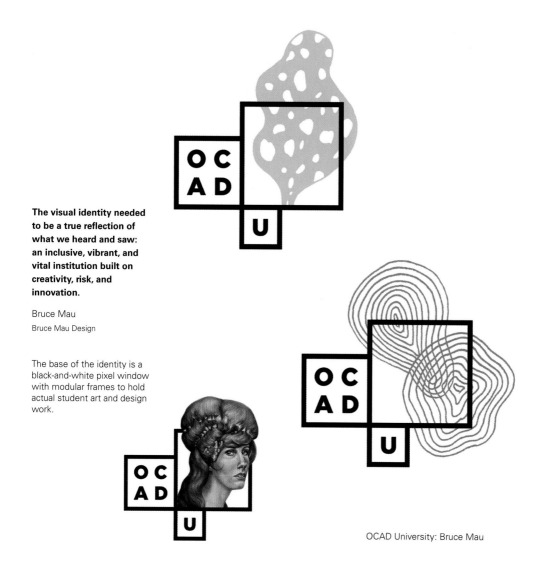

The visual identity needed to be a true reflection of what we heard and saw: an inclusive, vibrant, and vital institution built on creativity, risk, and innovation.

Bruce Mau
Bruce Mau Design

The base of the identity is a black-and-white pixel window with modular frames to hold actual student art and design work.

OCAD University: Bruce Mau

Philadelphia Museum of Art

Philadelphia Museum of Art

Philadelphia Museum of Art

Philadelphia Museum of Art

Philadelphia Museum of Art: Pentagram

Characters

It's alive! A character trademark embodies brand attributes or values. Characters quickly become the stars of ad campaigns, and the best ones become cultural icons. Along with their distinctive appearance and personality, many characters have recognizable voices and jingles, enabling them to leap off the silent shelf space into your life.

While the ideas that drive the personification may be timeless and universal, characters rarely age well and usually need to be redrawn and dragged into contemporary culture. The Michelin Man, well over one hundred years old, has been modified numerous times. As moms became working women, Betty Crocker was caught between generations. The Columbia Pictures goddess received a major face-lift, but she has never looked happy and satisfied holding that torch. Each Olympics creates a mascot that will be animated and reanimated in thousands of stuffed animals. Who knew a gecko could sell car insurance?

Poppin' Fresh, more widely known as the Pillsbury Doughboy, is an advertising icon and mascot of the Pillsbury Company. In 1965, Rudolph Perz, a copywriter working on the Pillsbury account for Leo Burnett advertising agency in Chicago, came up with the idea for the brand mascot, who would pop out of a can of refrigerated dough. The character's name was a nod to the product's quality and freshness.

Image courtesy of Pillsbury and General Mills

Historic characters

Character	Company	Year created
Uncle Sam	US Government	1838
Aunt Jemima	PepsiCo.	1893
Michelin Man	Michelin	1898
Mr. Peanut	Planters	1916
Betty Crocker	General Mills	1921
Reddy Kilowatt	Electric company	1926
Jolly Green Giant	B&G Foods	1928
Leo the Lion	MGM Pictures	1928
Mickey Mouse	Walt Disney Co.	1928
Windy	Zippo	1937
Rosie the Riveter	US Government	1943
Smokey the Bear	US Forest Service	1944
Elmer the Bull	Elmer's Glue	1947
Tony the Tiger	Kellogg	1951
Trix the Bunny	General Mills	1960
Charlie the Tuna	StarKist	1961
Columbia Goddess	Columbia Pictures Corporation	1961
Ronald McDonald	McDonald's	1963
Pillsbury Doughboy	General Mills	1965
Ernie Keebler & the elves	Kellogg	1969
Nesquik Bunny	Nesquik	1970s
Energizer Bunny	Eveready Energizer	1989
Jeeves	Ask Jeeves	1996
AFLAC duck	AFLAC Insurance	2000
Gecko	GEICO	2002

The Gecko has a Cockney accent and has starred in television and advertising campaigns. Geico was the first auto insurance company to invest in advertising.

The GEICO Gecko: The Martin Agency

Trends

The next big thing is already happening. Society is evolving unpredictably from moment to moment. As the market transforms itself, the best brands innovate continuously in response to social change, technology, popular culture, research, and the political landscape. Great brands acknowledge our paradoxical nostalgia for a simpler past to cushion us from relentless change.

Change almost never fails because it's too early. It almost always fails because it's too late.

Seth Godin
Tribes

A fusion of technologies is blurring the lines between the physical, digital, and biological spheres.

Sergei Brin
Google Cofounder and Alphabet President

Technology changes faster than people.

Derek Thompson
Hit Makers: The Science of Popularity in an Age of Distraction

Samsung's Gear VR helps customers do and discover what they've only dreamed about and go where they've never been.

Photo: © 2017 Jason Nocito; Design: Turner Duckworth

70

Artificial intelligence
AlphaGo
Google
Spotify

Big data
IBM Watson
Starbucks
T-Mobile

Chatbots
Mitsuku
Meekan for Slack
Chatshopper for Facebook

Cloud services
Amazon Web Services
Microsoft Azure
IBM Cloud

Crowdsourcing
DonorsChoose
Kickstarter
Indiegogo

Drones/personal video
DJI
GoPro

Gender fluidity
Cover Girl
David Bowie
Louis Vuitton
Saint Harridan

Functional fabrics
Mood sweater
Sensoree GER

Internet of things
Amazon Echo
Google Home
Nest

Mindfulness
Buddhify
Calm
Headspace

Mobile health
Asthmapolis
Personal KinetiGraph

New friends
Alexa
Siri

On demand
Enjoy
Shyp
Postmates

Online reviews
Angie's List
TripAdvisor
Yelp

Quantified self
Mint
MoodPanda

Robotics
Robosapien
Roomba
Sphero SPRK

Scrapbooks
Curalate
Pinterest
Tumblr

Sharing economy
Airbnb
DogVaCay
Lyft

Space
SpaceX
Virgin Atlantic

Subscription boxes
Birchbox
Blue Apron
Stitch Fix

Virtual reality
Magic Leap
Microsoft HoloLens
Oculus Rift

Wearable technology
Apple Watch
Snapchat Spectacles

3-D printing
Formlabs
LulzBot
MakerBot

Social robots will interact with people, not just replace them. Human and machine will partner to provide products and services in ways we haven't before—each providing its own strengths.

Richard Yonck
Futurist
Intelligent Future Consulting

Top 25 Unicorns 2016

Unicorns are start-up companies valued at more than a billion dollars.

Making a difference

Making a difference has become essential to building a brand. Consumers are shopping their values, and businesses are rethinking their value propositions. The triple bottom line— people, planet, profit—is a new business model that represents a fundamental shift in how businesses measure success.

Historically, the purpose of business has been to create shareholder value. The new imperative integrates economic prosperity with protecting the environment and demonstrating care for communities and employees. For many, sustainability will require radical innovation: retooling what they make, how they make it, and how it is distributed. A new generation of companies envisions sustainability as the core purpose of their brand promise. Authenticity is critical. Social networks quickly broadcast brands that don't stand true to their promise.

The least I can do is speak out for those who cannot speak for themselves.

Jane Goodall
Founder
The Jane Goodall Institute

Sustainability

Develop new business model.
Innovate responsibly.
Build community and volunteer.
Reduce carbon footprint.
Design smarter.
Rethink product life cycle.
Create long-term value.
Redesign manufacturing process.
Eliminate waste.
Do no harm.
Instigate meaningful change.
Make theory action.
Use energy efficiently.
Look at material alternatives.
Use renewable resources.
Value health and well-being.
Evaluate supply chain.
Rethink packaging and products.
Promote environmental awareness.
Do business with integrity.
Educate about sustainability.
Reuse, recycle, renew.
Promote credible certification.
Think people, planet, profit.
Revisit your mission.
Commit to core values.
Set environmental policy.
Demand transparency.
Evaluate business practices.
Set benchmarks for progress.
Create healthy workspaces.
Redefine prosperity.
Buy fair and buy local.

The Jane Goodall Institute has fought to protect apes and primates from disease and trafficking.

In 2004, a group of Guatemalan leaders of the Fundación Proyecto de Vida asked Bruce Mau Design to assist in producing a vision for the future of Guatemala, as a way to galvanize action and create a positive movement for the country going forward, after three decades of civil war. The multifaceted vision needed to embrace many initiatives across different regions in Guatemala, incorporate many partners, and resonate internationally.

Although the work began as a visual identity and communications strategy, it is an example of how creative and analytical thinking in the design process can be applied to cultural, political, and behavioral problems.

Of course, we can't solve Guatemala's problems—that can only be accomplished by Guatemalans. But by sharing our communication tools, we can help. What could be better than that?

Bruce Mau

Guateamala: Bruce Mau Design

CULTURA DEL APRENDIZAJE
Expandiendo nuestra capacidad para aprender continuamente.

Join the mass teaching session for mothers. Learn

Big data analytics

As you design the brands of the future, armies of algorithms will be eager to work in your stead. Big ideas and brand strategy still require strategic imagination, and need a human-in-the-loop. Big data is getting bigger every nano-second (think zettabytes). Each advance in brand analytics, machine learning, and artificial intelligence brings us closer to predicting the future, and making better decisions for designing and optimizing the customer experience.

Big data is arriving from multiple sources at an alarming velocity, volume, and variety.

www.ibm.com

Be familiar with your organization's priorities and objectives in data gathering. Designers do not need to be data scientists, but building an agile brand requires knowing how to interpret the data and having a seat at the table.

Gaemer Gutierrez
Creative Director
Store Brand Portfolio
CVS Health

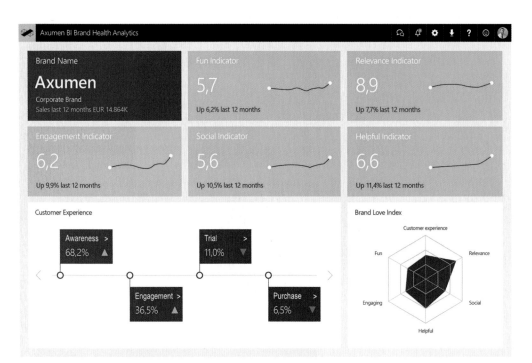

Brand touchpoints leave digital fingerprints, transforming brands into clusters of data. Advanced analytics and artificial intelligence transform these clusters into actionable insights and predictions.

Anders Braekken
CEO & Founder
Axumen Intelligence

Data visualization is crucial for both discovering patterns and behavior, and obtaining unique and compelling insights.

Digital fingerprints

Axumen Intelligence

Post ratings and reviews of products and services

Publish own website

Publish own blog

Write and edit articles on Wikipedia

Read customer reviews and ratings

Social media likes, follows, and shares

Write comments and updates on social media

Recommend and refer sites and posts to friends and family

Participate in online forums

Comment on other people's blogs

Read, write, and retweet on Twitter

Publish photos on media like Instagram

Listen to podcasts and webinars

Use news aggregators such as Google News

Upload video content to YouTube

Post own online articles and stories

Data basic concepts
Developed by Ramesh Dontha, Managing Partner, Digital Transformation Pro

Descriptive analytics

Descriptive analytics describe the past and provide historical insights into an organization's operations (brand performance, marketing ROI, finance, sales, human capital, inventory, and so on).

Predictive analytics

Predictive analytics are not about predicting the future accurately, but rather forecasting with probabilities of what might happen.

Prescriptive analytics

Prescriptive analytics advise on possible courses of action given the probable outcomes and what might happen with those courses of action.

Algorithm

An algorithm is a mathematical formula or statistical process used to perform an analysis of data.

Data mining

Data mining is about finding meaningful patterns and deriving insights in large sets of data using sophisticated pattern recognition techniques.

Cloud computing

Cloud computing is essentially software and/or data hosted and running on remote servers and accessible from anywhere on the internet.

Machine learning

Machine learning is a method of designing systems that can learn, adjust, and improve based on the data fed to them.

Structured vs. unstructured data

Structured data is any information that can be put into relational databases. Unstructured data is everything that can't—email messages, social media posts, recorded human speech, and so on.

The analytics continuum

© 2014 Gartner

Social media

Social media has become the fastest-growing budget in the marketing arsenal. While there is still much debate about how to measure the financial return on social, one thing is clear: consumers have become active participants in the brand-building process. Retweets work at speeds much faster than the rollout of a global marketing campaign. Everyone is a player, producer, director, and distributor.

And in the end, the love you take is equal to the love you make.

The Beatles

Earn the respect and recommendation of your customers. They will do your marketing for you, for free. Great service starts great conversations.

Andy Sernovitz
Word of Mouth Marketing

Measuring success

Quantitative
Fans/followers
Shares
Likes
Comments
Traffic/visitors
Clicks/conversions
Views

Qualitative
Engagement
Conversation quality
Fan loyalty
Insights/research value
Word of mouth
Brand reputation
Influence

Social media categories

Communication
Blogs
Microblogs
Forums
Social networks
Collaboration
Wikis
Social bookmarks
Social news aggregators
Reviews
Messaging
Chat rooms

Entertainment
Photo sharing
Video sharing
Livecasting
Audio and music sharing
Virtual worlds
Games

Rules for brands on social

Developed by Caroline Tiger, Content Strategist

Be choosy

Depending on resources and objectives, limit your number of platforms. Where does your target audience live? How many channels can your team handle well?

Calendar, calendar, calendar

Plan your messaging and your editorial and social schedules side-by-side a year out. (This calendar is a living document.)

Have sub-strategies

Beneath your umbrella strategy, devise clear ones for each channel. Maybe Facebook is for employee engagement, LinkedIn is for sharing industry news, and Twitter is for customer service.

Repeat after me: Repurpose!

One video interview can yield a blog series, a podcast episode, short video clips, a download, quotes for #mondaymotivation on Instagram, and so on.

Hire former journalists

They know how to find the golden nuggets.

Adhere to the 80/20 rule

80 percent content curation and community building; 20 percent self-promotion.

Watch the auto-posting

Be ready to jump in and turn off auto-updates during times of crisis or opportunity.

Establish a brand voice and stick to it

Your tone may vary, but your company's voice needs to remain consistent across all channels.

Add bling

Ideally each post you send out has a visual. (A graphic designer or someone with basic design skills is essential to a social media team.)

Always be learning

This field is ever-changing—cultivate a hunger for discovery and a willingness to evolve.

Tessa Wheeler on Snapchat

Smartphones

Devices have become second nature. Wherever we go, they go. We text like mad, check email at midnight, compare prices, watch Netflix, read the news, and conduct business. Everything we need fits in our pockets. Devices are our shopping malls, mini-universities, and spas for our minds. Siri eagerly waits to serve us, while armies of algorithms watch our every move.

What did people do with their idle time in supermarket lines and trains before there were apps?

Kevin Lee
Technologist

The web has moved beyond the desktop, and it's not turning back.

Ethan Marcotte
Responsive Web Design

A successful interaction should be easy and intuitive, but success differs depending on method of interaction and device you're designing for—voice, wearable, touch, mobile, desktop, or a future technology yet to be invented.

Vijay Mathews
Creative Director and Partner
W&CO

Fundamentals of responsive design
Developed by Vijay Mathews, Creative Director and Partner, W&CO

Adopt a flexible approach to web design to address the variety of current device formats and to adapt to future formats.

Maintain a clear relationship between the families of resolutions to reinforce a visual recognition of the site.

Design for the device and format with the greatest constraints to define parameters that will roll out to the other resolutions.

Take advantage of each device's physical properties and inputs to develop more native experience. (Not everything is point-and-click now).

Structure the access of content to respond to environments and behaviors. The user's environment can dictate the user's content needs, be it on the go or sitting at home.

Establish a clear hierarchy of information that lends itself to an intuitive user experience and a fluid relationship between formats.

While the identity for the AIGA 2016 Design Conference was being designed by Mother NY, W&CO began developing a flexible, customizable event site builder and native (iOS/Android) app platform. Included were videos, social integration, and detailed speaker and event information with search and filter functionality. The app experience utilizes mobile features such as adding events to your calendar, real-time voting and feedback, and using GPS to view your location on a venue map.

AIGA Conference:
W&CO and MotherNY

79

Apps

Apps have become a necessity. Like the best brands, you can't imagine life without them. Housed in a digital curio cabinet of collectibles, our choices reveal who we are, what we value, and how we manage our priorities. More than two million small bits of affordable software have a wide range of functionality and interactivity.

The best apps are the ones that become part of your daily routine and life.

Kevin Lee
Technologist

Best app qualities

Developed by Andrew Gazdecki
CEO, Bizness Apps

Reliable and consistent performance; carefully tested and tried

Compatible with whatever mobile platform and device you choose

Fast loading time

Continuous and uninterrupted performance

Useful and/or entertaining

App categories

Books
Business
Catalogs
Education
Entertainment
Finance
Games
Health and fitness
Lifestyle
Medical
Music
Navigation
News
Newsstand
Photo and video
Productivity
Reference
Social networking
Sports
Travel
Utilities
Weather

The best apps focus on one task, and do it very, very well. The single easiest way to screw up an app is to make it try and do too many things.

The Johnson & Johnson Official 7-Minute Workout app integrates audio and video to give users a great personalized workout experience. With more than 2 million downloads, the fast, simple, and science-based app is also on the Apple Watch.

Iconic	Illustrative	Realistic	Wordmark	Letterform	Abstract
Twitter	Evernote	Evernote Food	Five Guys	Airbnb	Flickr
Target	Chipotle	FatBooth	MoMA	Shazam	Pic Stitch
Starbucks	Lynda	Deluxe Moon	TED	Flipboard	Fitbit
Google Chrome	The New Yorker	Geo Walk	i.TV	NYT Now	7M Workout
Expedia	Instagram	Eebee's Baby	UNIQLO	Pinterest	Spotify

Iconic

Brands build on the equity of their trademarks in this approach. The best ones work at this scale.

Illustrative

A range of illustration styles are used to communicate the character and personality of the brand.

Realistic

Lifelike imagery is used as a differentiator that may relate to an app feature or character.

Wordmark

The entire brand name logotype is legible on the app icon. MoMA uses color to differentiate a family of apps.

Letterform

A single bold letter may be the actual trademark, or one letter of the name. Pinterest uses a circular icon with the letterform of its wordmark.

Abstract

The most unique app icon design expresses an attribute or a brand idea.

Private labeling

For many retailers, private labeling is a powerful marketing strategy to build brand equity that gives customers more reasons to shop at their stores. Retailers are leveraging better-designed packaging to attract upscale customers and increase profit margins.

The days when you could recognize a private label brand immediately because it looked generic, cheap, and low quality are over. Initially, private labeling was a business strategy aimed at higher profit margins per product and increased revenues. A private label product line is created and branded by a store, usually a large retail chain.

The products themselves are produced by a third-party supplier, which usually makes other name brand products for established national brands. Companies like IKEA use the master brand on all of their products, while companies like Target create multiple sub-brands. CVS does both.

We upped the quality, upped the price, and we're selling more units. Because it's the best tuna you could buy.

Richard Galanti
Chief Financial Officer
Costco

Since it exists in branded environments, private label can devote less energy to brand recognition, and more to great product stories.

Bruce Duckworth
Principal
Turner Duckworth

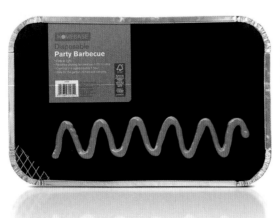

Homebase: Turner Duckworth

Private label brand architecture

Single master brand
Monolithic brand architecture

Best Buy

Carrefour

CVS

IKEA

Tesco

Trader Joe's

Multiple sub-brands
Pluralistic brand architecture

Costco
Kirkland Signature
Loblaws
Joe Fresh
President's Choice

Nordstrom
Classiques Entier
Halogen
Treasure and Bond

Safeway
Eating Right
O Organics
Waterfront Bistro

Target
Archer Farms
Market Pantry
Merona
Mossimo Supply Co.
Room Essentials
Threshold
Up&Up

Urban Outfitters
BDG
Kimchi Blue
Silence & Noise
Sparkle & Fade

Waitrose
Essential Waitrose
Love Life
Good to Go
Waitrose 1

Whole Foods
365 Organic
Engine 2 Plant-Strong
Whole Trade

Brand licensing

Licensing is a strategy for established brand owners to generate revenue from royalties on sales of products bearing their brand's logo, name, slogan, or other legally protected asset. It's an opportunity to attract new customers and delight existing brand champions.

The world of brand owners seeking new distribution channels for their intellectual property assets is expanding beyond consumer and entertainment brands to include nonprofits, branded destinations, and cultural venues.

Whether a property is a consumer brand, a media personality, a comic character, an artist, or a designer (dead or alive), the business imperative is the same: protecting and preserving the brand asset, being clear about what the brand stands for, and ensuring that each licensing opportunity is strategic.

Licensing can reinforce core brand attributes, promote brand exposure, and reach new consumers.

IMG Licensing

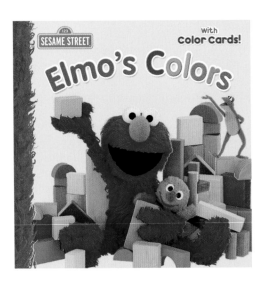

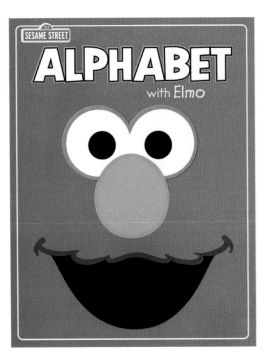

Sesame Workshop, the nonprofit organization behind Sesame Street, grants licenses to a variety of trusted licensees and manufacturers who create toys, apparel, and other products featuring its characters.

Sesame Street books, videos, and educational toys extend the learning beyond the television viewing experience. The royalties Sesame Workshop receives from the sale of these items are used to support its programs and initiatives around the world.

Benefits of brand licensing
Developed by Perpetual Licensing

Licensors or brand owners

Enhances the brand image

Grows the value of the brand

Increases awareness of the brand

Reinforces brand positioning and brand message

Attracts new consumers to the brand

Builds competitive advantage

Builds stronger relationships with customers

Gains entry into new distribution channels

Lets consumers exhibit their love of the brand

Protects the brand via trademark registration and policing of marketplace

Provides consumers genuine alternatives for illegal and unauthorized products

Generates incremental revenues through increased sales of core product and royalties from the sales of licensed products

Licensees or manufacturers

Increases market share

Opens new retail channels

Gains shelf space at retail

Increases awareness of their products

Attracts new customers to their products

Builds competitive advantage

Increases sales through a wider assortment of products

Lends credibility to their products

Generates incremental revenues through the sale of licensed products

Brand roles
Developed by Perpetual Licensing

Licensor

Set licensing goals and establish objectives

Approve annual strategic licensing plan

Approve prospective licensees

Approve licensed products, packaging, marketing, and collateral materials

Provide access to licensable assets and/or develop style guide

Register trademarks in appropriate categories

Pursue trademark infringers

Execute license agreements

Licensee

Set licensing goals and establish objectives

Approve annual strategic licensing plan (brand acquisition)

Approve prospective licensors

Develop, manufacture, and market approved products

Monitor marketplace for trademark infringers

Deliver quarterly royalty reports and payments

Agent

Develop strategic licensing program for presentation and approval

Create sales materials to solicit interest from licensees or licensors

Prospect qualified licensees or licensors

Negotiate terms of license agreement

Guide contract management process

Lead the acquisition and/or development of licensable assets, or the creation of a style guide

Manage product, packaging, and collateral material approval processes

Administer royalties

Police marketplace for trademark infringement

Handle daily program needs

We are very judicious about how we approach the licensing business. It's about the history and the heritage of the brand.

Ruth Crowley
Former VP, General Merchandise
Harley-Davidson

Consumers find comfort in brands they're familiar with—and have a greater propensity to purchase new products from those brands.

David Milch
President
Perpetual Licensing

Certification

As the proliferation of choices grows exponentially, consumers are looking for ways to facilitate their decisions and align their values with their purchases. Which products and companies should they trust? Which brands are environmentally and socially responsible? Which products are safe? Is their privacy protected?

To qualify for certification, products must undergo a series of rigorous tests by government bodies or professional associations. As the world continues to shrink and the number of certification symbols continues to grow, it will be essential to develop clear and trustworthy symbols that communicate across cultures.

B Corporations earn certification by meeting higher standards of social and environmental performance, accountability, and transparency. B Corps earn a minimum score on the B Impact Ratings System, which measures their impact on their employees, suppliers, community, consumers, and environment, legally expanding their corporate responsibilities to include consideration of stakeholder interests.

Jay Coen Gilbert
Cofounder
B Corporation

Certification matters because we all want to tell the difference between "good companies" and just good marketing.

Jay Coen Gilbert
Cofounder
B Corporation

Green building	Green products	Sustainable business

Efficiency

Social justice

No animal testing

Rainforest Alliance Certified

Data and privacy

Product safety

Food

Heart-healthy

Responsible forestry

Recycling

Environmental responsibility

Crisis communications

It takes years to build a brand, but only a nanosecond for a poorly managed crisis to ruin it. A crisis is an event—either internal or external—with the potential to negatively affect the brand. The most effective reputation management begins long before a crisis ever occurs. It's about what you do *before you must respond.*

Reputation management is the art of advancing and protecting a brand among its various audiences. A well-designed crisis communications plan is your best defense during the high-stakes communications challenges of the digital age. It includes proactive planning, message development, strategic communications counsel, and media training, all of which will help an organization manage an issue before it escalates into a crisis. However, such a plan is merely step one.

You need to train against the plan and update it on a regular basis.

No organization can afford to underestimate the potential impact of seemingly short-term decisions on its long-term reputation and business fortunes. The media and public have long memories, and will remember how a crisis was handled—or not.

Be thoughtful, measured, and strategic when planning for and responding to potentially damaging reputational issues.

Virginia Miller
Partner
Beuerman Miller Fitzgerald

If it's not important to senior management, it will not be important to middle management or line management at all.

Denny Lynch
SVP of Communications
Wendy's

If you lose money for the firm, I will be very understanding. If you lose reputation for the company, I will be ruthless.

Warren Buffett

Principles of crisis communications
Developed by Tavani Strategic Communications

Amat Victoria Curma! (Victory favors the prepared.)

Virginia Miller

By the time you hear the thunder, it's too late to build the ark.

Unknown

Critical planning questions

Do you have a crisis team leader and team?

Do you have a crisis communications plan that is regularly reviewed?

Are all of your senior leaders familiar with the plan and trained against it?

Have you included in-house and outside legal counsel in plan development and training?

Do you have an organizational protocol for determining a crisis?

Have you assessed where opportunities exist for potential crises within your organization?

Are you prepared with key messages and FAQs about your organization?

Has your organization identified and trained a spokesperson?

Do you have a social media policy, including a well-developed protocol for online forums such as blogs, Facebook, and Twitter?

Have you considered which audiences may be affected by your crisis, and have you identified the vehicles you will use to communicate with each of them?

Proactive planning steps for leadership

Identify and retain outside communications counsel.

Organize an internal crisis team to develop a plan with outside communications and legal counsel.

Conduct an audit of various threats to your organization's reputation.

Familiarize yourself with the plan and conduct regular training sessions against the plan for your crisis team.

Participate in a simulated crisis.

Establish organizational and media monitoring systems.

Track emerging issues on an ongoing basis.

Align your key messages across the enterprise.

Ensure that everyone in your organization understands the key messages.

Practice, assess, and refine the plan on an annual basis.

Imperatives

Be prepared: Have a plan on which you and the leadership team have been trained. Make sure that it's updated regularly.

Be quick: Get ahead of the story by getting your statement out first. Don't be forced into reacting to false or negative information floating around in cyberspace.

Define the issue: Get your message out there before the story breaks or as soon as possible afterward so you define the issue rather than the media, your adversaries, and other opinion makers.

Be forthright: Acknowledge action steps with strong rhetoric.

Be helpful: Don't speculate. If you know, say so. If you don't know, say you don't know. Provide the media and the public with information to make an informed decision.

Be transparent: Monitor, engage, and update information on a timely and consistent basis in both traditional and social media forums.

Social media

Have a social media policy: Create a social media policy before a crisis occurs, when you and your communications and legal counsel can think about it objectively.

Provide continuous updates: Establish a microsite to provide 24/7 updates.

Be available 24/7: Establish a round-the-clock social media monitoring schedule.

Respect all opinions: Do not delete negative comments on your organization's Facebook page or blogs.

Prepare your team: Train your organization's crisis team on social media.

Personal branding

The idea of personal branding encourages us to stay in touch with who we truly are. Our humor, style, and personal ideals influence every social media comment, text, or email. Facebook, Twitter, LinkedIn, and Instagram let us express ourselves in our own words and images, reflecting not just what we see but how we see it.

Personal branding (think Sun King, Napoleon Bonaparte, and Cleopatra) used to be for indulgent monarchs. Now it's de rigueur whether you are a corporate exec, a design guru, an aspiring entrepreneur, or a sales associate. We are all rock stars now. And the competition is fierce. Being authentic is critical because the web never forgets.

Why has personal branding become so important? We live in a global economy where changing employment is the norm. Forty percent of US workers do not have traditional full-time jobs. Social media and digital devices have accelerated the blur between business and life, work and leisure, and public and private. And we are all connected 24/7.

Be yourself; everyone else is already taken.

Oscar Wilde

You have got to find your own voice.

Frank Gehry
Architect

Six career secrets

1. There is no plan.
2. Think strengths, not weaknesses.
3. It's not about you.
4. Persistence trumps talent.
5. Make excellent mistakes.
6. Leave an imprint.

Daniel H. Pink
The Adventures of Johnny Bunko

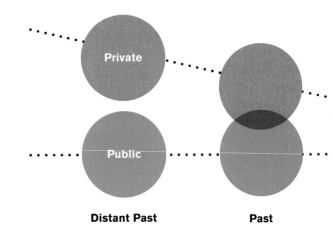

Distant Past · · · · · · · · **Past**

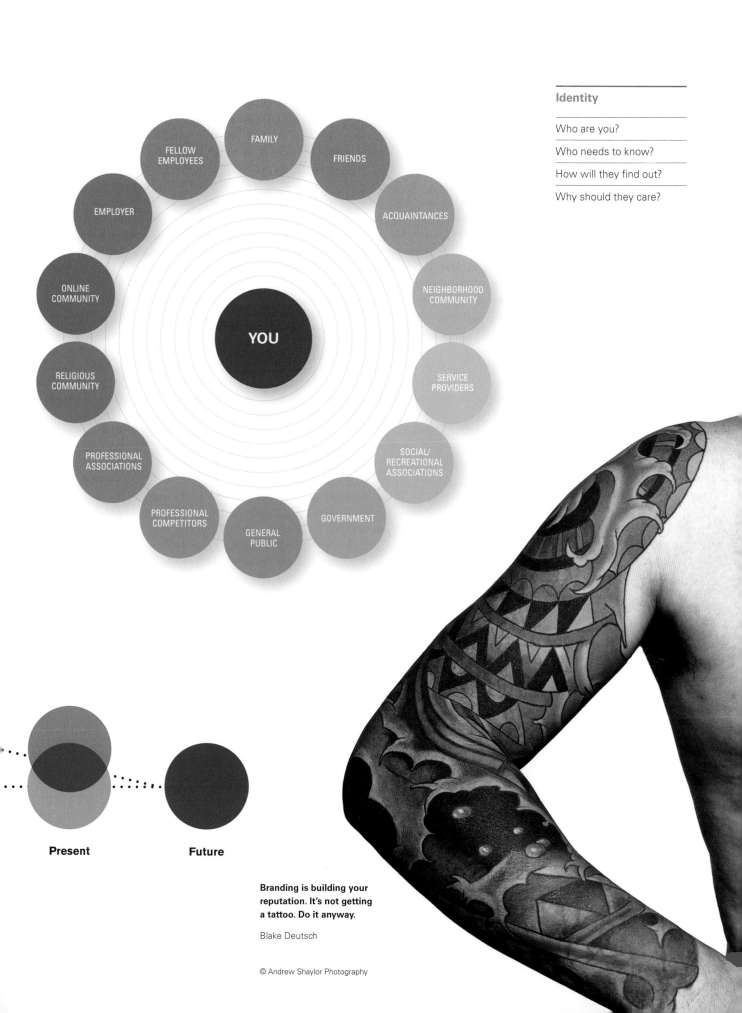

FELLOW EMPLOYEES

FAMILY

FRIENDS

EMPLOYER

ACQUAINTANCES

ONLINE COMMUNITY

NEIGHBORHOOD COMMUNITY

YOU

RELIGIOUS COMMUNITY

SERVICE PROVIDERS

PROFESSIONAL ASSOCIATIONS

SOCIAL/ RECREATIONAL ASSOCIATIONS

PROFESSIONAL COMPETITORS

GOVERNMENT

GENERAL PUBLIC

Identity

Who are you?

Who needs to know?

How will they find out?

Why should they care?

Present

Future

Branding is building your reputation. It's not getting a tattoo. Do it anyway.

Blake Deutsch

China

As brand builders rush into emerging markets, they most covet China, which represents the largest consumer market in the world. However, from a branding perspective, China is the most complex. Its vast diversity of regional, linguistic, and cultural nuances and its relative newness to branding demand extensive research, native advisors, and local partners.

The multinational companies that are most successful in China are the ones that don't rush. They begin by finding in-country native partners and advisors, taking the necessary time to build relationships based on trust, respect, and understanding. Perhaps no branding activity reflects the complexity of these cultures more than naming—whether to blend and balance the East and West or to emphasize one over the other, and if so, which? What the name sounds like and means in which dialects further contributes to the challenge of multilingual branding.

Decoding China's cultural codes is essential for creating successful and memorable brands.

Denise Sabet
Managing Director
Labbrand

Succeeding in China is adapting to China. When a brand innovates in China, it opens pathways for global innovation.

Vladimir Djurovic
President
Labbrand

Kleenex brand: Kimberly-Clark

The Chinese name for Kleenex means clean and comfort.

Fundamental branding principles in China
Developed by Labbrand

General

The need for cultural understanding impacts naming, product design, identity design, taglines, and color selection.

Due to the rapid rate of development in China, it is vital to monitor cultural and economic changes.

China is a place where diverse influences converge, where local and foreign brands coexist, and where changes are local and international.

Cultural heritage is important for Chinese consumers. It is an ancient culture.

Mandarin and Cantonese are the main, but not the only, Chinese dialects.

China's trademark registration is competitive. Brands must be aware of the intellectual property regulations in China and incorporate this into their brand development process.

Naming

Chinese is a character-based language with essentially small picture icons conveying both meaning and pronunciation.

A Chinese name should reflect brand attributes, and does not need to be a direct translation of the original name.

The pronunciation and connotations of the Chinese language vary greatly by region. Testing in the main Chinese dialects to avoid negative associations is critical.

Creating a local- or foreign-sounding Chinese name depends on the brand's target consumer, competitors, cities, industry, and other marketplace dynamics.

Sometimes Chinese names are chosen for the similarity of sound to the original brand name, but more often for an associative and relevant meaning.

The emphasis on auspiciousness, good fortune, happiness, power, and status is important in Chinese culture.

Nongfu Spring: Mouse Graphics

Before and after

As organizations grow, their purpose becomes more lucid. The creative team is challenged by three crucial questions: What is the business imperative for the change? What elements need to be maintained to preserve brand equity? Should the change be evolutionary or revolutionary? The majority of branding initiatives involve repositioning and redesign.

Change brings opportunity.

Nido Qubein

Before

After

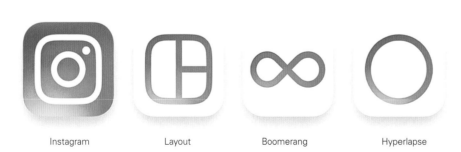

| Instagram | Layout | Boomerang | Hyperlapse |

We needed to strike a balance between recognition and versatility. We created a new Instagram app icon and a set of unified icons for Hyperlapse, Layout, and Boomerang. We've also refreshed the user interface with a simpler, more consistent design that helps people's photos and videos shine.

We hope that we've captured some of the life, creativity, and optimism people bring to Instagram every day—while staying true to Instagram's heritage and spirit.

Ian Spalter
Head of Design
Instagram

AMERICAN ASSOCIATION
OF MUSEUMS

**American
Alliance of
Museums**

**The American Alliance of
Museums logo unites
concepts of group strength
and diversity though the
colorful weave design.**

AAM Press Release

American Alliance of Museums:
Satori Engine

**We're proud to introduce the
Bélo: It's a symbol for people
who want to welcome into
their home new experiences,
new cultures, and new
conversations.**

Brian Chesky
Cofounder
Airbnb

Airbnb: DesignStudio

**We are excited to share a
new brand identity that
aims to make Google more
accessible and useful to our
users as they embrace an
expanding, multi-device,
multi-screen world.**

Jonathan Jarvis
Creative Lead
Google

**Tennis Australia wanted a
new identity to reflect the
Open's transformation into
a future-focused
entertainment brand.**

Nick Davis
Managing Partner
Landor

**Mastercard's new symbol
returns the brand to its
fundamental roots.**

Luke Hayman
Pentagram

Brandmark redesign

Before	After

The challenge was to create an identity system to communicate beyond shopping.

Joe Duffy
CEO
Duffy & Partners

Our goal was to reposition Alaska Airlines from a trusted regional airline to a trusted national carrier.

David Bates
Creative Director
Hornall Anderson

Columbus Salame was repositioned to appeal to more sophisticated, upscale customers.

Kit Hinrichs
Partner
Pentagram

We wanted to help the ACLU look like the guardians of freedom.

Sylvia Harris
Design Strategist

Our new logo symbolizes the focus we have on our customers.

Tiffany Fox
Senior Director, Corporate Communications
OpenTable

OpenTable: Tomorrow Partners

96

Before	After

Before After

Paperless Post needed a clearer logo that could live primarily online. In a makeover, I always try to maintain one or two key elements from the original. In this case it was the color, the postage stamp, and the bird.

Louise Fili

Our new brand evolves from a single vision: real transformation begins within.

Michelle Bonterre
Chief Brand Officer
Dale Carnegie

Dale Carnegie:
Carbone Smolan Agency

We wanted the design to evoke both the spirit and science of true discovery.

Michael Connors
VP Creative
Hornall Anderson

We modernized the mark to signal a newfound optimism in the brand.

Blake Howard
Cofounder
Matchstic

A new name and logo reflect the largest manufacturer of blast resistant buildings while respecting the equity of their former mark.

Bill Gardner
President
Gardner Design

Brandmark redesign

Before	After

By freeing the Siren from the band, we enabled customers to have a more personal connection.

Jeffrey Fields

Vice President
Global Creative Studio
Starbucks

Aetna's refreshed brand promise reflects our goal of creating a health care system that is more connected, convenient, and cost-effective.

Belinda Lang

VP, Brand, Digital and Consumer Marketing
Aetna

Aetna: Siegel + Gale

The new Bala logotype is streamlined and simple, just like the best engineering solutions.

Jon Bjornson

Founder
Jon Bjornson Design

The new logo increases the perception that the brand is up-to-date, cheerful, and innovative.

Christine Mau

Brand Design Director
Kimberly-Clark

We created a monolithic brand architecture for this market leader organized under the Santos Brasil master brand.

Marco A. Rezende

Director
Cauduro Associates

Kodak

We returned Kodak to their
ubiquitous and beloved
brand roots, the K symbol,
and reinvented the
typography to be both
modern and metaphorical.

Keira Alexandra
Partner
Work-Order

social media
business council

Social
Media
•ORG

A more concise and
memorable name was a
strategic triumph for the
brand.

Craig Johnson
President
Matchstic

 **Pitney Bowes**

pitney bowes

We wanted our new brand
strategy and identity to
reflect not only who we are
today, but also where we
are going in the future.

Marc Lautenbach
President and CEO
Pitney Bowes

Pitney Bowes: FutureBrand

Unilever's new brand
identity expressed a core
brand idea aligned with the
mission "Adding Vitality to
Life."

Wolff Olins

CONSERVATION
INTERNATIONAL

A simple blue circle
underlined with green
symbolizes our blue
planet—emphasized,
supported, and sustained—
as well as a unique human
form.

Sagi Haviv
Partner
Chermayeff & Geismar & Haviv

Packaging redesign

Topo Chico's new logo and typeface reinterpret the original 1895 identity, and reinvigorate its essence to appeal to both young adults and hardcore consumers alike.

Interbrand

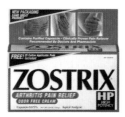

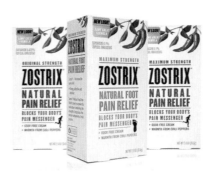

The Zostrix redesign capitalizes on the brand's powerful and effective natural pain relieving ingredient—as well as making the portfolio easier to navigate at shelf.

Little Big Brands

The new Better Together identity and packaging creates a versatile and ownable brand toolkit to support its current product and future innovation plans.

Chase Design Group

To communicate this new frozen treat had no added sugar but tasted great, the pack was designed to look tasty rather than light or boring.

Snask

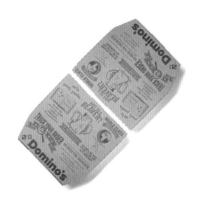

The brand's iconic red and blue domino logo was made pivotal to the redesign while leveraging the brand's pizza combo deal as a canvas.

Jones Knowles Ritchie

Budweiser needed to reconnect with what the brand stood for; the global redesign communicates the exceptional level of craft and quality in every pack.

Jones Knowles Ritchie

Klondike was in danger of being de-listed; the new design focuses heavily on taste appeal and leverages the brand's assets in a more indulgent manner.

Little Big Brands

Drawing inspiration from the original brandmark, Swiffer's new logo retains equity elements while modernizing the letterforms; the updated package also simplifies the overall brand expression.

Chase Design Group

Swiffer: Chase Design Group + P&G Design

Work with talented people to create something that will be of compelling benefit to the customer.

Susan Avarde

Head of Global Brand, Enterprise-wide
Citigroup

2 Process

Part 2 presents a universal process that underlies every successful branding initiative, regardless of its complexity. Why does it take so long? How should we decide?

A process for success

The branding process demands a combination of investigation, strategic thinking, design excellence, and project management skills. It requires an extraordinary amount of patience, an obsession with getting it right, and an ability to synthesize vast amounts of information.

Regardless of the nature of the client and the complexity of the engagement, the process remains the same. What changes is the depth with which each phase is conducted, the length of time and the number of resources allocated, and the size of the team, on both the identity firm and client sides.

The process is defined by distinct phases with logical beginnings and endpoints, which facilitate decision making at the appropriate intervals. Eliminating steps or reorganizing the process might present an appealing way to cut costs and time, but doing so can pose substantial risks and impede long-term benefits. The process, when done right, can produce remarkable results.

The process is the process, but then you need a spark of genius.

Brian P. Tierney, Esq.
Founder
Tierney Communications

The branding process

1 : conducting research

Clarify vision, strategies, goals, and values

Interview key management

Research stakeholders' needs and perceptions

Conduct marketing, competitive, technology, legal, and message audits

Evaluate existing brands and brand architecture

Present audit readout

2 : clarifying strategy

Synthesize learnings

Clarify brand strategy

Develop a positioning platform

Create brand attributes

Develop key messages

Write a brand brief

Achieve agreement

Create a naming strategy

Write a creative brief

Process is a competitive advantage

Assures that a proven method is being used to achieve business results

Accelerates understanding of the investment of necessary time and resources

Engenders trust and confidence in the team

Positions project management as smart, efficient, and cost-effective

Builds credibility and strengthens identity solutions

Sets expectations for the complexity of the process

Navigating through the political process—building trust—building relationships—it's everything.

Paula Scher
Partner
Pentagram

Most processes leave out the stuff that no one wants to talk about: magic, intuition, and leaps of faith.

Michael Bierut
Partner
Pentagram

3 : designing identity

Visualize the future

Brainstorm the big idea

Design brand identity system

Explore key applications

Finalize brand architecture

Present visual strategy

Achieve agreement

4 : creating touchpoints

Finalize identity design

Develop look and feel

Initiate trademark protection

Prioritize and design applications

Develop system

Apply brand architecture

5 : managing assets

Build synergy around the new strategy

Develop launch plan

Launch internally first

Launch externally

Develop standards and guidelines

Nurture brand champions

Managing the process

A branding project has to be managed effectively to accomplish desired outcomes throughout each phase of the process. Astute project management builds confidence and mutual respect among stakeholders, fostering the teamwork and commitment necessary for success. Synchronizing a wide range of skills and resources with goals requires patience and enthusiasm. It will enable the company's leadership and their brand consultants to work hand in hand with planning, coordinating, analyzing, understanding, and managing time, resources, and money.

Time factors

The length of a branding project is affected by the following factors:

Size of organization

Complexity of business

Number of markets served

Type of market: global, national, regional, local

Nature of problem

Research required

Legal requirements (merger or public offering)

Decision-making process

Number of decision makers

Number of platforms and applications

How long will it take?

All clients have a sense of urgency, regardless of the size and nature of the company. There are no shortcuts to the process, and eliminating steps may be detrimental to achieving long-term goals. Developing an effective and sustainable identity takes time. There are no instant answers, and a commitment to a responsible process is imperative.

Pay as much attention to the process as to the content.

Michael Hirschhorn
Organizational Dynamics Expert

Your goal is to identify the most appropriate talent for your business, your brands, your organization, and your culture. You need the right skills, for the right challenges, at the right time, for the right value.

John Gleason
President
A Better View Strategic Consulting

Process: Project management

> **Team protocol**

Identify client project manager and team

Identify firm contact and team

Clearly define team goals

Establish roles and responsibilities

Understand policies and procedures

Circulate pertinent contact data

> **Team commitment**

Team must commit to:
Robust debate
Open communications
Confidentiality
Dedication to brand
Mutual respect

> **Benchmarks + schedule**

Identify deliverables

Identify key dates

Develop project schedule

Update schedules as necessary

Develop task matrix

> **Decision-making protocol**

Establish process

Determine decision makers

Clarify benefits and disadvantages

Put all decisions in writing

> **Communications protocol**

Establish document flow

Decide who gets copied how

Put everything in writing

Create agendas

Circulate meeting notes

Develop online project site

Who manages the project?

Client side

For a small business, the founder or owner is invariably the project leader, the key decision maker, and the visionary. In a larger company, the project manager is whomever the CEO designates: the director of marketing and communications, the brand manager, or maybe the CFO.

The project manager must be someone with authority who can make things happen, given the enormous amount of coordination, scheduling, and information gathering. He or she must also have direct access to the CEO and other decision makers. In a large company, the CEO usually forms a brand team, which may include representatives from different divisions or business lines. Although this team may not be the ultimate decision-making group, they must have access to the key decision makers.

Identity firm side

In a large brand consultancy, a dedicated project manager is the key client contact. Various tasks are handled by specialists, from market researchers and business analysts, to naming specialists and designers. In a small to midsize firm, the principal may be the main client contact, senior creative director, and senior designer. A firm may bring on specialists as needed, from market research firms, to naming experts, to create a virtual team that meets the unique needs of the client.

Project leadership best practices
Developed by Dr. Ginny Vanderslice,
Praxis Consulting Group

Commitment: Create a culture in which people feel inspired and able to do their best work, and each member feels accountable to the other team members and to the project outcome. Build trust.

Focus: See and maintain the big picture while also breaking it down into smaller, ordered pieces. Keep moving despite challenges and constraints.

Discipline: Plan, track numerous tasks, and balance time and cost factors.

Strong communication skills: Communicate clearly and respectfully, include both the big picture and the details, and keep team members informed in a timely manner.

Empathy: Understand and respond to the needs, values, viewpoints, and perspectives of all players in the project.

Effective management skills: Define needs, priorities, and tasks. Make decisions. Flag problems. Clarify expectations.

Flexibility (adaptability): Stay focused and in control when things go wrong. Change in midstream when the situation requires it.

Creative problem-solving ability: See problems as challenges to address rather than as obstacles.

Insight: Understand policies, procedures, corporate culture, key people, and politics.

> **Documentation**

Date all documents

Date each sketch process

Assign version numbers to key documents

> **Information gathering**

Determine responsibilities

Determine dates

Identify proprietary information

Develop task matrix

Develop audit

Determine how you will collect audit materials

> **Legal protocol**

Identify intellectual property resource

Understand compliance issues

Gather confidentiality statements

> **Presentation protocol**

Circulate goals in advance

Hand out agenda at meeting

Determine presentation medium

Develop uniform presentation system

Obtain approvals and sign-offs

Identify next steps

Brand initiatives

Is your organization ready to invest the time, capital, and human resources to revitalize your brand? Take the time to plan, build trust, and set expectations. Ensure that your team understands brand fundamentals. Develop a set of guiding principles to keep you on point throughout the process.

Sustainable brands stay true to their core purpose, are agile, and stay relevant.

Shantini Munthree
Managing Partner
The Union Marketing Group

Our brand and reputation are driven by employees that sit side by side with clients every day. Our job is to empower those employees to be brand ambassadors every day.

Grant McLaughlin
VP Marketing & Communications
Booz Allen Hamilton

Guiding principles
Developed by Shantini Munthree, Managing Partner, The Union Marketing Group

A brand is an asset that holds reputational and commercial value.

Nurturing and protecting a brand is a long-term investment in building brand equity. Like other assets, a brand needs care and protection to hold its value and to appreciate over time.

A brand's job is to cohesively express a company's core purpose.

The design of brand messages and identity is an art, grounded in science. The art is about connecting the brand with customers where they are, responding to data and experiments to guide brand choices on what is said, and how it is expressed.

A brand is built from the inside out.

By placing employees at the heart of your brand experience, you enable them to help bring the brand to life. It takes everyone, from leaders to frontline staff, to help a customer on their brand journey.

Your customers amplify your brand in ways you're unable to.

When a customer loves your brand, they're more likely to tell others about it. In their circle of trust, your brand receives undivided attention during moments your marketing spend could never reach.

Every touchpoint matters, but only a handful matter the most.

A brand experience is the collective result of individual customer experiences, making every interaction in the customer journey count. Research shows that making a few specific moments of truth delightful is what drives client affinity.

Brands, like humans, are organic in nature.

A good brand strategy constructs the DNA of a brand. As customer needs change, or, as brands root themselves in both real and virtual worlds, a brand will selectively highlight attributes.

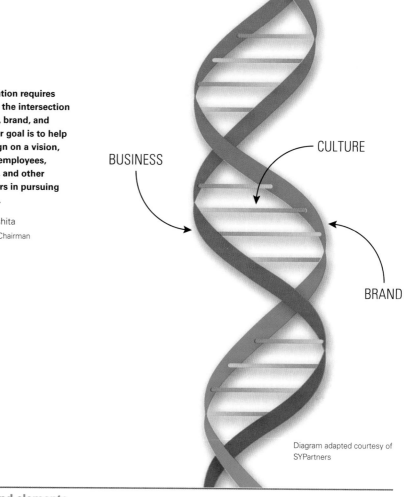

Transformation requires working at the intersection of strategy, brand, and culture. Our goal is to help leaders align on a vision, and enlist employees, customers, and other stakeholders in pursuing that vision.

Keith Yamashita
Founder and Chairman
SYPartners

BUSINESS

CULTURE

BRAND

Diagram adapted courtesy of SYPartners

Ten imperatives for success

Ensure that your leadership team endorses the brand initiative and process

Set goals, responsibilities, and a clear endpoint

Communicate throughout the process

Use a disciplined process with realistic benchmarks

Stay consumer centric

Commit to a small decision making group

Determine your readiness to make a commitment

Determine how you will measure success

Explain why the brand is important

Keep moving

Core brand elements
Developed by Shantini Munthree, Managing Partner, The Union Marketing Group

Core purpose	The reason the company exists beyond making a profit
Vision	The story a leader tells to explain "how" a company will achieve its mission
Values	Core cultural beliefs and philosophies
Personality	Brand tone and voice for receptivity and resonance
Capabilities & features	Measure of the ability of the brand to achieve its mission
Core competencies	A cluster of related abilities, commitments, knowledge, and skills that enable a brand to perform effectively
Competition	Points of parity and difference
Target audience	The addressable population, focusing on decision makers
Needs & objections	Needs: Unmet needs we hope to fulfill Objections: Top reasons audience may reject us, or not act
Big idea/brand essence	Evergreen, differentiating phrase that provides inspiration and focus
Value proposition	Set of functional, emotional, and social benefits (how we fulfill audience needs)
Proof points	Why should they believe we do this best? Why should they act?
Desired outcome	In consumer language, a single statement most desired from stakeholders

Measuring success

Brand identity systems are a long-term investment of time, human resources, and capital. Each positive experience with a brand helps build its brand equity and increases the likelihood of repeat purchasing and lifelong customer relationships. A return on investment is achieved, in part, through making it easier and more appealing for the customer to buy, making it easier for the sales force to sell, and being vigilant about the customer experience. Clarity about the brand, a clear process, and smart tools for employees fuel success.

Decision makers frequently ask, "Why should we make this investment? Can you prove to me that it has a return?" It's difficult to isolate the impact of a new logo, a better brand architecture, or an integrated marketing system. It is critical that companies develop their own measures of success. Those who don't expect instant results, and think in the cumulative long term, understand the value of incremental change and focus.

Businesses are now only as strong as their brands, and nothing else offers business leaders so much potential leverage.

Jim Stengel
Grow: How Ideals Power Growth and Profit at the World's Greatest Companies

Pride
Wow factor
I get it
Confidence
Your boss is happy
The CEO gets it

Human capital	Demand	Growth	Leadership
Once they understood our vision, our employees accepted responsibility enthusiastically, which sparked numerous simultaneous and energetic developments in the company.	**Brands are powerful assets for creating desire, shaping experience, and shifting demand.**	**In any competitive market, what drives margin and growth and separates one business from another—for employees, customers, partners, and investors— is the brand.**	**A well-timed and creatively well-executed corporate rebranding can be the most powerful single tool at a leader's command—broadly effective in commanding new attention, resetting direction, and renewing employee commitment.**
Jan Carlzon	Rick Wise	Jim Stengel	Tony Spaeth
Former CEO Scandinavian Airlines Group *Moments of Truth*	Chief Executive Officer Lippincott	*Grow: How Ideals Power Growth and Profit at the World's Greatest Companies*	Identity Consultant

Metrics for brand management Source: Prophet

Perception metrics

Awareness

Are customers aware of your brand?

Saliency

Brand recognition

Familiarity + consideration

What do customers think and feel about the brand?

Differentiation

Relevance

Credibility

Likability

Perceived quality

Purchase intent

Performance metrics

Purchase decision

How do customers act?

Customer leads

Customer acquisition

Trial

Repeat

Preference

Price premium

Loyalty

How do customers behave over time?

Customer satisfaction

Retention

Revenue per customer

Share of wallet

Customer lifetime value

Referrals

ROI

Cost savings

Financial metrics

Value creation

How does customer behavior create tangible economic value?

Market share

Revenue

Operating cash flow

Market cap

Analyst ratings

Brand valuation

Metrics for isolated touchpoints

Websites

Total visits + percent new visits

Unique visitors

Time on site + bounce rate

Search engine landing pages

Key performance indicators

Referral traffic from backlinks

Average conversion rate

Order value + per-visit value

Visitor demographics + frequency

Visitor flow

Page views by page

Site search tracking

Keywords + bounce rate per landing page

Visits + visitor engagement by keyword

Search engine impressions, queries, clicks

Social media

Quantitative

Fans/followers

Shares

Likes

Comments

Traffic/visitors

Clicks/conversions

Qualitative

Engagement

Conversation quality

Fan loyalty

Insights/research value

Word of mouth

Brand reputation

Influence

Intellectual property

Protecting assets

Preventing litigation

Adhering to compliance

Direct mail

Response rate

Trade shows

Number of leads generated

Number of sales

Number of inquiries

Licensing

Revenues

Protecting assets

Product placement

Reach

Impressions

Awareness

Public relations

Buzz

Awareness

Advertising

Awareness

Conversion

Revenues

Packaging

Market share vis-à-vis competition

Sales change after new packaging

Compare sales change to overall project cost

Money saved because of engineering and materials

Eye-tracking studies, to track what they see first (shelf impact)

More shelf space

Home usage/observation consumer/field test

Entrée to a new retailer

Press coverage; buzz

Number of line extensions

Product placement

Sales cycle time

Consumer feedback

Influence on purchasing decision

Web analytics

Online brand center

Number of users

Number of visits per user

Time per visit session

Number of downloaded asset files

Actual ROI on site usage

Faster decision making

More efficient ordering

Better compliance

Standards + guidelines

More consistent implementation

More effective content management

More efficient use of time

Faster decision making

Right the first time

Reduction in legal involvement

More efficient protection of brand assets

Metrics rethought

Design

The Design Council study of share prices of UK quoted companies over the last decade found that a group of companies recognized as effective users of design outperformed key FTSE indices by 200 percent.

Steady investment in, and commitment to, design is rewarded by lasting competitiveness rather than isolated successes.

The Design Council

Evidence-based design

Evidence-based design quantifies the effect of design on outcomes (e.g., health, satisfaction, safety, efficiency) by basing design decisions on credible research, generating new evidence about the built environment.

Ellen Taylor, AIA, MBA, EDAC
Director of Pebble Projects
The Center for Health Design

Mergers

In the UK, over 70 percent of what was paid in the acquisition of companies was for the goodwill from intangibles including corporate brand value.

Turnbridge Consulting Group

Sustainability

Eco-friendly packaging

Reducing e-waste and trash

Reducing hazardous materials in product design

Saving energy

Reducing carbon footprint

Commitment to an environmental policy

Collaboration

Great outcomes require vision, commitment, and collaboration. Collaboration is not consensus or compromise. It evolves from a thoughtful and genuine focus on problem solving, generating an interdependent, connected approach. It also acknowledges the tension between different viewpoints and different disciplines.

Most branding projects involve individuals from various departments with different agendas. Even small organizations have silos that stand in the way of achievement. Collaboration requires the ability to suspend judgment, listen carefully, and transcend politics.

Open source is a new model of collaboration, creativity, and problem solving, now used in product development and brand innovation. It is characterized by open sharing of information for mutual benefit between customers and merchants, creators and end users, employees and volunteers, and competitors. Wikipedia and Linux are the most well-known examples of the open source methodology.

Let go of stereotypes. Intellectual property lawyers do have creative thoughts, investment bankers can feel compassion, and designers can do math.

Blake Deutsch

You may have the greatest bunch of individual stars in the world, but if they don't play together, the club won't be worth a dime.

Babe Ruth

Organizing your teams conversations, apps, tools, and information sharing, through software like Slack, streamlines collaboration.

Great brand design evolves from a collective acknowledgment of all that is good, and also incomplete, about a brand. It's a team commitment to let go of all fears, and to forge new paths.

Shantini Munthree
Managing Partner
The Union Marketing Group

Like King Arthur's Round Table, effective teams acknowledge and respect diverse expertise, share power, actively debate, unite around a common purpose, and use their collective intelligence to achieve ambitious goals.

Moira Cullen
Vice President,
Global Beverage Design
PepsiCo

When I work with a writer, we shed our own passionate and personal viewpoints, listen deeply, and allow a third person to emerge with a new vision.

Ed Williamson
Art Director

Leadership must believe in collaboration and its organizational benefits.

Listen to all perspectives; share your viewpoint honestly; put all issues on the table.

Promote participation.

Everyone's contribution is important.

Develop strong professional relationships, building high levels of trust and rapport; suspend titles and organizational roles.

Engage in dialogue; find a common purpose and language for learning and communicating; construct guiding principles for decision making.

Provide equal access to information; create a common work process; examine assumptions and data objectively.

Create team protocols.

Guarantee cooperation, engagement, and ownership; recognize that rewards are earned for the group, not for individuals; shed any competitive "win-lose" mentality.

To optimize brand customer experience, CEOs are playing a critical role to decentralize branding decisions while breaking the silos either through corporate restructuring (P&G), increasing operational efficiencies (Amazon), enhancing the workplace environment (Google), or through unifying the brand around a common goal as in the case of Apple.

Dr. Salah S. Hassan

Professor, Strategic Brand Management
School of Business
The George Washington University

Decision making

The decision making process needs to build trust and help organizations make the right choices to build their brands. Most people can recall when the wrong decision was made because of politics, entrenched thinking, or too many decision makers. Social science experts believe that decisions made by large groups tend to be less inspired than ones made by small groups. Organizational development experts think that consensus can result in higher-quality decisions because the organization uses the resources of its members.

The process needs a leader who can elicit ideas and opinions from a wider group without succumbing to group-think. The final decision makers, regardless of the size of the organization, should include the CEO. Participation should be mandatory at key decision points throughout the process, for example, agreement on goals, brand strategy, names, taglines, and brandmarks.

The branding process frequently refocuses key stakeholders on the vision and mission of the organization. When it is done well, people throughout the organization feel empowered and begin to "own" the new brand.

Decision making requires trusting yourself, your process, and your team.

Dr. Barbara Riley
Managing Partner
Chambers Group LLC

A brand consultancy that invests the effort to really empathize with the organization and its customers builds the trust needed to transcend from being outsider to an insider.

Andrew Ceccon
Executive Director
FS Investments

Critical success factors

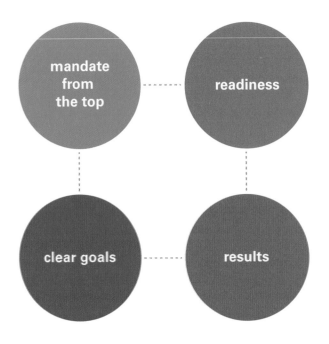

The CEO (or global brand manager) does not have time to meet with you.

I will know it when I see it.

We are going to show all the partners to see if they like it.

We are going to use focus groups to help us make the right decision.

We know that is the better design, but the CEO's husband does not like it.

We want to show the entire list of 573 names to the CEO and let her decide what she likes best.

Let's vote on our favorites.

Decide how you are going to decide and stick to it.

Essential characteristics

The CEO leads a small group that includes marketing brand champions.

The entire process is clearly communicated to key stakeholders.

Decisions are aligned with vision and goals.

All members are trusted and respected.

Agreement on goals and positioning strategy precedes creative strategy.

All relevant information and concerns are voiced and tracked.

Pros and cons are always fully discussed.

A commitment is made to communicate about the brand through all levels of the organization.

Focus groups are used as a tool, not as a thought leader.

Decisions are communicated internally first.

Confidentiality is honored.

Challenging scenarios

The CEO is not involved.

New decision makers get involved in the middle of the process.

Team members' opinions are not respected.

Critical steps in the process are eliminated to save money and time.

Personal aesthetics get confused with functional criteria.

Mergers and acquisitions

Financial stakes are high.

Difficult to gather input when confidentiality is critical.

Time frame is compressed and atmosphere is tense.

Names and marks used in a symbolic chess match.

Everyone needs attention of leadership.

Critical to maintain focus on customer benefit.

Critical success factors

The CEO supports this initiative.

The company is ready to invest time, resources, and brainpower.

There is an endpoint that everyone understands and agrees on.

There is value to the outcome, and all agree what success looks like.

If you have gone through a process with people you respect, a decision is not a leap of faith. It's planning.

Dr. Barbara Riley
Managing Partner
Chambers Group LLC

A lot of decisions are made in quiet conference rooms where new work can look radical or intimidating. But the work— the branded experience— needs to work OUT THERE. It's a noisy and busy world. You can spend a lot of money and discover that the customer doesn't know the difference. When you build things by consensus, you can lose your distinctiveness.

Susan Avarde
Head of Global Brand,
Enterprise-wide
Citigroup

Intellectual property

Brands outperform their rivals by establishing a difference that they can express, sustain, and legally protect. Distinctive product and packaging designs, improved functionality, and brand identifiers such as logos, names, slogans, colors, and even sounds may be protected as trademarks. Long-term value is increased when brand identifiers are immediately recognizable and memorable.

Patents encourage the development and disclosure of new inventions, copyrights promote and protect creativity, and trademarks help ensure that the consumer is not confused or misled by a similar source identifier. Although common law trademark rights arise from mere use of the mark as a source identifier in the US, federal trademark registration is needed to achieve exclusive nationwide rights in certain circumstances. Goods and services are categorized within forty-five industry classes, and a trademark may be registered in more than one class.

Intellectual property is the legal discipline that provides protection for brand assets by obtaining, monitoring, enforcing, and monetizing various forms of intellectual property rights. A trademark search and analysis at the outset of the branding process is an invaluable means of identifying and mitigating risks. Trademark owners are responsible for monitoring the marketplace for misuse or infringement by others. Many brands utilize trademark watch services to proactively protect their assets.

Trademarks and service marks

Protect brand identifiers such as names, logos, slogans, and jingles

Trade dress

Protects the visual appearance of a product, product packaging, or a business's interior design—recognized by consumers as brand identifiers

Copyrights

Protect original creative expression, such as visual art, literature, music, choreography, computer software

Utility patents

Protect the functional aspects of new and useful inventions, including machines, and processes

Design patents

Protect the unique ornamental aspects of a product, such as the shape or appearance

Trade secrets

Protect valuable secret information like customer lists, methods, processes, and formulations

A single item can be protected under multiple forms of IP

Don't fall in love with an idea for a new mark or tagline before making sure that it is legally available.

Cassidy Merriam
Trademark and Copyright Attorney

Process: Trademark search and registration

> **Establish brand differentiation**

Determine how a new brand will best stand out in the marketplace

Develop differentiators that define unique and innovative brand elements

Conduct market research to assess the competitive landscape

Determine alternative options and don't fall in love with a trademark before it is cleared

> **Develop legal strategy**

Decide what should be protected: name, symbol, logotype, product design, etc.

Determine the types of registrations needed: copyright?, trademark?, federal, state, foreign countries

Identify the goods or services with which trademarks will be used

Identify any regulatory constraints

> **Employ legal resources**

Identify intellectual property counsel and trademark search services

Assign intellectual property counsel to the branding team

Integrate intellectual property actions into the branding process

Ensure that contracts state that the company, not the branding firm, owns the copyright for a logo design

> **Conduct searches**

Conduct comprehensive searches for prospective trademarks

Search pending and granted trademark registrations as well as common-law usage

Obtain an opinion on whether prospective trademarks are likely to be registrable or infringe others' rights

Determine whether you need to search in foreign countries

Trademark basics

Nontraditional trademarks

Levi Strauss's distinctive jean pocket stitching

Tiffany's robin-egg blue packaging

Coca-Cola's iconic bottle design

Intel's sonic bing

Post-it's canary yellow

Law & Order's "bang bang" sound effect

Darth Vader's breathing

The word "superhero"

Hermès Birkin bag

Starbucks Frappuccino

T-Mobile's magenta

UPS brown

The more differentiated a brand is from competitors, the easier it is to protect from a legal perspective.

Certain brand names, packages, labels, and marketing materials for regulated industries like health care, pharmaceuticals, and financial services require approvals by governing bodies prior to launch.

The owner of the mark—whether an individual, a corporation, a partnership, or other type of legal entity—controls the use of the mark and the nature and quality of the goods or services with which it is used, either by the owner's own use, or by ensuring that license agreements are in place with third parties.

Trademark rights are jurisdictional. Establishing rights in one country does not provide protection in other countries. Rights need to be assessed in each country where business is or will be conducted.

One can establish rights in a mark in the US based on use of the mark in commerce, without a registration, because common law rights in a limited geographic region arise from actual use of a mark and allow the common law user to challenge another's registration or application. In the majority of other countries, however, registration is required.

Federal trademark registration provides advantages, including the owner's exclusive right to use the mark nationwide in connection with identified goods and services, the ability to bring an action concerning the mark in federal court, and the ability to prevent importation of infringing foreign goods by registering the mark with Customs.

Because many brand owners conduct clearance searches before adopting or filing an application to register a mark, federal registration often prevents third parties from inadvertently adopting a similar or identical mark to one discovered in a search.

The US Patent and Trademark Office (USPTO) database can be used to search for existing federal trademark applications and registrations, but intellectual property lawyers are needed to assess legal opportunities and risks.

Trademark applications in the US can be filed based on an "intent to use," giving the owner priority dating back to the application filing date, rather than when the mark is first used.

Trademark rights can exist in perpetuity as long as the mark is in use, however, they must be renewed. In the US, a registration must be renewed every ten years.

Registered trademark: Federal registration symbol that may be used only after the USPTO actually registers a mark, and not while an application is merely pending.

TM

Trademark: Used to alert the public to your claim of owner-ship of a mark. It may be used while an application is pending, or if you have not filed an appli-cation with the USPTO.

SM

Service mark: Used to alert the public to your claim of owner-ship of a unique service. It may be used regardless of whether you have filed an application with the USPTO.

> **Pursue trademark protection**

Finalize list of trademarks needing registrations

Apply for state, federal, or country trademark registrations as appropriate

Develop standards for appropriate trademark usage

Monitor activities of competitors to identify possible trademark infringements

Ensure that agreements with third parties cover how intellectual property is used

> **Consider**

IP adjacent issues:

Domain names
Social media accounts
Publicity rights
Consumer privacy issues
Employee policies
Contracts
Regulatory agencies

> **Educate + audit**

Educate employees and vendors

Publish standards that clarify proper usage

Conduct annual intellectual property audits

Make it easy to adhere to proper trademark usage

Consider trademark watch services

Design management

Increasingly, experienced design directors are joining senior management teams to oversee and build the brand, manage the design group, and identify specialists needed. Companies that value design as a core competency tend to be more successful in their marketing and communications.

Brand identity programs are usually developed by outside firms who have the right qualifications, experience, time, and staffing. The biggest mistake that external consulting firms make is not including the internal design group in the initial research phase. The internal group has insight into the challenge of making things happen. In addition, successful implementation of the program is dependent on the internal group embracing and implementing the system. The internal team must have ongoing access to the external firm for questions, clarifications, and unforeseen circumstances. The external firm should come in for periodic reviews of new work, as well as participate in annual brand audits to ensure that brand expression remains fresh and relevant.

If you think that good design is expensive, you should look at the cost of bad design.

Dr. Ralf Speth
CEO
Jaguar Land Rover

In-house teams live and breathe the brands they work on, and often have more clarity about what the brand stands for.

Alex Center
Design Director
The Coca-Cola Company

Internal creative teams need to seize their insider advantage by using deep knowledge of the brand to leverage their strategic value to the corporation.

Moira Cullen

Vice President, Global Beverage Design
PepsiCo

WGBH recognized that design needed to be a function that reported directly to the CEO.

Chris Pullman

Vice President of Design
WGBH

Characteristics and challenges of internal design teams

Essential characteristics

Managed by a creative or design director

Valued by senior management

Staffed by experienced designers (creative and technical expertise)

Multifunctional (experience across all media)

Multilevel experience (senior level and junior level)

Clearly defined roles and responsibilities

Clearly defined processes and procedures

Commitment to brand identity standards

Ability to be creative within a system

Ability to explain the rationale behind solutions

Open channels of communication with senior management and within the group

Systems to track progress and projects

Biggest challenges

Lack of understanding what brand strength delivers

Overcoming political hurdles

Getting access to senior management

Getting management's respect

Overcoming design-by-committee

Debunking the myth that high quality means high cost

Not being at the table when critical branding decisions are being made

Too much work for too small a staff

An in-house studio becomes indispensable to a brand when knowledge, investment, and pride fuse with vision, creativity, and a mastery of expression.

Jeffrey Fields
Vice President, Global Creative Studio
Starbucks

Design management model
Developed by Jen Miller, consultant

Design groups within organizations often operate at and grow to different levels of maturity depending on the needs of their internal clients as well as their own internal capabilities.

The design team's level of growth is based on their ability to share knowledge through well-defined standards, training, and communication.

Jen Miller
Consultant
Jen Miller Solutions

Internal design department drives company priorities and brand vision, and leads development of brand standards. Brand standards are regularly updated and audited for usability. Brand adherence is measured.

Brand builders

Internal design team collaborates with external agency in brand development, and serves as primary counsel to executive team and clients in developing branding initiatives. Team includes dedicated brand ambassador role.

Innovators

External agency develops brand standards. Internal design department helps set company priorities and leads efforts based on brand knowledge. Creative directors monitor brand adherence.

Strategists

Internal design department designs and executes against brand standards, measures effectiveness, and adds value through best practices.

Advisors

Internal design department executes brand vision at request of business and against available brand standards.

Service providers

Conducting research

Building a brand requires business acumen and design thinking. The first priority is to understand the organization: its mission, vision, values, target markets, corporate culture, competitive advantage, strengths and weaknesses, marketing strategies, and challenges for the future.

1 : conducting research

Answering questions is relatively easy. Asking the right question is more difficult.

Karin Cronan
Partner
CRONAN

Face-to-face conversation is the new luxury.

Susan Bird
Founder + CEO, Wf360
TED Resident

Learning must be focused and accelerated. Clients hire firms with the intellectual capacity to understand the business as a way of ensuring that the solutions are linked to business goals and strategies.

Understanding comes from various sources—from reading strategic documents and business plans to interviewing key stakeholders. Requesting the appropriate information from a client is the first step; it should precede interviewing of any key management or stakeholders. Listening to the organization's vision and strategies for the future forms the nucleus of the creative process for a new identity.

Interviewing key stakeholders provides invaluable insight into the voice, cadence, and personality of an organization. Frequently, ideas and strategies that may never have been recorded before emerge during an interview.

Understanding is also achieved by experiencing the organization from a customer's perspective, and seeing how easy it is to understand the product offerings, receive a sales pitch, or use the products. The goals are to uncover the essence of the company and to understand how the organization fits into the larger competitive environment.

Baseline information to request

Request these business background materials to learn more about the organization prior to any interviews. If it is a public company, examine what financial analysts say about the company's performance and future prospects.

Mission
Vision
Values statement
Value proposition
Organization chart
Strategic planning documents
Business plans
Marketing plans
Annual reports

Existing marketing research
Cultural assessments
Employee surveys
CEO speeches
Press releases
News clippings
History
Domains and trademarks
Social media accounts

Interviewing key stakeholders

Interviewing key management is best done face-to-face. Recording the interview facilitates eye contact and a better interview. If necessary, interviewing can be done over the telephone. Building trust is another agenda. The quality of the questions and the rapport established in the interview set the tone for an important relationship. Encourage individuals to be brief and succinct. Do not provide questions in advance, if possible, since spontaneous answers may be more insightful. It is

absolutely critical for you to read through the baseline information about the company before conducting any interview.

It is important to convey that you have already examined the documents provided. The list of who should be interviewed is cocreated with a client. It is best to keep interviews under forty-five minutes in length. The following questions should be customized before the interview.

Core interview questions

What business are you in?

What is your mission? What are your three most important goals?

Why was this company created?

Describe your products or services.

Who is your target market?

Prioritize your stakeholders in order of importance. How do you want to be perceived by each audience?

What is your competitive advantage? Why do your customers choose your product or service? What do you do better than anyone else?

Who is your competition? Is there a competitor that you admire most? If so, why?

How do you market your products or services?

What are the major trends and changes that affect your industry?

Where will you be in five years? In ten years?

How do you measure success?

What values and beliefs unify your employees and drive their performance?

What are the potential barriers to the success of your products or services?

What keeps you up at night?

Place yourself in the future. If your company could do anything or be anything, what would it be?

If you could communicate a single message about your company, what would it be?

We have two eyes, two ears, and one mouth. We should use them in that proportion.

Ilse Crawford
Designer + Creative Director
StudioIlse

Insight Phase 1

Observing the world and listening without judgment to the ideas of others opens up possibilities. The work itself becomes the hero.

Although research is the business discipline for gathering and interpreting data, insight comes from a more personal and intuitive place.

Design is a dance between the intuitive and intentional. The greatest challenge of the branding process is to realize that you cannot control anything other than your focus and attention. Trusting the process and keeping the ball in the air will always deliver extraordinary outcomes.

Just breathe.

Work to envision, believe in, and fight for greatness. One leader, one person, one challenge at a time.

Keith Yamashita
Founder
SYPartners

Your superpower is what you do better than anyone else on your team. One way for a team to draw on all its strengths is to know and activate each member's superpower.

Superpower Card Deck
SYPartners

We are moving from an economy and a society built on the logical, linear, computer-like capabilities of the Information Age to an economy and a society built on the inventive, empathic, big picture capabilities of what's rising in its place, the Conceptual Age.

Daniel H. Pink
A Whole New Mind

Questions to ponder

Peter Drucker, Management Consultant

What is your business?

Who is the customer?

What is the value to the customer?

What will our business be?

What should our business be?

Keith Yamashita, Chairman, SYPartners

Why do we exist?

What will we become?

What makes employees passionate about their work?

What excites our customers?

What are the ideas that drive our company?

What are we doing that's different from what everyone else in our industry is doing?

What do we need to be successful?

What is holding us back?

Jim Collins, *From Good to Great*

What are you passionate about?

What can you be best in the world at?

What drives your economic engine?

Marcel Proust, Author

If you could change one thing about yourself, what would it be?

What do you consider your greatest achievement?

What is your most marked characteristic?

What is your idea of perfect happiness?

Basekamp

Why are we doing this?

What problem are we solving?

Is this actually useful?

Are we adding value?

Will this change behavior?

Is there an easier way?

What's the opportunity cost?

Is it really worth it?

Chris Hacker, Professor, Art Center College of Design

Do we really need it?

Is it designed to minimize waste?

Can it be smaller or lighter or made of fewer materials?

Is it designed to be durable or multifunctional?

Does it use renewable resources?

Are the product and packaging refillable, recyclable, or repairable?

Does it come from a socially and environmentally responsible company?

Is it made locally?

Danny Whatmough, Blogger

What is the objective?

How will you build a community?

What are you going to say?

Who's going to manage it?

How will you measure success?

Stanisław Radziejowski, Sea Captain

What do you want to be when you grow up?

Insights appear when we stop thinking and let go. Answers to an intractable problem can come on a walk, in a dream, or in the shower. When we least expect it, fragmented thinking falls away and the whole appears.

Lissa Reidel
Consultant

Insight leads to compelling new customer experiences.

Michael Dunn
CEO
Prophet

Market research Phase 1

Smart research can be a catalyst for change; misguided research can stand in the way of innovation. Market research is the gathering, evaluation, and interpretation of data affecting customer preferences for products, services, and brands. New insights about attitudes, awareness, and behavior of prospects and customers often indicate opportunities for future growth. Usability research has finally become more mainstream.

Although anyone can access secondary research on the web, data alone does not provide answers. Interpretation is a skill in itself. There are many proprietary research tools and client intelligence competencies to help global corporations develop brand strategy. Smaller branding firms often partner with market research firms and, in many cases, are provided with existing research reports about customer preferences or marketing segments. Every member of the branding team should be a mystery shopper.

The best market researchers see the big picture, are diligent about the details, and know how to produce actionable results.

Laurie C. Ashcraft
President
Ashcraft Research

Research is to see what everybody else has seen, and to think what nobody else has thought.

Albert Szent-Györgyi

Qualitative research

Qualitative research reveals customers' perceptions, beliefs, feelings, and motives. Findings may offer new insights about the brand and are often a prelude to quantitative research.

Bulletin boards

Participants take part in online panels where they can post anything they want. During mergers, employees can reply anonymously.

Ethnography

Customer behavior is observed in everyday life in work, home, environment, or retail.

Focus groups

Group discussions about a predetermined subject are led by a moderator with selected participants who share common characteristics.

Mystery shopping

Trained mystery shoppers anonymously pose as customers, and evaluate the shopping experience, salesmanship, professionalism, closing skills, follow-up, and overall satisfaction.

One-on-one interviews

Individual in-depth interviews with company leaders, employees, and customers are ideally conducted face-to-face. Information and anecdotes yielded by this method can be rich and particularly valuable to the branding process.

Social listening

Social listening is monitoring conversations about a brand on social networks.

Primary research
Collection of new qualitative or quantitative information designed to fit specific needs.

Quantitative research

Quantitative research creates statistically valid market information. The aim is to provide enough data from enough different people to enable companies to predict—with an acceptable level of confidence—what might happen.

Images of dominant brands, such as the IPod, stimulate the same side of the brain activated by religious symbols.

Martin Lindstrom
Buyology

When it comes to evaluating concepts, it's more valuable to understand how consumers feel than what they think.

Emelia Rallapalli
Founder
Pebble Strategy

Online surveys

Information is gathered via the web from respondents who are clustered around commonalities. Typically, potential respondents receive an email inviting them to take a survey, with a link to the survey itself.

Usability testing

Designers and human-factor engineers observe and monitor participants using software or screen sharing. Users are selected carefully, and results are analyzed in depth.

Product testing

Products are tested to replicate real life or to get a point-in-time user experience. Whether it is preparing and eating a food product or driving a new vehicle, product testing is critical to the long-term success of a brand.

Neuromarketing

Neuromarketing applies the principles of neuroscience and uses biometrics to study how consumers' brains respond to marketing stimuli.

Segmentation

Consumers and businesses are divided into clustered groups, each with its own special interests, lifestyles, and affinity for particular goods and services. Consumer segments are usually defined by demographic and psychographic information.

Equity tracking

Ongoing brand strength is monitored. Most large brands conduct continual in-market equity tracking that includes key brand ratings, brand and advertising awareness, and brand usage trended over time.

Digital analytics

Information is automatically collected from the web.

Secondary research

Interpretation and application of existing statistical, demographic, or qualitative data.

Researchers use information to quantify, qualify, define, benchmark, and cast a critical eye on a company and its brand, the markets they serve, and the opportunities they seek.

Dennis Dunn, PhD
Principal
B2BPulse

Competitive intelligence

Many business database services on the web provide data and information about industries, private and public companies, and their stock activity and management.

Market structure

This research defines how a category is structured. It provides a hierarchy for attributes such as size, form, or flavor. It identifies "white space" or market opportunities where no brands are currently competing.

Syndicated data

This kind of standardized data is regularly recorded and sold by suppliers such as Nielsen and IRI. It is used for determining market share and purchase cycle.

Usability testing Phase 1

Usability testing is a research tool used by designers, engineers, and marketing teams to develop and refine new and existing products. This method can be extended to any part of the customer experience, purchasing, delivery, and customer service. Unlike other research methods, usability testing relies on "live" customer experiences with a product. Through the careful observation of a handful of typical users, product development teams can acquire immediate feedback on the product's strengths and weaknesses. By documenting the actual experiences of people using the product, the development team can isolate and remedy any design flaws before releasing it to the market.

The benefit of this approach is that it makes the end user's needs central to the product development process, rather than an afterthought.

True usability is invisible. If something is going well, you don't notice it. If one thing doesn't work about it, you notice everything.

Dana Chisnell
Founder of UsabilityWorks
Co-Director of Center for Civic Design

Usability testing is a great tool throughout the process. Test early and often with small groups of representative users. If you are revising or updating something, test the current version first.

Dr. Ginny Redish
Redish & Associates, Inc.

Process: Usability testing From *Handbook of Usability Testing* by Jeffrey Rubin and Dana Chisnell

> **Develop test plan**

Review testing goals

Communicate research questions

Summarize participant characteristics

Describe the method

List the tasks

Describe the test environment, equipment, and logistics

Explain moderator role

List the data you will collect

Describe how the results will be reported

> **Set up environment**

Decide on location and space

Gather and check equipment, artifacts, and tools

Identify coresearchers, assistants, and observers

Determine documentation techniques

> **Find + select participants**

Define the behavior and motivation selection criteria for each user group

Characterize users

Define the criteria for each user group

Determine the number of participants to test

Screen and select participants

Schedule and confirm participants

> **Prepare test materials**

Develop a script for moderator

Develop task scenarios for participants to perform

Develop background questionnaire to collect demographic data

Develop pretest questionnaires and interviews

Develop post-test questionnaire about experience

What is needed for usability testing
Developed by Dr. Ginny Redish
Letting Go of the Words: Writing Web Content that Works

Benefits of usability testing
Developed by Dana Chisnell

There's no substitute for watching and listening to users as they interact with your design, whether it's a product, software, or a service.

Dana Chisnell
Founder of UsabilityWorks

Real issues: You have thought about what you want to learn and planned the test to give you answers to your questions.

Real people: Participants represent (at least some of) the site visitors or app users you want.

Real tasks: The stories (scenarios, conversations) you have them try out with the website or app are ones that they really want to do or that are realistic to them.

Real data: You watch, listen, ask neutral questions, and take notes as they work. (In remote unmoderated tests, you may get only what they did—clickstream data —without hearing why or being able to ask questions.)

Real insights: You put away your assumptions and biases as you review the data. You see what is working well and what is not.

Real changes: You use what you learned. You keep what is working well and improve what could be better.

Focus group results are what site visitors think they might do. Usability testing shows what visitors actually do.

Kelly Goto & Emily Cotler
Web ReDesign 2.0: Workflow that Works

Informs design solutions

Creates satisfying (and even delightful) products

Eliminates design problems and frustrations

Creates a historical record of usability benchmarks for future releases

Development teams employing usability methods are quicker to market

Puts customer at center of the process

Increases customer satisfaction

Creates products that are useful and easy to use

Features are more likely to be popular among users

Improves profitability

Reduces development costs over the life of a product

Increases sales and the probability of repeat sales

Minimizes risk and complaints

> Conduct test sessions

Moderate the session impartially

Probe and interact with the participant as appropriate

Don't "rescue" participants when they struggle

Have participants fill out pretest questionnaires

Have participants fill out post-test questionnaires

Debrief participants

Debrief observers

> Analyze data + observations

Summarize performance data

Summarize preference data

Summarize scores by group or version

Identify what causes errors and frustrations

Conduct a source of error analysis

Prioritize problems

> Report findings + recommendations

Focus on solutions that will have the widest impact

Provide short- and long-term recommendations

Take business and technology constraints into account

Indicate areas where further research is required

Create a highlights video

Present findings

Marketing audit Phase 1

Marketing audits are used to methodically examine and analyze all marketing, communications, and identity systems, both existing systems and those out of circulation. The process takes a magnifying glass to the brand and its multiple expressions over time. To develop a vision for an organization's brand in the future, you must have a sense of its history.

Inevitably, something of worth has been tossed out over time—a tagline, a symbol, a phrase, a point of view—for what seemed to be a good reason at the time. There might be something from the past that should be resuscitated or repurposed. Perhaps a color or a tagline has been in place since the founding of the

company. Consider whether this equity should be moved forward.

Repositioning an organization, revitalizing and redesigning an existing identity system, or developing a new identity for a merger requires an examination of the communications and marketing tools an organization has used in the past. Identifying what has worked and what has been successful or even dysfunctional provides valuable learning in the creation of a new identity. Mergers present the most challenging audit scenarios because two companies that were competitors are now becoming aligned.

Examine customer experience first and move to the intersection of strategy, content, and design.

Carla Hall
Creative Director
Carla Hall Design Group

Process: Marketing audit

> Understand the big picture	> Request materials	> Create a system	> Solicit information	> Examine materials
Markets served	Existing and archival	Organization	Contextual/historical background	Business papers
Sales and distribution	Identity standards	Retrieval	Marketing management	Electronic communications
Marketing management	Business papers	Documentation	Communications functions	Sales and marketing
Communications functions	Sales and marketing	Review	Attitudes toward brand	Internal communications
Internal technology	Electronic communications		Attitudes toward identity	Environments
Challenges	Internal communications			Packaging
	Signage			
	Packaging			

Request materials

The following is the broad range of materials to request. It is important to create an effective organization and retrieval system since in all probability you will be amassing a large collection. It is important to have someone provide background about what has worked and what has not worked.

Organizing audits: Create a war room

Create a war room and curate the walls. Devise a standard system to capture findings. Take a "before" picture.

Brand identity

All versions of all identities ever used
All signatures, marks, logotypes
Company names
Division names
Product names
All taglines
All trademarks owned
Standards and guidelines

Business papers

Letterhead, envelopes, labels, business cards
Invoices, statements
Proposal covers
Folders
Forms

Sales and marketing

Sales and product literature
Newsletters
Advertising campaigns
Investor relations materials
Annual reports
Seminar literature
Presentations

Digital communications

Website
Intranet
Extranet
Video
Banners
Blogs
Social networks
Apps
Email signatures

Internal communications

Employee communications
Ephemera (T-shirts, baseball caps, pens, and so on)

Environmental applications

External signage
Internal signage
Store interiors
Banners
Trade show booths

Retail

Packaging
Promotions
Shopping bags
Menus
Merchandise
Displays

> ### Examine identity

Marks
Logotypes
Color
Imagery
Typography
Look and feel

> ### Examine how things happen

Process
Decision making
Communications responsibility
In-house and webmaster
Production
Advertising agency

> ### Document learnings

Equity
Brand architecture
Positioning
Key messages
Visual language
Epiphanies

Competitive audit Phase 1

A competitive audit is a dynamic, data-gathering process. Audits examine the competition's brands, key messages, and identity in the marketplace, from brandmarks and taglines to ads and websites. More than ever, it is easy to gather information on the internet; however don't stop there. Finding ways to experience the competition as a customer often provides valuable insights.

The greater the insight into the competition, the greater the competitive edge. Positioning the company in relationship to the competition is both a marketing and a design imperative. "Why should the customer choose our products or services over those of others?" is the marketing challenge. "We need to look and feel different" is the design imperative.

The breadth and depth of this audit can vary widely depending on the nature of the company and the scope of the project. Frequently, a company has its own competitive intelligence. Qualitative or quantitative research that can be a source of critical data need to be reviewed.

An audit is an opportunity to build a complete understanding of the business and establish a context for the branding solution.

David Kendall

Principal, User Experience Design, Digital Design and UX
AT&T

Process: Competitive audit

> Identify competitors	> Gather information + research	> Determine positioning	> Identify key messages	> Examine visual identity
Who are leading competitors?	List information needed	Examine competitive positioning	Mission	Symbols
What is their category?	Examine existing research and materials	Identify features/benefits	Tagline	Meaning
Who most closely resembles the client, and in what ways?	Determine if additional research is required	Identity strengths/ weaknesses	Descriptors	Shape
Which companies compete indirectly?	Consider interviews, focus groups, online surveys	Examine brand personality	Themes from advertising and collaterals	Color
		Examine category		Typography
				Look and feel

Using the competitive audit

Present audit at the end of the research phase.

Use learning to develop new brand and positioning strategy.

Use audit to inform the design process.

Consider meaning, shape, color, form, and content that the competition does not use.

Use audit when presenting new brand identity strategies to demonstrate differentiation.

Understanding the competition

Who are they?

What do their brands stand for?

What markets/audiences do they serve?

What advantages (strengths) do they have?

What disadvantages (weaknesses) do they have?

What are their modes of selling and cultivating customers/clients?

How do they position themselves?

How do they characterize their customers/clients?

What are their key messages?

What is their financial condition?

How much market share do they hold?

How do they use brand identity to leverage success?

What do they look and feel like?

Competitive audit of meal kit subscription services

Meal kit subscription services have transformed the task of making dinner into an easy culinary experience.

Robin Goffman
Entrepreneur

> **Document identity**

Identity signatures

Marketing collateral materials and website

Sales and promotional tools

Brand architecture

Signage

> **Examine naming strategy**

Core brand name

Naming system for products and services

Descriptors and domains

> **Examine brand hierarchy**

What type of brand architecture?

How integrated or independent is the core brand in relation to subsidiaries or sub-brands?

How are the products and services organized?

> **Experience the competition**

Navigate websites

Visit shops and offices

Purchase and use products

Use services

Listen to a sales pitch

Call customer service

> **Synthesize learnings**

Make conclusions

Start seeing opportunities

Organize presentation

Language audit Phase 1

A language audit may be called a voice audit, message audit, and content audit. Regardless of the moniker, it is the Mount Everest of audits. Every organization aspires to conduct one, but very few accomplish it or go beyond base camp one. Even though language is an intrinsic part of the marketing audit, many companies do not tackle "voice" until after they have designed a new brand identity program.

The courageous look at content and design at the same time, revealing the entire spectrum of how language is used. Analyzing the intersection of customer experience, design, and content is an intensive and rigorous endeavor that demands the left brain and right brain to work in tandem.

"Dear World...Yours, Cambridge" provides a verbal and visual format with which the University of Cambridge can talk about past and present global achievements and introduce what's next. The letters appear on banners and posters across the campus; the framework is used on the university's giving portal; and the verbal theme extends across speeches, animations, and films.

Vigorous writing is concise.

William Strunk, Jr. and E.B. White
The Elements of Style

Dear
World...

**Yours,
Cambridge**

Process: Examining language

Company name–formal
Company name–informal
Descriptors
Taglines
Product names
Process names
Service names
Division names

Identification

Mission
Vision and values
Key messages
Guiding principles
Customer pledges
History
Elevator pitch
Boilerplate

Aspiration

Meaning
Voice
Tone
Emphasis
Accuracy
Clarity
Consistency
Positioning
Framework
Hierarchy
Punctuation
Capitalization
Style

Foundation

Criteria for evaluating communications
Developed by Siegel + Gale

Adherence to brand values

Is the tone and look of the information consistent with your brand attributes?

Customization

Is content based on what you already know about the customer?

Structure and navigational ease

Is the purpose of the communication readily apparent, and is the communication easy to use?

Educational value

Did you take the opportunity to anticipate unfamiliar concepts or terminology?

Visual appeal

Does the communication look inviting and in keeping with the company's positioning?

Marketing potential

Does the communication seize the opportunity to cross-sell products in a meaningful, informed way?

Loyalty support

Does the communication thank customers for their business or in some way reward them for extending their relationship with you?

Utility

Is the communication well suited to its function?

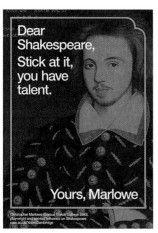

University of Cambridge: Johnson Banks

The campaign celebrates eight centuries of achievement in order to attract world-class academics and to fund world-changing initiatives.

Michael Johnson
Founder
Johnson Banks

Call to action   Phone numbers   URLs   Email signatures   Voicemail messages   Titles   Addresses   Diagrams   Forms   Directions

Navigation

News releases   FAQs   Press kits   Annual reports   Brochures   Shareholder communications   Call center scripts   Customer service scripts   Sales scripts   Presentations   Announcements   Web content   Blog content   Blast emails   Advertising campaigns   Direct mail

Information

Audit readout Phase 1

An audit readout signals the end of the research and analysis phase. It is a formal presentation made to the key decision makers that synthesizes key learnings from the interviews, research, and audits. The biggest challenge is organizing a vast amount of information into a succinct and strategic presentation. The audit readout is a valuable assessment tool for senior management, and a critical tool for the creative team to do responsible, differentiated work. It is a tool used as a reference throughout the entire process.

It is rare that an audit readout does not engender epiphanies. Although marketing and communications may not be top of mind for some management teams, seeing a lack of consistency across media, or seeing how much more discipline the competition uses in its marketing systems, is a real eye-opener. The objective of the audit is to open up the possibilities.

I can't believe we are using the same stock images as our biggest competitors.

Anonymous

We see the opportunity. Others see how far the brand voice has strayed.

Joe Duffy
Chairman
Duffy & Partners

Analysis requires an ability to listen, read between the lines, observe what others don't see, see patterns, make connections, and identify opportunities.

Blake Deutsch

Process: Synthesize learnings

> Interviews	> Brand essence	> Marketing research	> Marketing audit	> Language audit
Stakeholder categories	Strategy	Brand recognition	Logos and signatures	Voice and tone
Key learnings	Positioning	Survey results	Brand architecture	Clarity
Customer insights		Focus group findings	Across marketing channels, media, product lines	Naming
Excerpts		Perceptual mapping	Look and feel	Taglines
		SWOTs	Imagery	Key messages
		Gap analysis	Color	Navigation
		Benchmarking	Typography	Hierarchy
				Descriptors

Essential characteristics

Focuses leaders on the possibilities	Adds value and sense of urgency to the process
Jumpstarts robust conversations	Informs the creative team
Identifies gaps between positioning and expression	Unearths brilliant, forgotten ideas, images, and words
Uncovers inconsistencies	Builds commitment to doing things right in the future
Reveals the need for more differentiation	

Action Against Hunger serves over 45 countries. A visual audit shows the complicated mixture of local country names and acronyms.

Michael Johnson
Founder
Johnson Banks

Action Against Hunger audit readout: Johnson Banks

> **Competitive audit**

Positioning
Logos
Brand architecture
Taglines
Key messages
Look and feel
Imagery
Color
Typography

> **Intellectual property audit**

Trademarks
Compliance issues

> **Process audit**

Existing guidelines
Technology
Collaboration

Clarifying strategy

Phase 2 involves both methodical examination and strategic imagination. It is about analysis, discovery, synthesis, simplicity, and clarity. This combination of rational thinking and creative intelligence characterizes the best strategies, which go where others have not.

2 : clarifying strategy

Look into a microscope with one eye and a telescope with the other.

Blake Deutsch

In Phase 2, all of the learnings from the research and audits are distilled into a unifying idea and a positioning strategy. Agreement is solidified about target markets, competitive advantage, brand core values, brand attributes, and project goals. More often than not, the definitions of the problem and its challenges have evolved. Although many companies have their values and attributes in place, they may not have taken the time to articulate and refine them, or to share them beyond an off-site management retreat. The role of the consultant here is to identify, articulate, illuminate, weave, and play back the possibilities.

Phase 2 can lead to a number of possible outcomes. In a merger, a new brand strategy for the combined enterprise is necessary. Other scenarios require a unifying idea that will be effective across business lines. A brand brief is created, and a discussion about findings and epiphanies follows. When there is openness and candor between the client and the consultant, true collaboration can produce exceptional results. Key success factors during this phase are trust and mutual respect.

A clearly defined business strategy

When Turner Duckworth first met with Jeff Bezos in 1999, their client needed a logo to reflect the visionary's business strategy to sell more than just books. The strategy was clear, and the design firm's goals were to position Amazon.com as customer-focused and friendly.

A need for brand strategy

In 2003, the V&A did not have a strong or distinctive brand. The museum worked with Jane Wentworth Associates (JWA) to develop a brand strategy. Its vision was to be the world's leading museum of art and design. JWA then developed a long-term staff engagement program to help everyone understand what the strategy represented and give them the confidence to put it into practice.

A need to activate business strategy

Landor worked with the Mint team to develop an identity system to embody the spirit of the brand, and to make sure that the brand work activated the business strategy. In 2014, Landor helped Intuit translate Mint's business strategy to stand for a bigger, emotional idea.

Starting from a blank page

NIZUC Resort & Spa started as nothing more than a destination and a developer that had a burning desire to compete with established luxury brands. In 2014, Carbone Smolan Agency created the story that would act as the foundation for the NIZUC brand and transform its property into a sought-after luxurious escape.

A joint venture needs a name and strategy

VSA Partners created a brand strategy and a new name, Cingular, for the joint venture of Bell South Mobility and SBC Wireless in 2000. The new name would represent eleven former brands and more than 21 million customers. The brand strategy positioned Cingular as the embodiment of human expression since VSA viewed the wireless space evolving from a features-and-functions buying decision to a lifestyle choice.

To spark a conversation with the founders of a start-up about their strategy, I composed their brand attributes in an image of their product category.

Jon Bjornson
Jon Bjornson Art & Design

Narrowing the focus Phase 2

It is never enough to examine a company's current business strategy, core values, target markets, competitors, distribution channels, technology, and competitive advantage. It is crucial to stand back and look at the big picture—what are the economic, sociopolitical, global, or social trends that will affect the brand in the future? What are the drivers that have made the company successful in the past?

Interviews with senior management, employees, customers, and industry experts will provide an intimate glance into the uniqueness of a company. Often, the CEO has a clear picture of an ideal future and all its possibilities. A good consultant will hold up a mirror and say, "This is what you have told me and I heard it again from your customers and your sales force. And this is why it is powerful." It is important to look for the gold.

A brand becomes stronger when you narrow the focus.

Al Ries and Laura Ries
The 22 Immutable Laws of Branding

If you want to build a brand, you must focus your branding efforts on owning a word in the prospect's mind. A word that no one else owns. What prestige is to Mercedes, safety is to Volvo.

Al Ries and Laura Ries
The 22 Immutable Laws of Branding

As the mass and volume of information increases, people search for a clear signal—one that gives pattern, shape, and direction to the voice.

Bruce Mau
Designer

Vision
Values
Mission
Value proposition
Culture
Target market
Segments
Stakeholder perceptions
Services
Products
Infrastructure

Understanding

Marketing strategy
Competition
Trends
Pricing
Distribution
Research
Environment
Economics
Sociopolitics
Strengths/weaknesses
Opportunities
Threats

Engage in meaningful dialogue

Companies frequently do not take the time to revisit who they are and what they are about. The beauty of this process is that it gives senior managers an explicit reason to go off-site and spin a dream. It is a worthwhile exercise. Superb consultants know how to facilitate a dialogue between core leaders in which various brand scenarios are explored and brand attributes surface.

Uncover brand essence (or simple truth)

What does a company do that is best in world? Why do its customers choose it over its competition? What business are they in? How is it really different than its most successful competitor? What are three adjectives that summarize how this company wants to be perceived? What are its strengths and weaknesses? The clarity of these answers is an important driver in this phase.

Develop a positioning platform

Subsequent to information gathering and analysis are the development and refinement of a positioning strategy. Perceptual mapping is a technique that is frequently used to brainstorm a positioning strategy. On which dimension can a company compete? What can it own?

Create the big idea

The big idea can always be expressed in one sentence, although the rationale could usually fill a book. Sometimes the big idea becomes the tagline or the battle cry. The big idea must be simple and transportable. It must carry enough ambiguity to allow for future developments that cannot be predicted. It must create an emotional connection, and it must be easy to talk about, whether you are the CEO or an employee. Big ideas are hard to develop.

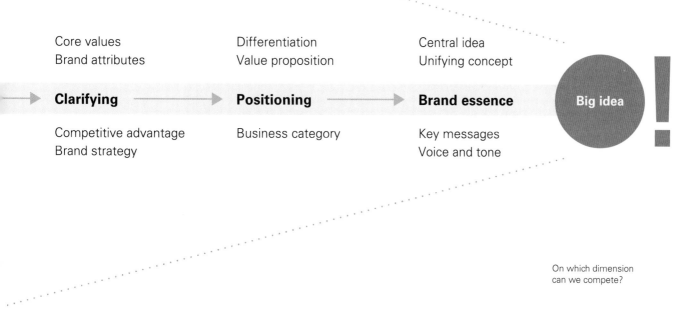

Core values
Brand attributes

Clarifying ⟶

Competitive advantage
Brand strategy

Differentiation
Value proposition

Positioning ⟶

Business category

Central idea
Unifying concept

Brand essence

Key messages
Voice and tone

Big idea

!

On which dimension
can we compete?

139

Positioning Phase 2

A brand's positioning is influenced by every encounter—not just with customers, but with employees, stakeholders, competitors, regulators, suppliers, legislators, journalists, and the public. Understanding customer needs, the competition, the brand's advantage, changes in demographics, technology, and trends is critical.

Today, a brand's positioning evolves continually, influenced by Facebook posts and Twitter trends, social and political shifts, and the constant micro-changes in the business climate internationally. The ability to diversify, change, and reposition is essential. New opportunities emerge as disruptions make yesterday's products and services obsolete. Brands like Trader Joe's, Southwest Airlines, and Amazon have convinced their customers that they truly understand their lifestyle. Airbnb, Lyft, and Craigslist have transformed consumers' habits and disrupted the economy. Crowdfunding has altered the way people relate to friends, strangers, and the possibilities they pursue.

Great brands are in command and out of control. Twenty-first century brands won't be built by telling; they will be built by being.

Chris Grams
The Ad-Free Brand

Positioning has the potential to create new openings in an oversaturated, continually changing marketplace.

Lissa Reidel
Consultant

The onliness exercise
Marty Neumeier, *ZAG*

This exercise helps brand builders discover their radical differentiation. "If you can't say why your brand is both different and compelling in a few words, don't fix your statement—fix your company," says Neumeier. Cirque de Soleil, the only circus that doesn't have animals, is a great example.

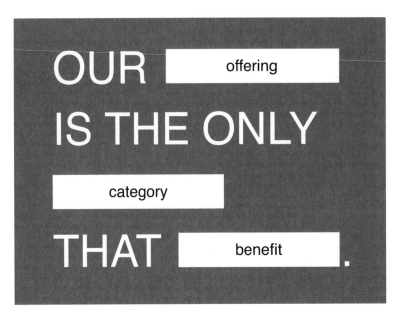

OUR [offering] IS THE ONLY [category] THAT [benefit].

@MartyNeumeier

Superior competitive positioning

Excerpted from *Brand Planning* by Kevin Lane Keller

Determine competitive frames of reference

The competitive frame of reference defines which other brands a brand competes with and therefore which brands should be the focus of analysis and study.

Develop unique brand points-of-difference

Attributes or benefits that consumers strongly associate with a brand, positively evaluate, and believe they could not find to the same extent with a competitive brand.

Establish shared brand points-of-parity

Associations designed to negate competitors' points-of-difference and demonstrate category credentials.

Create a brand mantra

Short, three- to five-word phrases that capture key points of difference and the irrefutable essence or spirit of the brand.

Imperatives for the positioning process

Developed by Chris Grams, *The Ad-Free Brand*

Understand that it matters what everyone thinks about the brand, not just customers.

Empower as many people as possible to listen and to speak on behalf of the brand.

Bring the community in and allow the brand out.

Encourage people to live the brand, not just talk about it.

Achieve results with a collaborative and engaging process.

Signal that branding is an ongoing conversation and a work in progress.

Acknowledge that building a brand in a digital and connected world is about guiding, influencing, and being, not telling.

Test ideas with communities of prospects, partners, and contributors.

Brand pillars

Developed by Matchstic

Purpose
What is your purpose beyond making money?

What gets you out of bed in the morning?

What motivates your employees?

Difference
What do you do or deliver that your competition doesn't?

What is your unique personality?

Why should your customers choose you over others?

Value
What do your customers truly need? Why?

What are their functional and emotional drivers?

How do you connect on a deeper level?

Execution
How do you demonstrate your benefits?

How do you consistently reinforce your position in the marketplace?

How do you ensure a positive customer experience?

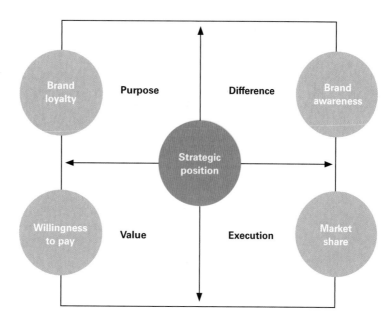

© Matchstic 2017

Brand brief Phase 2

Getting key decision makers to have a shared understanding of the brand is a critical step, and often hard to do. Culling the brand down to a simple, one-page document, rather than a twenty-page treatise that no one wants to read, let alone try to remember, makes it easier to facilitate robust discussions and make decisions. The best briefs are succinct, strategic and approved by the most senior people in an organization early in the process.

When a brief is approved, the project is more likely to be on track and successful. The brief is the result of a collaborative process—collective thinking and agreement on a brand's attributes and positioning, desired endpoint and criteria of the process. Once the brand brief is agreed upon, the next step is to write the creative brief, which is a road map for the creative team. Never write it until the brand brief has been approved.

The brand brief is a foundational document, that clearly articulates who we are and why we exist.

Matt Hanes
Founder
Acru

We use the brand brief to focus the conversation on building leadership alignment around the brand's core components.

Blake Howard
Cofounder
Matchstic

Matchstic was engaged by the Arthritis Foundation to reignite its purpose, and increase engagement between staff and volunteers.

Arthritis Foundation Brand Brief

Big Idea

Champion of Yes

Core Purpose: We exist to...

Conquer arthritis.

Attributes: We Are...

All-in
Driven by passion and commitment to work beyond the call of duty

Expert
Daily applying and strengthening our long-standing track record of leadership

Bold
Tenacious and aggressive persistence in attacking arthritis and its effects

Ever Present
When, where and how you need us—in a relevant way and for the long haul

Brave
Optimistic outlook and winning spirit together in the face of darkness

Primary Target Audience

Resilient Mother

Arthritis has shattered her ability to live and thrive in the day to day. Limits abound. Frustration mounts. She needs a partner, a community and a reason to believe that this will not destroy the small moments of joy that life has in store.

Value Proposition

The Arthritis Foundation anchors my family's fight against arthritis by helping me build a plan to live fully today and find hope for tomorrow.

Secondary Target Audience

Arthritis Care Provider

As a specialist, he is this population's number one trusted resource. He needs a partner to help him develop and deliver patient-focused resources. *This is the first domino in reaching the broader arthritis care community.*

Value Proposition

The Arthritis Foundation enhances my patient care with the how-to's of living a thriving life with arthritis.

Positioning: What makes us different?

We are the Arthritis Nonprofit Health Organization that fights for people with arthritis by cocreating a personalized plan to live their best life, one Yes at a time.

Arthritis Foundation: Matchstic

The components of a brand brief
Developed by Shantini Munthree, Managing Partner, The Union Marketing Group

	Purpose	What to include
Core purpose/ mission statement	Explain why the company exists beyond making a profit	Short, readable, memorable sentence or two
Audience	Define the target audience and ideal customers	Target audience, their highest-level needs, and key insights into aspirations and challenges
Value proposition	Outline functional, emotional, and social benefits (how we fulfill audience needs)	Highest-level benefits that tie to highest-level needs
Values	Document the core beliefs and values that define our culture	Selective words to describe brand values
Personality attributes	Guide brand expression strategies and personality	Selective words to describe brand personality, voice, and distinctive character
Key competitors	Compare points of difference and parity	Leading competitors who serve same target
Business/product/services	Describe the deliverables being offered	Top three to four offers
Proof points	State reasons why we will be successful	Irrefutable evidence to support value proposition
Big idea	Express a compelling, central, unifying concept	Succinct, memorable phrase

The difference between a brand brief and a creative brief
Developed by Shantini Munthree, Managing Partner, The Union Marketing Group

	Brand brief	Creative brief
Primary purpose	Brand equity/reputation management/clarity	Achieve project goals
Timeline	Evergreen	Product/service, business goal-specific
Decision owner	CEO/leadership team	Marketing/creative director/design team
Metrics	Brand health, tied to business goals	Goal tied to project goal
Key audience	Leadership team and all employees	Creative team
Used for	Organizational agreement, brand strategy, staying on brand	Brand messaging, identity design, redesign or naming

Create a succinct and strategic diagram

Creating a brand brief that everyone agrees on is a hard task but well worth the time invested because it is a sustainable tool. Make it visual. Hand out 11 x 17 prints of the brief to jumpstart conversations. The number of versions may surprise you. It's okay.

Brief variations

Large companies create briefs for marketing segments or business lines.

Version control

Writing a brief is an iterative process. Save each version with a date and version number.

Naming Phase 2

Naming is not for the faint of heart. It is a complex, creative, and iterative process requiring experience in linguistics, marketing, research, and trademark law. Even for the experts, finding a name for today's company, product, or service that can be legally protected presents a formidable challenge.

Various brainstorming techniques are used to generate hundreds, if not thousands, of options. Culling the large list takes skill and patience.

Names need to be judged against positioning goals, performance criteria, and availability within a sector. It is natural to want to fall in love with a name, but the bottom line is that meaning and associations are built over time. Agreement is not easy to achieve, especially when choices seem limited. Contextual testing is smart and helps decision making.

Naming is 20% creative and 80% political.

Danny Altman
Founder and Creative Director
A Hundred Monkeys

Naming digital assets is like playing three-dimensional Scrabble. You need to play with words from more points of view, and you need to decide how much you can spend before you start grabbing letters, because the words that look best from the most points of view will have a price tag attached to them.

Howard Fish
Founder
Fish Partners

Process: Naming

> Revisit positioning

Examine brand goals and target market needs

Evaluate existing names

Examine competitor names

> Get organized

Develop timeline

Determine team

Identify brainstorming techniques

Determine search mechanisms

Develop decision-making process

Organize reference resources

> Create naming criteria

Performance criteria

Positioning criteria

Legal criteria

Regulatory criteria, if any

> Brainstorm solutions

Create numerous names

Organize in categories and themes

Look at hybrids and mimetics

Be prolific

Explore variations/iterations on a theme

Inspiration

Language
Meaning
Personality
Dictionaries
Googling
Thesauruses
Latin
Greek
Foreign languages
Mass culture
Poetry
Television
Music
History
Art
Commerce
Colors
Symbols
Metaphors
Analogies
Sounds
Science
Technology
Astronomy
Myths
Stories
Values
Dreams

Naming basics

Brand names are valuable assets.

When you are brainstorming, there are no stupid ideas.

Always examine a name in context.

Consider sound, cadence, and ease of pronunciation.

Be methodical in tracking name selections.

Determine smartest searching techniques.

Review all the criteria before you reject a name.

Meaning and association are built over time.

Voice of the stakeholders exercise

Create one page for each name candidate.

Develop five to ten statements using the name in context.
Example: New Name is the product I trust.

Attribute each statement to a key stakeholder.
Example: New Name is the product I trust. Tessa Wheeler, customer

Have each decision maker read one statement out loud.

Discuss what you like about this name first.

Discuss what challenges the name presents next.

> ## Conduct initial screening

Positioning
Linguistic
Legal
Common-law databases
Online search engines
Online phone directories
Domain registration
Creating a short list

> ## Conduct contextual testing

Say the name
Leave a voicemail
Email the name
Put it on a business card
Put it in an ad headline
Put it into the voice of the stakeholders

> ## Testing

Determine methods to trust
Check for red flags
Unearth trademark conflicts
Check language connotations
Check cultural connotations
Do linguistic analysis

> ## Final legal screen

Domestic
International
Domain
Regulatory
Registration

Ten principles for renaming
Developed by Marshall Strategy

Be clear about why change is needed. You should have a compelling reason, and clear business benefits, for going through the name change process. Making a strong case for change—whether legal, market-based, or other—will help everyone involved rise above emotional issues and enable a more successful and meaningful effort.

Assess the impact of change. A name change is more complicated than creating a new name because it affects established brand equity and all existing brand communications. A thorough audit of equity and communication assets should be conducted, to fully understand how a name change will affect your investments and operations.

Know what your choices are. Depending on your reason for change, it can be very difficult to consider change in the abstract. It is much easier to commit to a change when you have alternative names to consider that solve your communication issues.

Know what you are trying to say before you name it. Naming is a highly emotional issue that can be hard to judge objectively. By first agreeing on what your new name should say, you concentrate your efforts on choosing the name that says it best.

Avoid trendy names. By definition, these are names that will lose their appeal over time. Choosing a new name simply because it sounds "hip" or "cool" generally results in names that wear quickly.

"Empty vessel names" require filling. Made-up or meaningless names will require more investment to build understanding, memorability, and proper spelling than names that have some inherent meaning. Compare the immediate meaning and relevance of names like Google and Amazon to empty vessels like Kijiji and Zoosk.

Avoid names that are too specific. This may be the reason that change was necessary in the first place. Names that identify a specific geography, technology, or trend might be relevant for a period of time, but in the long run they could restrict your ability to grow.

Understand that a new name can't do everything. Names are powerful tools, but they do not tell the whole story. A name change alone—without rethinking of all brand communications—could risk being seen as superficial. Consider how new taglines, design, communications, and other context-building tools should work with the new name to build a rich new story that you can own.

Ensure you can own it. Check patent and trademark offices, common-law usages, URLs, Twitter handles, and regional/cultural sensitivities before you decide, and make the investment to protect your name. This is best done by an experienced intellectual property attorney.

Transition with confidence. Make sure you introduce your new name as part of a value-oriented story that conveys clear benefits to your employees, customers, and shareholders. The message "we've changed our name" on its own generally falls flat. Commit to the change with confidence and implement as quickly and efficiently as possible. Having two names in the market at the same time is confusing to both internal and external audiences.

If you wish to make a meaningful statement, a name change is not enough. The name should represent a unique, beneficial, and sustainable story that resonates with customers, investors, and employees.

Philip Durbrow
Chairman and CEO
Marshall Strategy

Companies change their names for many reasons, but in every case, a clear rationale for change with strong business and brand benefits is critical.

Ken Pasternak
Managing Director
Marshall Strategy

Notable renaming

Old name	New name
Andersen Consulting	Accenture
Apple Computer	Apple
BackRub	Google
The Banker's Life Company	Principal Financial Group
Brad's Drink	Pepsi-Cola
Ciba Geigy + Sandoz (merger)	Novartis
Clear Channel	iHeartRadio
Comcast (Consumer Services)	Xfinity
Computing Tabulating Recording Corporation	International Business Machines (renamed IBM)
Datsun	Nissan
David and Jerry's Guide to the World Wide Web	Yahoo!
Diet Deluxe	Healthy Choice
Federal Express	FedEx
GMAC Financial Services	Ally Financial
Graphics Group	Pixar
Justin.tv	twitch
Kentucky Fried Chicken	KFC
Kraft snacks division	Mondelez
Lucky Goldstar	LG
Malt-O-Meal	MOM Brands
Marufuku Company	Nintendo
MasterCharge: The Interbank Card	Mastercard
Mountain Shades	Optic Nerve
MyFamily.com	Ancestry
Philip Morris	Altria
Service Games	SEGA
ShoeSite.com	Zappos
TMP Worldwide	Monster Worldwide
Tribune Publishing	tronc
Tokyo Telecommunications Engineering Corporation	Sony
United Telephone Company	Sprint

Effective shortening

Many organizations look at shortening their names in order to make it easier to talk about them.

YMCA: the Y

Flextronics: Flex

California Institute of Technology: Caltech

Designing identity

Investigation and analysis are complete; the brand brief has been agreed upon, and the creative design process begins in Phase 3. Design is an iterative process that seeks to integrate meaning with form. The best designers work at the intersection of strategic imagination, intuition, design excellence, and experience.

3 : designing
identity

We never know what the process will reveal.

Hans-U. Allemann
Cofounder
Allemann, Almquist & Jones

Form and counterform.
Light and tension.
Expanded meaning that is
not exhausted at first
glance. You need to know
the enterprise inside
and out.

Malcolm Grear

You design for durability, for
function, for usefulness, for
rightness, for beauty.

Paul Rand

The best identity designers
understand how to
communicate effectively
through the use of signs and
symbols, a keen sense of
form and letterforms, and the
history of design.

Hans-U. Allemann

The trademark, although a
most important element, can
never tell the whole story. At
best it conveys one or two
aspects of the business. The
identity has to be supported
by a visual language and a
vocabulary.

Steff Geissbuhler

First things first

Understand what the brand stands for, what it offers, who its customers are, how it is different from its competitors, and its competitive advantage. Be clear about design goals, constraints, timelines, deliverables, and communications protocols. The creative brief does not replace the brand brief.

Review all research

It is critical that the design team has reviewed all internal and competitive audits. If the design team has not conducted the interviews or led any workshops, it's imperative to revisit the key findings. Immerse yourself in the brand, its possibilities, and challenges.

Identify key applications

Make sure that you have a list of the most important applications, so you can test the viability of your solutions in real-world scenarios. This is helpful in the design process and critical when you present to the final decision makers. Show the solution as if it already exists.

Look at top-level identification

Will it be a wordmark or a symbol? Will that symbol be abstract? Pictorial or based on a letterform? If it's a symbol, what kind of logotype will it need? When is the tagline used? If this is a redesign, think about ways to extend existing brand equity.

Brand architecture

Depending on the complexity of organization, this is the right time to design a logical and cohesive brand architecture for brand extensions and sub-brands. Think about how this architecture could anticipate future growth.

Color

You are examining the way that color will function—first looking at top-level elements, and then proceeding to look at the whole integrated system. A family of colors needs to work across real and digital applications, and for global companies, the colors need to have positive associations in different cultures.

Typography

Most brands have one or two typeface families that are used consistently across platforms. Keep in mind that there will be licensing fees down the road for certain choices. The typeface family is not necessarily the font used in the logotype. Some companies choose to design their own proprietary font.

Look and feel

Content, color, typography, iconography, and imagery are part the brand's cohesive visual language. Michael Bierut, Pentagram partner, said it best: "You should be able to cover up the logo and still identify the company because the look and feel is so distinctive."

Visual assets

The visual assets that the brand needs should anticipate content strategy considerations. Determine the types of visuals that will help the company tell its stories. Will it be photography, illustration, video, abstract patterns? You are designing a unique visual language.

Presentation

Careful planning is essential to ensure successful outcomes. Present each design approach as a unique strategy. Talk about meaning, not aesthetics. Never show more than three. (Paul Rand would just show one.) Show your solutions in real applications and next to the competition.

My best idea is always my first idea. It took me a few seconds to draw it, but it took me thirty-four years to learn how to draw it in a few seconds.

Paula Scher

A logo is a typographic portrait—the face of a business. I talk to clients at length, learning everything about who they are and what is important to them, and then translate it. A great logo appears effortless—and is, of course, anything but.

Louise Fili

A logotype or a symbol should express the fundamental essence of an organization or a product or a service—the visual manifestation of its nature, its aspirations, its culture, its reason for being.

Bart Crosby

Identity system design Phase 3

Symbol design

Reducing a complex idea to its visual essence requires skill, focus, patience, and unending discipline. Designers examine hundreds of ideas before focusing on a final choice. Even after a final idea emerges, testing its viability begins yet another round of exploration.

In some offices, numerous designers work on the same idea; in other offices, each designer develops a different idea or positioning strategy. Each preliminary approach can be a catalyst to a new approach. Since an identity needs to be a workhorse, it's important to look at trial applications early in the process. In symbol redesign projects, designers examine the equity of the existing trademark and understand what it has symbolized to a company's culture.

Examine

Meaning
Attributes
Acronyms
Inspiration
History
Form
Counterform
Abstract
Pictorial
Letterform
Wordmark
Combination
Time
Space
Light
Still
Motion
Transition
Perspective
Reality
Fantasy
Straight
Curve
Angle
Intersection
Patterns

Getting a large, diverse group of people to agree on a single new global identity requires being a strategist, psychiatrist, diplomat, showman, and even a Svengali.

Paula Scher
Partner
Pentagram

Logotype design

A logotype is a word (or words) in a determined font, which may be standard, modified, or entirely redrawn. If it is freestanding, it is called a wordmark. When a logotype is juxtaposed with a symbol in a formal relationship, it is called a signature. The best signatures have specific isolation zones to protect their presence.
A company may have numerous signatures: horizontal, vertical, with and without tagline.

The best logotypes are a result of thoughtful typographic exploration. Legibility at various scales and in a range of media is imperative. Each typographic decision is driven by visual and performance considerations, as well as by what the typography itself communicates.

Should the name be in all caps or caps and lowercase? Roman, italic, or bold? Classic or modern?

Hornall Anderson knew that the new logo needed to communicate that Fred Hutch does the scientific research and development that leads to cancer cures. One of the design approaches explored was as if you were observing a cell culture through a microscope. The dots and dashes could also read as data and a modern approach to research. Some also saw a globe, cueing the global impact of the organization.

As Hornall Anderson began to refine this concept, the design team came across a quote from their initial research. One of the research scientists had mentioned that looking for cancer is looking for a moment of change —when cells begin to behave differently than they should. This insight made it all click together. The joiner between the two stems of the H became the catalyst moment that ultimately brought the mark to its final state.

Fred Hutchinson Cancer Research Center: Hornall Anderson

Brandmark

Logotype   Signature

Look and feel Phase 3

Look and feel is the visual language that makes a system proprietary and immediately recognizable. It also expresses a point of view. This support system of color, imagery, typography, and composition is what makes an entire program cohesive and differentiated.

In the best programs, designers create an overall look that resonates in the mind of the customer and rises above the clutter of a visual environment. All elements of a visual language should be intentionally designed to advance the brand strategy, each doing its part and working together as a whole to unify and distinguish.

You should be able to cover up the logo and still identify the company because the look and feel is so distinctive.

Michael Bierut
Partner
Pentagram

Look is defined by color, scale, proportion, typography, and motion. Feel is experiential and emotional.

Abbott Miller
Partner
Pentagram

Look and feel basics

Design

Design is intelligence made visible. The marriage of design and content is the only marriage that lasts.

Color palettes

Systems may have two color palettes: primary and secondary. Business lines or products may have their own colors. A color palette may have a pastel range and a primary range.

Imagery

Within the category of content, style, focus, and color all need to be considered, whether the imagery is photography, illustration, or iconography.

Typography

Systems incorporate typeface families, one or sometimes two. It is not unusual for a special typeface to be designed for a high-visibility brand.

Sensory

There are also material qualities (how something feels in your hand—texture and weight), interactive qualities (how something opens or moves), and auditory and olfactory qualities (how something sounds and smells, respectively).

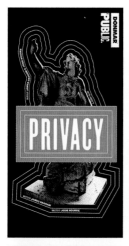

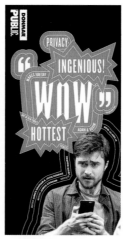

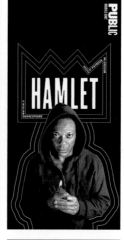

Developing these mini-identities within the Public branding helps keep it fresh. Next year, we'll do it all over again.

Paula Scher
Partner
Pentagram

Pentagram partner Paula Scher has designed the graphics for the Public Theater since 1994, including a refresh of the identity in 2008. Each year, as the campaigns evolve, the work always celebrates the institution as a whole and reaffirms the Public's tradition of merging art and popular taste.

Public Theater: Pentagram

Color is used to evoke emotion and express personality. It stimulates brand association and accelerates differentiation. As consumers we depend on the familiarity of Coca-Cola red. We don't need to read the type on a Tiffany gift box to know where the gift was purchased. We see the color and a set of impressions comes to us.

In the sequence of visual perception, the brain reads color after it registers a shape and before it reads content. Choosing colors requires a core understanding of color theory, a clear vision of how the brand needs to be perceived and differentiated, and an ability to master coherence and meaning over a broad range of media.

While some colors are used to unify an identity, other colors may be used functionally to clarify brand architecture, through differentiating products or business lines. Families of color are developed to support a broad range of communications needs.

Color creates emotion, triggers memory, and gives sensation.

Gael Towey
Creative Director
Gael Towey & Co.

Color is subjective and emotional. It is often the most volatile element of a project.

Sean Adams
The Designer's Dictionary of Color

Color brand identity basics

Use color to facilitate recognition and build brand equity.

Colors have different connotations in different cultures. Research.

Color is affected by various reproduction methods. Test.

The designer is the ultimate arbiter for setting color consistency across platforms. It's hard.

Ensuring consistency across applications is frequently a challenge.

Sixty percent of the decision to buy a product is based on color.

You can never know enough about color. Depend on your basic color theory knowledge: warm, cool; hue, value, saturation; complementary colors, contrasting colors.

Quality insures that the brand identity asset is protected.

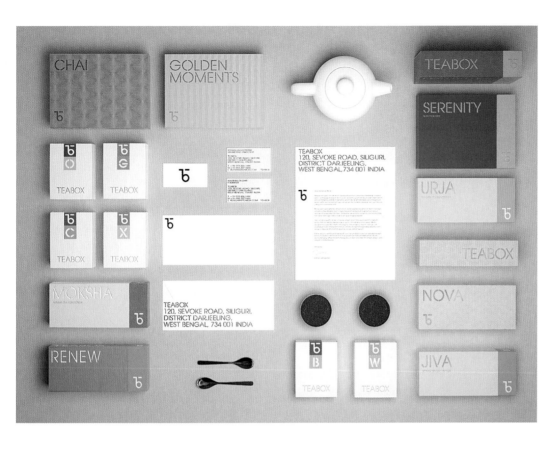

Teabox wanted to demystify tea and present it in more approachable way, so consumers can explore different varieties, regions, and flavors. Like wine, tea is incredibly complex. The company sought to elevate the tea-drinking experience, treating tea like fine wine, but building in an element of accessible connoisseurship that would help educate consumers, attract new generations of tea lovers, and appeal to the booming artisanal food market.

Teabox is a tea-commerce company that is seeking to revolutionize the experience of one of the oldest drinks in history by bringing it directly to the consumer.

Kaushal Dugar
Founder
Teabox

We wanted to create a luxurious, tactile, personal experience of the brand. The color system indicates the specific type of tea, and the custom-made typeface emulates the traditional tea-crate aesthetic.

Natasha Jen
Pentagram

Black Tea	Green Tea	White Tea	Oolong Tea	Chai Tea	Blends

Teabox: Pentagram

155

More color Phase 3

Testing the effectiveness of a color strategy

Is the color distinctive?

Is the color differentiated from that of competitors?

Is the color appropriate to the type of business?

Is the color aligned with brand strategy?

What do you want the color to communicate?

Will the color have sustainability?

What meaning have you assigned to the color?

Does the color have positive connotations in the target markets?

Does the color have positive or negative connotations in foreign markets?

Is the color reminiscent of any other product or service?

Will the color facilitate recognition and recall?

Did you consider a specially formulated color?

Can the color be legally protected?

Does the color work on white?

Can you reverse the mark out of black and still maintain the original intention?

What background colors are possible?

How does scale affect the color?

Can you achieve consistency across media?

Have you tested the color on a range of monitors, PC and Mac, and devices?

Are you aware that color reproduces differently on all production methods?

Have you examined the Pantone Matching System color on coated and uncoated stock?

Will this color work in signage?

What are the color equivalents on the web?

Have you tested the color in the environment in which it will be used?

Have you created the appropriate color electronic files?

Our range of colors is not only visually exciting, it represents the diversity, energy, and passion of our community. No single color is favored above the rest—the entire spectrum works together in unison to bring cohesion to the brand, and vibrancy to our messages.

Glaad Brand Guidelines

Glaad: Lippincott

Color systems

Will the color system be flexible enough to allow for a range of dynamic applications?

Does the color system support a consistent experience of the brand?

Does the color system support the brand architecture?

Is the color system differentiated from that of the competition?

Have you examined the benefits and disadvantages of:

Using color to differentiate products?

Using color to identify business lines?

Using color to help users navigate decisions?

Using color to categorize information?

Can you reproduce these colors?

Have you developed both a web palette and a print palette?

Have you named your colors?

Have you created identity standards that make it easy to use the color system?

Mergers, acquisitions, redesign

Have you examined the historical use of color?

Is there equity that should be preserved?

Is the color aligned with the new brand strategy?

Is there a symbolic color that communicates the positive outcome of the merged entities?

Will developing a new color for the company send a new and immediate signal about the future?

Will retiring an existing color confuse existing customers?

Five Guys is a fast-casual restaurant that promises a better burger and great fries. The color red is dominant—the restaurants have red-and-white checkered tile walls, red light fixtures, and the employees wear red T-shirts and baseball caps. Five Guys has grown to almost 1,500 locations spanning the US, Canada, United Kingdom, Europe, and the Middle East. The name originates from the founder's five sons.

Typography Phase 3

Typography is a core building block of an effective identity program. Many brands are immediately recognizable in great part due to their distinctive and consistent typographic style. Typography must support positioning strategy and information hierarchy.

Hundreds of thousands of fonts have been created by renowned typographers, designers, and type foundries over the centuries, and new typefaces are being created each day. Some identity firms routinely design a proprietary font for a client. Choosing the right font requires a basic knowledge of the breadth of options and a core understanding of how effective typography functions. Issues of functionality differ dramatically on a form, a pharmaceutical package, a magazine ad, and a website. The typeface needs to be flexible and easy to use, and it must provide a wide range of expression. Clarity and legibility are the drivers.

Type is magical. It not only communicates a word's information, but it conveys a subliminal message.

Erik Spiekermann
Stop Stealing Sheep

Great typography heightens and enriches our knowledge of things, and redefines the way we read.

Eddie Opara
Partner
Pentagram

The Cooper Hewitt typeface is a contemporary sans serif. Initially commissioned by Pentagram to evolve his Polaris Condensed typeface, Chester Jenkins created a new digital font to support the newly transformed museum. The font, which is used on all museum communications and signage, can be downloaded free of charge for unrestricted public use.

Cooper Hewitt font:
Pentagram + Chester Jenkins

Typeface family basics

Typefaces are chosen for their legibility, their unique character, and their range of weights and widths.

Intelligent typography supports information hierarchy.

Typeface families must be chosen to complement the signature, not necessarily to replicate the signature.

The best standards identify a range of fonts but give the users flexibility to choose the appropriate font, weight, and size for the message conveyed.

Limiting the number of fonts that a company uses is cost-effective since licensing fonts is legally required.

The number of typeface families in a system is a matter of choice. Many companies choose serif and sans serif faces; some companies choose one font for everything.

Basic standards sometimes allow special display faces for unique situations.

A company website may require its own set of typefaces and typography standards.

The best typographers examine a level of detail that includes numerals and bullets.

Many companies identify separate typefaces for internally produced word-processed documents and electronic presentations.

Certain industries have compliance requirements regarding type size for certain consumer products and communications.

Type considerations

Serif
Sans serif
Size
Weight
Curves
Rhythm
Descenders
Ascenders
Capitalization
Headlines
Subheads
Text
Titles
Callouts
Captions
Bulleted lists
Leading
Line length
Letter spacing
Numerals
Symbols
Quotation marks

Typeface imperatives

Conveys feeling and reflects positioning

Covers the range of application needs

Works in a range of sizes

Works in black and white and in color

Differs from the competition's

Compatible with the signature

Legible both online and off

Has personality

Sustainable

Reflects culture

Type trivia

The Obama political campaign used Gotham, designed by Tobias Frere-Jones. It's also the typeface used for the 9/11 Memorial.

Frutiger was designed for an airport.

Matthew Carter designed Bell Gothic to increase legibility in the phone book.

Meta was designed by Meta Design for the German post office but never used.

Wolff Olins designed Tate for Tate Modern in London.

There is a documentary film about the typeface Helvetica.

Licensing fonts

It is vital to understand the licensing terms for any font used on a website, an app, a package, or any other part of a brand identity system.

Sound Phase 3

As bandwidth increases, sound is quickly becoming the next frontier for brands. Many of our appliances and devices talk to us. Voice-activated prompts let us schedule a FedEx pickup without human interface. The sound of silence is a has-been.

Whether you are at the Buddha Bar in Paris or the shoe department at Nordstrom, sound puts you in the mood. Sound also sends a signal: "Hail to the Chief" announces the president's arrival, and Looney Tunes cartoons always end with a "Tha-a-a-t's all folks." A foreign accent adds cachet to almost any brand. Being put on hold might mean a little Bach cantata, a humorous sound sales pitch, or a radio station (don't you hate that?).

Logos should be heard as well as seen.

Geoff Lentin
New Business Manager
TH_NK

Amazon could eliminate the existence of brands with voice technology. If you look at search terms on Google and voice commands on Amazon's Alexa, the percentage of time that brand prefixes are used in a request is declining.

Scott Galloway
Marketing professor
NYU Stern School of Business

Google's interactive, playable logo celebrated the birthday of musician and inventor Les Paul. Within 48 hours, 40 million songs were recorded, which were played back 870,000 times.

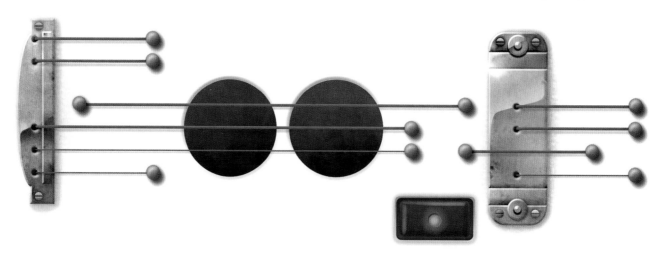

Google Doodle Design: Ryan Germick and Alexander Chen; engineers: Kristopher Hom and Joey Hurst

Branding sound

Chatbot

A computer program that simulates how a human would behave as a conversational partner.

Also known as:

Talkbots

Chatterbots

Bots

Chatterbox

IM bot

Interactive agent

What is audio architecture?

Audio architecture is the integration of music, voice, and sound to create experiences between companies and customers.

Muzak

Motors

Harley-Davidson motorcycles tried to trademark its distinctive purr. When Miata designed the first hot sports car in the moderate price category, the sound of the motor was reminiscent of a classic upscale sports car.

Retail environments

From cafés, to supermarkets, to fashion boutiques, music is used to appeal to a particular customer and put him or her in the mood to shop or revel in the experience.

Jingles

Catchy messages set to music will stick in the mind of the consumer.

Signals

The Intel chip has its own musical bleeps, and AOL's "You've got mail" ditty became so much a part of the culture that it was used as the title of a 1998 romantic comedy with Meg Ryan and Tom Hanks.

Websites and games

Sound is being used increasingly to aid navigation, as well as to delight the user. Sound effects on computer games heighten the adventure, and avatars can be customized by the user.

Talking products

Technology is making the way for pill dispensers that gently remind you to take a pill, and cars that remind you to fill the tank, get service, or turn left. A Mercedes will definitely sound different than a Volkswagen.

Multimedia presentations

Interactivity and new media require the integration of sound. Testimonials are given by real customers. Video clips of company visionaries are shown to employees.

Spokespersons

Famous people have been used throughout advertising history to endorse a product. Also, a receptionist with a great voice and a friendly personality can become the spokesperson of a small firm.

Recorded messages

Great museums are paying attention to the voices they choose for audio tours. Companies specialize in targeted messages while you're on hold.

Characters

While the AFLAC duck has a memorable quack, many characters, like Elmer of Elmer's Glue, are still silent.

No one who saw *2001: A Space Odyssey* will ever forget the voice that said, "Open the pod bay doors, HAL."

Fundamentals of sonic branding
Excerpted from "Sonic Branding Finds Its Voice" by Kim Barnet, on Interbrand's Brand Channel

Sound needs to complement the existing brand.

Sound can intensify the experience of a brand.

Music can trigger an emotional response.

Sound, especially music, heightens the brain's speed of recall.

Music can transcend cultures and language.

Aural and visual branding are becoming increasingly complementary.

Many businesses compose original music.

Many audio effects are subliminal.

Trial applications **Phase 3**

It's important to choose a group of real applications to test the viability of concepts to work within a system. No mark should ever be shown on a blank piece of paper. Decision makers need to see the identity the way that a customer would see it. They need to see how it will take them into the future. Designers need to conduct rigorous testing before any concepts are shown and to demonstrate flexibility and durability.

A typical list for a small engagement might include a business card, a home page, an advertisement, a brochure cover, a letterhead, and something fun, like a baseball cap. On larger projects, the designer needs to demonstrate the effectiveness of brand extensions and the ability of the identity to work across business lines and markets served.

The possibilities are endless.

David Bowie

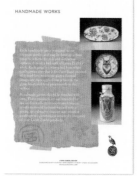

Testing the concept

Choose the most visible applications.

Choose the most challenging applications.

Examine the flexibility of the identity.

Examine how to express coherence.

Does the signature work?

Is it differentiated enough from the competition?

Is it scalable?

Is it legible at a small scale?

Will it work in different media?

How will it work digitally?

Will it be conducive to brand extensions?

It works with the parent; will it work with the divisions?

Can it accommodate a tagline in the signature?

Will it work in other cultures?

Identity design testing basics

Use real scenarios and real text for application testing.

Continue asking the big questions in regard to appropriate meaning, sustainability, and flexibility.

Start thinking about the implications for the entire system of color and typeface families.

Always examine best- and worst-case scenarios.

Remember, this is an iterative process.

If something does not work, deal with it now. Go back to the beginning if necessary to examine the core concept. The signature might need to be reworked.

Date and assign a version number to the entire sketch process; be obsessive about organization of this phase.

Think ahead to production: How will this look on a smartphone?

Solicit feedback from trusted colleagues—designers and nondesigners—to reveal any connotations that may not be apparent.

Anticipate what you will need to present the design strategy; start envisioning the presentation.

Continue to actively think about the future: five or ten years out is sooner than you think.

Building on Laura Zindel's passion for naturalist illustration, I developed a visual language that was both simple and scalable.

Jon Bjornson
Founder
Jon Bjornson Art + Design

Laura Zindel: Jon Bjornson Art + Design

Presentation Phase 3

The first major design presentation is the decisive moment—the culmination of months of work. The expectations and stakes are high. Clients are usually impatient during the planning and analysis phase since they are so focused on the end goal. There is usually a sense of urgency around scheduling this meeting. Everyone is ready to hit the ground running, even though the implementation phase of the work is not imminent.

Careful planning is essential. The smartest and most creative solutions can get annihilated in a mismanaged presentation. The larger the group of decision makers, the more difficult the meeting and the decision are to manage. Even presenting to one decision maker alone demands planning in advance.

The best presentations stay focused on the agenda, keep the meeting moving within the scheduled time, set out clear and reasonable expectations, and are based on a decision-making process that has been predetermined. The best presenters have practiced in advance. They are prepared to deal with any objections and can discuss the design solutions strategically, aligning them with the overall brand goals of the company. Larger projects routinely involve numerous levels of building consensus.

Wow with emotion and defend with rationale.

Blake Howard
Cofounder
Matchstic

Presentation concepts Developed by Matchstic

Introducing a new app to outbound the rest—a new peer-to-peer delivery service for city dwelling urbanites that lets you ship same-day with local drivers. But what to call it?

Inspired by boisterous marsupials, the name has some serious bounce. We needed a great character to match.

That's when a burly brawler named "Hank" was born. He likes to kick butt, move some stuff, and hug it out.

The visual identity is a heavy lifting blend of vibrant colors, custom retro script, and our lovable hunk Hank.

164

Presentation basics

Agree in advance about the agenda and the decision-making process.

Clarify who will attend the meeting and the roles they will play. Individuals who have not participated in the early part of the process may derail the process.

Circulate the agenda in advance. Be sure to include the overall goals of the meeting.

Create an in-depth outline of your presentation and practice in advance.

Look at the room's physical layout in advance to decide where you want to present from and where you want others to sit.

Arrive well in advance to set up the room and be there to greet all the attendees.

If the company is going to provide any equipment for the meeting, test it in advance. Familiarize yourself with the lighting and temperature controls in the room.

Presentation strategies

Begin the meeting with a review of the decisions made to date, including overall goals, definition of target audience, and positioning statement.

Present each approach as a strategy with a unique positioning concept. Talk about meaning, not aesthetics. Each strategy should be presented within several actual contexts (home page, business card, and so on), as well as juxtaposed with the competition.

Always have a point of view. When presenting numerous solutions (never more than three), be ready to explain which one you would choose and why.

Be prepared to deal with objections: steer the conversation away from aesthetic criticism and toward functional and marketing criteria.

Never present anything that you do not believe in.

Never allow voting.

Be prepared to present next steps, including design development, trademarking, and application design.

Follow up the presentation with a memo outlining all decisions that were made.

Don't expect the work to speak for itself. Even the most ingenious solutions must be sold.

Suzanne Young
Communications Strategist

Kanga: Matchstic

Creating touchpoints

Phase 4 is about design refinement and design development. The brand identity design concept has been approved, and a sense of urgency generates a fusillade of questions: "When we will get business cards?," followed by, "How soon can we get our standards online?"

4 : creating touchpoints

Design is intelligence made visible.

Lou Danziger
Designer and Educator

It's never too late to be what you could have been.

George Elliot

Now that the major decisions have been made, most companies want to hit the ground running. The challenge to the identity firm is to keep the momentum going while ensuring that critical details are finalized.

In Phase 3, hypothetical applications were designed in order to test the ideas, and to help sell the core concepts. The highest priority now is to refine and finalize the elements of the identity and to create signatures. This work requires an obsessive attention to detail; the files created are permanent. Final testing of the signature(s) in a variety of sizes and media is critical. Decisions about typeface families, color palettes, and secondary visual elements are finalized during this phase.

While the design team is fine-tuning, the company is organizing the final list of applications that need to be designed and produced. Core applications are prioritized, and content is either provided or developed. The intellectual property firm begins the trademark process, confirming what needs to be registered and in which industry classes. The lawyers confirm that there are no conflicting marks.

A brand identity program encompasses a unique visual language that will express itself across all applications. Regardless of the medium, the applications need to work in harmony. The challenge is to design the right balance between flexibility of expression and consistency in communications.

Creative brief

The creative brief cannot be written until the brand brief is approved. Each member of the creative team must review the brand brief, the competitive audit, and the marketing audit.

The creative brief synthesizes what the creative team needs to know in order to do responsible work aligned with the overall objectives of the project. This brief must be signed off by key decision makers before any conceptual or creative work is done. The best briefs are a result of collaboration between the client and the consulting team. Creative work includes the range of brand identity from naming, logo redesign, key message development, brand architecture, and packaging design, to integrated system design.

Creative brief contents

Team goals

Communications goals of all brand identity elements

Critical application list

Functional and performance criteria

Mind map or SWOTs

Positioning

Protocols

Confidentiality statement

Documentation system

Benchmarks and presentation dates

Identity design is not about what one likes or dislikes. It's about what works.

Sagi Haviv
Partner
Chermayeff & Geismar & Haviv

Application design

Essentials

Convey the brand personality.

Align with positioning strategy.

Create a point of view and a look and feel.

Make the design system work across all media.

Demonstrate understanding of the target customer.

Pay attention to the details.

Differentiate. Differentiate. Differentiate.

Basics

Design is an iterative process between the big picture and minutiae.

Design real applications and the identity system simultaneously.

Ensure that all assumptions are achievable.

Be open to additional discovery as it gets more real.

Imperatives

Seize every opportunity to communicate the big idea.

Create a unified visual language.

Start thinking about launch strategy.

Create balance between consistency and flexibility.

Produce real applications before finalizing standards.

Work on the highest-visibility applications first.

Know when to identify outside experts for collaboration.

Keep track of numerous applications.

Never show any application without showing alignment with brand strategy.

Be obsessive about quality.

Gather notes during this phase for standards and guidelines.

Content strategy Phase 4

With a multitude of communications modalities and marketing channels, content creation and distribution has become an imperative for brands big and small. Whether the content is original or user-generated, and whether it entertains, enlightens, or educates, it strengthens the bond with your customers. Make it a priority: customers expect content that's fresh and engaging. Successful content marketing is authentic to your brand voice.

Distinct from content management systems (CMSs), which allow users to easily edit digital content, content strategy is an art that requires a keen understanding of your customers and a desire to distinguish your brand from the competition. Research shows that content incorporating videos and images is shared more and remembered better than text-only content.

Users now expect personalized and hyper-relevant content delivered instantly to them wherever they are engaging.

Amanda Todorovich
Content Marketing Director
Cleveland Clinic

Goals

Drive brand awareness

Fuel sharing

Invite customer participation

Provoke curiosity

Add value: be useful

Build affinity and trust

Spark the conversation

Make the customer a hero and a brand builder

Increase conversion rates

Engage employees as brand ambassadors

Channels

Facebook
Instagram
Snapchat
Twitter
YouTube
Vimeo
LinkedIn

168

Content types

Original

Thought leadership, glimpses into company culture, maybe even your own branded magazine—this forms the foundation of your content marketing. Ideally both informative and entertaining, this is the content you generate and that communicates your brand DNA.

Curated

Offering a carefully curated source of relevant material is a way to build customer loyalty. Aggregating the best content from multiple sources and crediting them elevates your brand's credibility and demonstrates commitment to transparency.

Evergreen

Customer testimonials, company histories, case studies, how-to's, and FAQs are evergreen—they don't expire or need frequent updating. Evergreen content is useful to customers; it is particularly SEO-friendly as it tends to generate high traffic.

Sponsored

Sponsored content includes posts, interviews, or videos you create for another brand's channel, that is republished, with appropriate crediting, by another brand, usually on its website, blog, or social media.

User-generated

The ubiquity of social media and the ease of content creation has shifted the balance of power from brands to customers. Whether photographs submitted for a contest or tweets in support of a new product, user-generated content (UGC) adds to a company's brand story.

Critical success factors

Develop customer personas so that your content speaks to them: Delve into the interests, fears, activities, and preferences of your customer.

Determine the balance of original, user-generated, and curated content.

Make it visual.

Maximize your user's mobile experience.

Invest in quality: customers will share great content.

See what your competitors are doing, then do your own thing.

Website Phase 4

Websites lead the top of the brand necessity list—no longer enslaved to the desktop, they migrate to wherever the consumer is, on her iPad or her smartphone, at the mall, on a hike, or under her pillow.

Engaging content and inviting interfaces have the potential to bring a brand to life. Websites just may be the next best thing to reality, and in some cases they are more efficient, more user friendly, and faster. Think retail.

The best websites know who their visitors are, and give them a reason to come back again and again. Videos have started to populate most websites with storytelling and testimonials.

A number of specialists work collaboratively to build a site, including graphic and user experience designers, information architects, developers, content authors, project managers, usability engineers, and search engine experts have become a critical part of the team.

Everyone needs food, shelter, love, and a website.

Lissa Reidel
Consultant

Transformation isn't just about our brand; it's how we make it real for people—that's so critical to how the world looks at us now.

Michelle Bonterre
Chief Brand Officer
Dale Carnegie

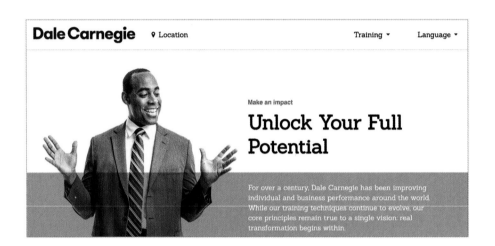

Process: Website design   Developed by Gavin Cooper

> **Initiate plan**

Reaffirm business goals

Establish team, roles, and responsibilities

Review brand brief and positioning

Identify critical success factors

Develop workflow, timeline, and budget

Establish communications protocol

Conduct competitive audits and SEO analysis

Establish best practices

> **Understand the users**

Identify users and build user personas

Assess user goals

Gain insights from key users

Create site use scenarios

Consider the mobile experience

Consider social experience

> **Build content strategy**

Conduct keyword research

Clarify content management responsibilities

Forecast twelve-month content rollout

Develop SEO content strategy

Evaluate possible social media outlets

Develop information architecture

Map content to approved navigation

> **Create prototypes**

Decide on information architecture

Examine interface possibilities

Build site wireframe

Conduct usability testing

Refine prototype based on usability results

Retest to measure improvement

Map content to wireframe

Start to outline development plan

Website basics

Keep site goals, audience needs, key messages, and brand personality central to each decision.

Anticipate future growth. Consider all platforms and devices.

Begin site structure with content, not a screen design. Write content specifically for the web.

Do not force content into counterintuitive groupings.

Conduct usability testing.

Don't wait to make it perfect. Get it out there and constantly make it better. Give users a reason to return.

Observe etiquette. Alert visitors where special technology is needed, where a screen may load slowly, or where a link leaves your site.

Comply with ADA: arrange for visually impaired visitors to use software to read the site aloud or greatly magnify text.

At each stage ask: Is the message clear? Is the content accessible? Is the experience positive?

Confront internal political agendas that may sabotage site goals.

This is an iconic American brand, but the footprint and the personality are global now.

Justin Peters
Executive Creative Director
Carbone Smolan Agency

Dale Carnegie: Carbone Smolan Agency (brand design) + Digital Surgeons (site design and development)

> **Visualize**

Review brand brief and design guidelines

Design master pages

Design social media pages

Consider all relevant devices

Utilize usability design principals

Produce all text, photography, and video

Refine and finalize design for consistency

Optimize content for search engines

> **Production**

Confirm development plan

Code the front end

Implement CMS

Implement on-page SEO

Populate site with content

Implement website reporting structure

Launch beta for key decision makers

Test design + functionality among browsers and devices

Make adjustments as necessary

> **Launch + monitor**

Promote site launch internally

Promote site launch externally

Disseminate user-friendly guidelines

Launch website

Implement analytics assessment

Communicate successes and impact

The best collateral communicates the right information at the right time with a customer or prospect. A unified system will increase brand recognition. By making information accessible, a company demonstrates its understanding of customer's needs and preferences.

Brand is more than a logo or a tagline; it is a strategic endeavor.

Michelle Bonterre
Chief Brand Officer
Dale Carnegie

Collateral system basics

Information should be easy for customers to understand and should help them make buying decisions.

System guidelines should be easy for managers, design professionals, and advertising agencies to understand.

Systems should include flexible elements but not waver on clear, absolute standards.

Great design is effective only if it can be reproduced at the highest quality.

The best collateral is well written and presents appropriate amounts of information.

Systems should include a consistent call to action, URL, and contact information.

Process: Collateral design

> Revisit the big picture	> Design a cover system	> Determine typographic system	> Determine visuals	> Design color family
Clarify objectives	Define grid for signature, content, and visuals	One typeface family or two	Define style qualities	Define set of approved colors
Examine positioning goals	Examine:	Title typeface	Photography	Evaluate production methods to align color across media
Examine competitive and internal audits	Signature in primary place	Cover descriptor typeface	Illustration	
Identify functional needs, usage, distribution and production methods	Split signature	Header typeface	Design elements	
Identify challenges	Signature not used on cover	Subhead typeface	Collage	
	Signature used on back only	Text typeface	Typographic	
	Product name in primary position	Caption typeface	Abstract	
			Identity derivative	

Our brand team was made up of franchisees that represented different regions from around the world. We worked hard to suspend our personal preferences, and to focus on the core brand principles that were shared by diverse perspectives.

Michelle Bonterre
Chief Brand Officer
Dale Carnegie

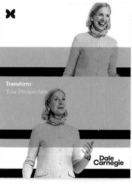

After doing a proof-of-concept on the visual approach to the collateral system, we decided to embrace a photo style that reflected the idea of transformation. The images are bold, emotionally open, and vibrant—and all about people.

Justin Peters
Executive Creative Director
Carbone Smolan Agency

Dale Carnegie: Carbone Smolan Agency

> **Choose standard formats**

US sizes

International sizes

Consider postage

Consider electronic delivery

> **Specify paper**

Examine functionality, opacity, and feel

Examine price points

Decide on family of papers

Have dummies made

Feel the paper

Consider weight

Consider recycled

> **Develop prototypes**

Use real copy

Edit language as needed

Demonstrate flexibility and consistency of system

Decide on signature configurations

> **Develop guidelines**

Articulate goals and value of consistency

Create grids and templates

Explain system with real examples

Monitor execution

Stationery Phase 4

Doing business in a digital world still requires paper. Although we can text our VCFs in a nanosecond, business cards are still a rite of passage used around the world to network. Even though we invoice via PayPal and write voluminous emails, letterhead still confers more professionalism and dignity.

Even to a pinging generation, a personal note via snail mail is usually met with delight. In a world filled with electronic communications, the way a business card feels sends a signal of quality and success. In the future, our business cards might include a fingerprint or other biometric data.

A good business card is like a kick-ass tie; it won't make you a better person, but it'll get you some respect.

Sean Adams
Founder
Burning Settlers Cabin

Business cards are a ritual that will last.

Andrew Hill
Leadership in the Headlines

JAGR began as a collaboration between experts in turn-of-the-century furniture, fine art, and interior design.

Process: Stationery design

> **Clarify use + users**	> **Determine need**	> **Revisit positioning**	> **Finalize content**	> **Develop design**
Business cards	Print +/or digital	Internal audit	Critical information	Use real content
Letterheads	Corporate	Competitive audit	Address	Examine whole system
Memos	Divisional	Brand architecture	Phone + email	Know your country sizes
Invoices	Personal	Logo, color + typeface	Web	Consider the back
Forms	Quantities		Tagline	Examine iterations:
Envelopes	Frequency		Regulatory info	Best-case scenario
Labels			Professional affiliation	Worst-case scenario
			Unify abbreviations	

Sandra K   Colleen K   Bethany S   John L   Dana L

I designed individual symbols for each person based on their initials. Inspired by the Japanese, each oversized card was placed in an envelope.

Jon Bjornson
Founder
Jon Bjornson Art + Design

JAGR: Jon Bjornson Art & Design

Most of the world uses letterhead and envelopes based on the metric system. Only the United States, Canada, and Mexico don't.

Stationery design basics

Think of a business card as a marketing tool.

Make it easy to retrieve information.

Minimize the amount of information.

Use the back for a marketing message.

Convey quality through the look, feel, and weight of the card.

Make sure that all abbreviations are consistent.

Make sure that the titles are consistent.

Make sure that the typographic use of upper- and lowercase is consistent.

Develop system formats.

> **Specify paper**

Surface
Weight
Color
Quality
Recycled
Budget

> **Choose production**

Offset printing
Digital printing
Engraving
Foil stamping
Embossing
Letterpress
Watermark

> **Manage production**

Proofread for accuracy + consistency
Develop digital templates
Review proofs
Print limited run if quantity is huge

Signage Phase 4

From city streets and skylines, through museums and airports, signage functions as
identification, information, and advertising.
Effective retail signage increases revenues, and
intelligent wayfinding systems support and
enhance the experience of a destination.

In the eighteenth century, laws required inn-
keepers to have their signs high enough to clear
an armored man on horseback. In the twenty-
first century, cities and towns around the world
routinely revise sign codes to create environments that support the image that a community
wants to portray, and to regulate standards to
protect public safety.

**Signage helps people
identify, navigate, and
understand environments.**

Alan Jacobson
Principal
Ex;it

Behind these walls, we're creating your new museum experience.

Philadelphia Museum of Art

Constructionism is an
installation that transforms
a construction fence into an
impromptu gallery of art
reproductions, showcasing
the Philadelphia Museum
of Art's permanent collection—reminding the public
that the museum is still
open during a major
expansion by architect
Frank Gehry.

Philadelphia Museum of Art: Pentagram

Process: Signage design

> **Establish goals**

Determine project scope

Understand audience needs and
habits

Clarify positioning

Clarify function

Develop time frame and budget

> **Build project team**

Client facilities manager

Information design firm

Fabricator

Architect or space designer

Lighting consultant

> **Conduct research**

Site audit: environment

Site audit: building type

User habits and patterns

Local codes and zoning

Consideration for the disabled

Weather and traffic conditions

Materials and finishes

Fabrication processes

> **Establish project criteria**

Legibility

Placement

Visibility

Sustainability

Safety

Maintenance

Security

Modularity

Signage basics

Signage expresses the brand and builds on understanding the needs and habits of users in the environment.

Legibility, visibility, durability, and positioning must drive the design process. Distance, speed, light, color, and contrast affect legibility.

Signage is a mass communications medium that works 24/7 and can attract new customers, influence purchasing decisions, and increase sales.

Exterior signage must consider both vehicular and pedestrian traffic.

Every community, industrial park, and shopping mall develops its own signage code; there are no universal codes.

Signage codes affect material, illumination (electrical), and structural choices; zoning or land use issues affect placement and size of signage.

Zoning constraints need to be understood prior to design development.

Permit and variance applications should include the benefit to the land-use planning scheme.

Signage requires a long-term commitment, and maintenance plans and contracts are critical to protecting the investment.

Developing prototypes minimizes risk by testing design prior to fabrication.

Signage should always complement the overall architecture and land use of a site.

Signage standards manuals include various configurations, materials, supplier selections, and production, installation, and maintenance details.

Constructionism **is a celebration of what the museum does, which is make art accessible to the city.**

Paula Scher
Partner
Pentagram

> **Begin design schematic**	> **Develop design**	> **Complete documentation**	> **Manage fabrication + maintenance**
Brand identity system	Begin variance process	Complete working drawings	Check shop drawings
Color, scale, format	Prepare prototypes or models	Construction, mounting, and elevation details	Inspect work
Typography	Finalize content	Final specifications	Manage fabrication
Lighting	Create drawings or renderings	Placement plans	Manage installation
Materials and finishes	Choose materials and color samples	Bid documents	Develop maintenance plan
Fabrication techniques		Permit applications	
Mounting and hardware			
Placement			

Product design Phase 4

The best products make everyday living easier and better, and fuse superior function, form, and brand. Think OXO, iPod, Google, Prius. Now products are also judged by their sustainability: Do I really need this? Will this product end up in a landfill? Is the company earth friendly and socially responsible? Satisfied consumers have become the new marketing department with blogs, Instagram, and texting. Disgruntled customers broadcast their dismay.

Behind every product innovation is a cross-functional team of experts who build on understanding customer needs, behavior, and desires. Research, design, human factors, and engineering experts work collaboratively with branding teams to satisfy unmet needs, build customer loyalty and lifelong relationships, and perpetuate the brand promise.

Bresslergroup developed a simple, intuitive UI for the groggy, early-morning coffee drinker wanting to brew the perfect cup.

Bruvelo: Bresslergroup

Utility that surprises and delights will be rewarded with love and loyalty.

Bill Horan
Creative Director, Interaction Design
Bresslergroup

The best consumer products

Anticipate customer needs and behavior	Meaningful differentiation
Express the brand promise	Sustainable considerations in supply chain
Deliver superior function, form, and value	Spark word-of-mouth referrals
Easy to use and easy to understand	Created by a cross-functional team
Reliable, friendly service and support	Consistent with pre- and post-sale touchpoints
Set expectation and desire for future products	

Product design process Developed by Bresslergroup

> Generative research	> Product definition/ planning	> Ideation	> Evaluative research	> Concept refinement
Clarify product brand strategy	Assemble cross-functional development team	Conduct multitier brainstorming	Develop research methodology	Synthesize customer feedback
Conduct competitive analysis	Develop user profiles	Explore configuration options	Recruit participants	Refine specification
Absorb client and secondary research	Define key features and differentiators	Explore 2-D and 3-D concepts	Conduct customer concept testing	Flesh out aesthetic and feature details
Identify information gaps	Clarify brand position	Build models to prove concepts	Analyze data	Create user interaction logic
Research new insights	Refine formal product spec	Refine concepts for team review	Develop recommendations for refinement	Engineer component resolution
Analyze ergonomic and usability issues	Build consensus with team	Narrow range of concepts and refine		Detail form and touchpoints
Survey market trends		Create testing presentation		Refine product info and graphic system
Search for any IP landmines				Review 2-D and 3-D touchpoints
Perform feasibility study				

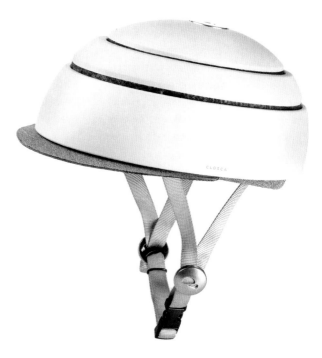

Closca Helmet: Closca & Culdesac

Closca was born to add a touch of style, design, and good taste to both their customers and the cities where they live.

We are with people who appreciate beauty, are not intimidated by change, and feel the inevitable need to transform things.

Carlos Ferrando
Founder & Enhancer
Closca

Closca Fuga is a foldable bike helmet that is safety certified, convenient, and chic. It's positioned as the bike helmet for smart citizens.

> **Engineering development**

Develop breadboards

Create manufacturing strategy

Build detailed parts list

Develop assembly design tasks

Analyze high-risk features and interfaces

Engineer for sustainability and cost optimization

Render mechanical, electrical, UI design in CAD

Fabricate prototypes

Conduct performance testing and customer validation

> **Evaluative research**

Validate product design

Examine customer experience

Evaluate aesthetics, usability, functionality

Perform engineering analysis

Ensure standards compliance

Review production strategy with manufacturers

Analyze results of testing

Create list of final changes

> **Production implementation**

Finalize production estimates

Complete mass production details

Fabricate final prototypes

Codify design improvements

Perform engineering tolerance study

Finalize engineering documentation for tooling and production

Finalize tooling and production plan

> **Production support**

Coordinate tooling fabrication

Do formal review of first production parts

Achieve final approval

Provide final production design changes

Assist with final compliance testing

Packaging Phase 4

Packages are brands that you trust enough to take into your home. We are continually comforted and cajoled by packaging shapes, graphics, colors, messages, and containers. The shelf is probably the most competitive marketing environment that exists, and we make our decisions about what to purchase in seconds. From new brands to extending or revitalizing existing product lines, considerations of brand equity, cost, time, and competition are often complex.

Packaging design is a unique discipline, and it routinely involves collaboration with industrial designers, packaging engineers, and manufacturers. In the food and pharmaceutical industry, it is regulated by the government. In addition to strong packaging, launching a new product requires many different facets. These include supply chain management, manufacturing, distribution or shipping, sales force meetings, marketing, advertising, and promotion.

Packaging, the only brand medium experienced 100 percent by consumers, provides a higher ROI than any other branding strategy.

Rob Wallace
Brand Advocate
Best of Breed Brand Consortium

First I bought it because it looked cool. Later I bought it because it tasted good.

Michael Grillo
Age 14

Packaging is the most potent blend of brand story with customer behavior.

Brian Collins
Chief Creative Officer
Collins

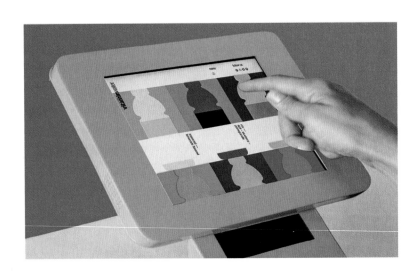

As a brand we've always embraced our design principles of vibrancy, minimalism, personality, and functionality. Our new identity system for vitaminwater reinvented those textures and brought them all together in an authentic, bold, and relevant way.

Alex Center
Design Director
The Coca-Cola Company

vitaminwater: Collins

Process: Packaging design

> Clarify goals + positioning	> Conduct audits + identify expert team	> Conduct research as needed	> Research legal requirements	> Research functional criteria
Establish goals and define problem	Competitive (category)	Understand brand equity	Brand and corporate standards	Product stability
Brand equity	Retail (point of sale)	Determine brand standards	Product-specific	Tamper or theft resistance
Competition	Online	Examine brand architecture	Net weight	Shelf footprint
Existing brands in product line	Brand (internal, existing product line)	Clarify target consumer	Drug facts	Durability
Price point	Packaging designer	Confirm need for product— does product benefit resonate?	Nutrition facts	Usage
Target consumer	Packaging engineer	Confirm language—how should benefit be expressed?	Ingredients	Packability
Product benefit	Packaging manufacturers		Warnings	Fillability
	Industrial designers		Claims	
	Regulatory legal department			

Packaging basics

Champagne in a can, tuna in a bag, wine in a box. The egg for me is still the perfect package.

Blake Deutsch

The shelf is the most competitive marketing environment in existence.

Good design sells. It's a competitive advantage.

Positioning relative to the competition and to the other members of the product line is critical for developing a strong packaging strategy.

A disciplined, coherent approach in planning leads to a unified, powerful brand presence in the marketplace.

Structure and graphics can be developed concurrently. It is a chicken-and-egg debate. Approach each agnostically and mutually.

Brand extensions are always a strategic tug-of-war between differentiation and coherence within a product line.

Consider the entire life cycle of the package and its relationship to the product: source, print, assemble, pack, preserve, ship, display, purchase, use, recycle/dispose.

Devise timetables involving packaging approval and production, sales force meetings, product sell in to stores, manufacturing, and distribution.

Developing a new structure takes a long time and is very expensive, but it offers a unique competitive advantage.

Brands like vitaminwater are now utilizing one consistent voice across every consumer touchpoint. All aspects of the brand communication, whether they live online, offline, in-store, or outdoor and whether they fall into the discipline of advertising, promotion, or packaging, must adhere to the integrity of one clear, telegraphic visual system. There should be as few anomalies presented to the public as possible.

> **Determine printing specifications**

Method: flexo, litho, roto

Application: direct, label, shrinkwrap label

Other: number of colors, divinyl, UPC code, minimums for knockouts

> **Determine structural design**

Design new structure or use stock?

Choose forms (e.g., carton, bottle, can, tube, jar, tin, blister packs)

Choose possible materials, substrates, or finishes

Source stock and get samples

> **Finalize copy + content**

Product name

Benefit copy

Ingredients

Nutrition facts/drug facts

Net contents

Claims

Warnings

Distributed by

Manufactured in

UPC code

> **Design + prototype**

Start with face panels (2-D renderings)

Get prototypes made

Narrow option(s)

Design rest of package

Simulate reality: use actual structure/substrate with contents

> **Evaluate solution + manage production**

In a retail/competitive environment + online

As a member of the product line

Consumer testing

Finalize files

Oversee production

Advertising Phase 4

Since Silk Road traders described the benefits of jade and silk in lyrical song, merchants have created a sense of longing and entitlement by communicating about their products. Today we call it advertising and, despite social media and the decline of print, it is still one of the ways consumers learn about new products, services, and ideas.

Our society has a love-hate relationship with advertising. Pundits issue warnings about its ubiquity and the cynicism of an increasingly skeptical audience. But who can resist the latest catalog or ignore sumptuous magazine ads? Advertising is influence, information, persuasion, communication, and dramatization. It is also an art and a science, determining new ways to create a relationship between the consumer and the product.

Brands should stop interrupting what people are interested in and become what they are interested in.

David Beebe
VP, Global Creative and
Content Marketing
Marriot International

Skip Ad ▶|

Leverage the power of seduction.

Pum Lefebure
Chief Creative Officer & Creative Director
Design Army

Unless your campaign contains a big idea, it will pass like ships in the night.

David Ogilvy
Ogilvy on Advertising

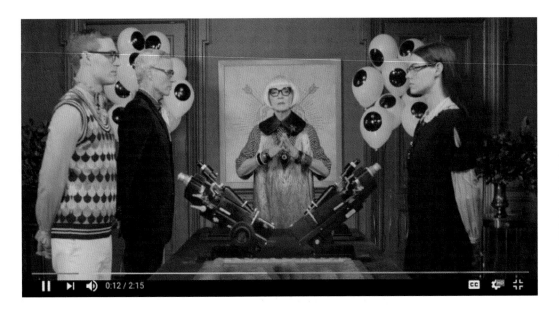

II ▶| ◀)) 0:12 / 2:15   CC ⚙ ⛶

The Eye Ball is a film that tells the story of the Voorthuis family, the optically obsessed owners of Georgetown Opticians. The highly stylized, whodunit stars an optical instrument heiress, a villainous butler, purloined heirlooms, and a cast of fifty hounds. Design Army and Dean Alexander oversaw every aspect of the film, from video style to casting talent to post-production color grading.

SHOP ONLINE AT OURFAMILYKNOWSGLASSES.COM

FOLLOW US ON FACEBOOK & INSTAGRAM @GEORGETOWNOPTICIAN

O
UR
FAMILY
KNOWS
GLASSES

GEORGETOWN
OPTICIAN

GEORGETOWN | 14TH STREET | TYSONS GALLERIA

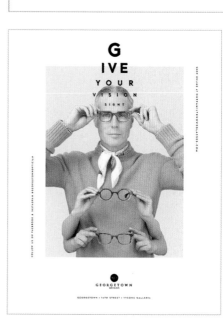

Georgetown Opticians, a venerable thirty-year-old retailer of fine eyewear, wanted to introduce its brand and luxury products to a wider audience. Design Army's multichannel campaign positioned the company as visionaries in the world of chic, original eyewear. An extensive social media takeover conveys the brand's fashion-centric point of view, with the quirky *The Eye Ball* film at its core.

Design Army created ads for print and digital, that juxtapose eye charts with portraits of the film's cast modeling the latest eyewear. The campaign extended the consumer segment to an older audience while integrating a larger range of product.

Georgetown Opticians: Design Army
Photography: Dean Alexander; Copy: Mark Welsh

183

Placemaking Phase 4

It's not unusual for the design and ambience of a restaurant to be a greater attraction than the culinary art, or for a financial services company to open a hip café to serve up good coffee and financial advice. Fabergé, the goldsmith known for the splendid jeweled eggs for the czar, was one of the first global entrepreneurs to understand that a well-conceived showroom appeals to customers and increases sales.

Exterior architecture represents yet another opportunity to stimulate immediate recognition and attract customers. In the 1950s, an orange tile roof in the distance sent an immediate and welcoming signal that there was a Howard Johnson's restaurant ahead. At the opposite end of the cultural spectrum, the architecture of the Guggenheim Museum in Bilbao, Spain, is the brand and a powerful magnet that draws millions of visitors.

Architects, space designers, graphic designers, industrial designers, lighting experts, structural and mechanical engineers, general contractors, and subcontractors collaborate with client development teams to create unique branded environments and compelling experiences. Color, texture, scale, light, sound, movement, comfort, smell, and accessible information work together to express the brand.

We're starved for Wow! For experiences that coddle, comfort, cajole, and generally show us a darn good time. That's what we want for the money. I want decent vittles, mind you, but food we can get anywhere.

Hilary Jay
Founder
DesignPhiladelphia

Understanding how people experience the places where they work, learn, heal, and discover advances an organization's mission.

Alan Jacobson
President
Ex;it

Photos: Steve Weinik

Branded environment imperatives

Understand the needs, preferences, habits, and aspirations of the target audience.

Create a unique experience that is aligned with brand positioning.

Experience and study the competition, and learn from their successes and failures.

Create an experience and environment that make it easy for customers to buy, and that inspire them to come back again and again.

Align the quality and speed of service with the experience of the environment.

Create an environment that helps the sales force sell and makes it easy to complete a transaction.

Consider the dimensions of space: visual, auditory, olfactory, tactile, and thermal.

Understand the psychological effect of light and lighting sources, and consider energy efficiency whenever possible.

Consider all operational needs so that the client can deliver on the brand promise.

Understand traffic flow, the volume of business, and economic considerations.

Align merchandising strategies with displays, advertising, and sales strategies.

Design a space that is sustainable, durable, and easy to maintain and clean.

Consider the needs of disabled customers.

Mural Arts Philadelphia's Open Source was a month-long, citywide celebration of innovation and global public artworks. A pop-up exhibit and meeting space was created in a vacant storefront of the Graham Building, a Center City high-rise.

Open Source: J2 Design, Ex;it, and Mural Arts

Vehicles Phase 4

Building brand awareness on the road is easier than ever. Vehicles are a new, large, moving canvas on which almost any type of communication is possible. Whether on an urban thruway at rush hour or a remote country road at sunset, the goal remains the same: make the brand immediately recognizable.

From trains, to planes, to large vans and small delivery trucks, vehicles are omnipresent. Vehicle graphics are experienced from ground level; from other vehicles, such as cars and buses; and from the windows of buildings.

Designers need to consider scale, legibility, distance, surface color, and the effects of movement, speed, and light. Designers also need to consider the life of the vehicle, the durability of the signage medium, and safety requirements and regulations that may vary state by state.

Many vehicles carry other messages, from taglines and phone numbers to graphic elements and vehicle identification numbers. Simplicity should rule the road.

Vehicle types

Buses
Airplanes
Trains
Ferries
Subways
Container trucks
Delivery trucks
Helicopters
Motorcycles
Jitneys
Hot-air balloons
Blimps
Drones

Get your motor runnin'.

Steppenwolf

Just Eat: Venturethree

Process: Vehicle branding

> **Plan**

Audit vehicle types
Revisit positioning
Research fabrication methods
Research installers
Receive technical specifications
Get vehicle drawings

> **Design**

Choose base color for vehicle
Design placement of signature
Determine other messages:
Phone number or domain
Vehicle ID number
Tagline
Explore other graphic elements

> **Determine**

Fabrication methods:
Decal and wrap
Vinyl
Magnetic
Hand-painted

Just Eat is an online food order and delivery service. As an intermediary between independent take-out food outlets and customers, it has recruited over 64,000 restaurants in thirteen markets.

We have new focus and momentum to take the business forward. The rebrand is part of a strategy to demand clear market leadership to drive sustainable profitability.

David Buttress
Chief Executive
Just Eat PLC

> **Examine**

Impact on insurance rates

Life of vehicle

Life of sign type

Cost and time

Safety or other regulations

> **Implement**

Create files done to spec

Prepare documentation for installer

Examine output

Test colors

Manage installation

Uniforms Phase 4

Clothing communicates. From the friendly orange apron at Home Depot, to a UPS delivery person in brown, a visible and distinctive uniform simplifies customer transactions. A uniform can also signal authority and identification. From the airline captain to the security guard, uniforms make customers more at ease. Finding a waiter in a restaurant may be as simple as finding the person with the black T-shirt and the white pants. On the playing field, professional teams require uniforms that will not only distinguish them from their competitors,

but also look good on television. A lab coat is required in a laboratory, as are scrubs in an operating room, and both are subject to regulations and compliance standards.

The best uniforms engender pride and are appropriate to the workplace and environment. Designers carefully consider performance criteria, such as durability and mobility. The way an employee is dressed affects the way that the individual and her organization are perceived.

> It was essential for our uniforms, just like our new aircraft livery, to stand out at the world's busiest airports.

Raelene Gibson
Manager Cabin Crew and Service Delivery
Fiji Airways

Designed by Alexandra Poenaru-Philp, the Fiji Airways uniforms prominently feature three distinct masi motifs created by celebrated Fijian masi artist Makereta Matemosi. The Qalitoka symbolizes the unity of people to complete a task, Tama symbolizes friendly service, and Droe means clear blue skies and cool breeze on beaches.

Fiji Airways: FutureBrand

Uniform performance criteria

Functional: Does the uniform take into consideration the nature of the job?

Durability: Is the uniform well made?

Ease: Is the uniform machine washable or easy to clean?

Mobility: Can employees do their tasks easily?

Comfort: Is the uniform comfortable?

Visibility: Is the uniform immediately recognizable?

Wearability: Is the uniform easy to put on?

Weight: Has the weight been considered?

Temperature: Does the uniform consider weather factors?

Pride: Does the uniform engender pride?

Respect: Does the uniform respect different body sizes?

Safety: Does the uniform adhere to regulations?

Brand: Is the uniform a reflection of the desired image?

Who needs uniforms?

Public safety officers
Security guards
Transportation personnel
Couriers
Bank tellers
Volunteers
Health care workers
Hospitality workers
Retail personnel
Restaurant personnel
Sports teams
Sports facilities personnel
Laboratory workers
Special events personnel

Methods

Off the shelf
Custom design
Custom fabrication
Embroidery
Screen printing
Patches
Striping

Uniform possibilities

Aprons	Boots
Belts	Helmets
Pants	Shoes
Shorts	Socks
Skirts	Tights
Turtlenecks	ID badges
Golf shirts	Accessories
T-shirts	Scarves
Vests	Fleece
Neckwear	Windwear
Outerwear	Visors
Rainwear	Pins
Blazers	Baseball caps
Blouses	Patient gowns
Bows	Lab coats
Gloves	Scrub apparel

Ephemera Phase 4

Ephemera is an object with a short life, or more simply put, stuff. Many nonprofits give branded gifts to donors to inspire giving, while companies frequently have marketing and promotion items with their logos. A trade show is not a trade show without giveaways. The best booths give you canvas bags to store all your goodies, from squeezy stress balls, to commuter cups, to baseball caps, to mouse pads.

Reproduction is rarely simple. Special techniques, such as embroidering a golf shirt or leather stamping a portfolio, usually require a custom signature that understands the needs of the production technique. The best way to control quality is to examine a proof, even if there is an additional cost.

Categories

Thank you
Appreciation
Recognition
Special event
Trade show
Grand opening
Affiliation
Pride
Motivation

Production methods

Silk screening
Imprinting
Embossing
Foil stamping
Color filled
Engraving
Etching
Embroidering
Leather stamping

Adanu builds schools in rural Ghana, using education to transform children's lives. 100 percent of all proceeds from purchases on the website go directly to development projects in Ghana.

Adanu: Matchstic

The possibilities

List provided by Advertising Specialty Institute

Alarm clocks
Albums
Aprons
Auto/travel stuff
Awards
Awnings
Badge holders
Badges/buttons
Bag clips
Bags
Balloons
Balls
Bandanas
Banks
Banners/pennants
Bar stuff
Barbecue stuff
Barometers/hygrometers
Baseball caps
Baskets
Bathrobes
Batteries
Beauty aids
Belt buckles
Beverage holders
Bibs
Binoculars
Blankets
Bookends
Bookmarks
Books
Bottle holders
Bottles
Bottle stoppers
Bowls
Boxer shorts
Boxes
Breath mints
Briefcases
Buckets
Bulletin boards
Bumper stickers
Business card holders
Business cards
Calculators
Calendar pads
Calendars
Cameras
Camping equipment
Candle holders
Candles
Candy
Canisters
Cans
Caps/hats
Carabiners

Carafes
Cards
Cases
Certificates
Chairs
Christmas decorations
Cigars
Clipboards
Clocks
Clothing
Coasters
Coffeepots
Coin holders
Coins/medallions
Coloring books
Combs
Compact discs
Compasses
Computer stuff
Condoms
Containers
Cookware
Corkscrews
Cosmetics
Coupon keepers
Covers
Crayons
Crystal products
Cups
Cushions
Decals
Decanters
Decorations
Desk stuff
Dials/slide charts
Diaries/journals
Dice
Dishes
Dispensers
Doctor/druggist aids
Dog tags
Drink stirrers/sticks
Drinkware
Easels
Electronic devices
Emblems
Embroidery
Emergency first aid kits
Envelopes
Erasers
Exercise/fitness
Eyeglasses
Eyeglasses 3-D
Fans
Fidget toys
Figurines

Flags
Flashdrives
Flashlights
Flasks
Flying saucers
Flyswatters
Foam novelties
Folders
Food/beverages
Frames
Games
Gauges
Gavels
Gift baskets
Gift cards/wrap
Glass specialties
Globes
Gloves
Glow products
Goggles
Golf stuff
Greeting cards
Handkerchiefs
Hangers
Hardware tools
Headbands
Headphones
Headrests
Highlighters
Holders
Holograms
Horseshoes
Hotel amenities
Ice buckets
Ice packs
Ice scrapers
ID holders
Inflatables
Invitations
Jackets
Jars
Jewelry
Jewelry boxes
Kaleidoscopes
Kazoos
Key cases/tags
Key holders
Kitchen stuff
Kites
Labels
Lamps/lanterns
Lanyards
Lapel pins
Lawn/garden stuff
Leather specialties
Leis
Letter openers
License plates/

frames
Lighters
Lights
Lint removers
Lip balm
Lipsticks
Liquid motion products
Locks
Luggage/tags
Lunch boxes/kits
Magnets
Magnifiers
Maps/atlases
Markers
Masks
Matches
Mats
Measuring devices
Medals
Medical information products
Megaphones
Membership cards
Memo cubes
Memo pads
Menus/menu covers
Metal specialties
Microphones
Miniatures
Mirrors
Money clips
Money converters
Mouse pads
Mugs
Musical specialties
Nameplates
Napkin rings
Napkins
Noisemakers
Office supplies
Openers
Organizers
Ornaments
Packaging
Pads
Pajamas
Pamphlets
Paper specialties
Paperweights
Party favors
Pedometers
Pen/pencil sets
Pepper mills
Pet stuff
Phone calling cards
Phones
Phone stuff

Photo cards
Photo cubes
Physical/therapeutic aids
Picnic coolers
Pictures/paintings
Pillows
Piñatas
Pins
Pitchers
Place mats
Planners
Plants
Plaques
Plates
Playing cards
Pointers
Poker chips
Portfolios
Postcards
Puppets
Purses
Puzzles/tricks
Radios
Rainwear
Recorders
Recycled products
Reflectors
Religious goods
Ribbons
Rubber stamps
Rulers
Safety products
Sandals
Scarves
Scissors
Scoops/scrapers
Scratch-off cards
Seals
Seats (folding)
Seeds
Sewing stuff
Shirts
Shoes/shoehorns
Shovels
Signs/displays
Slippers
Snow globes
Soap
Socks
Special packaging
Sponges
Spoons
Sports equipment
Sports memorabilia
Sports schedules
Squeegees
Stamp pads

Stamps
Staplers
Stationery/business forms
Stickers
Stones
Stopwatches
Stress relievers
Stuffed animals
Sun catchers
Sunglasses
Sun visors
Sweaters
Tablecloths
Tags
Tape measures
Tattoos
Teapots
Telescopes
Thermometers
Tiaras/crowns
Ties
Tiles
Timers
Tins
Tissues
Toolkits
Toothbrushes
Tops/spinners
Toys/novelties
Travel stuff
Trays
Trophies/loving cups
T-shirts
Umbrellas
Uniforms
USB/flash drives
Utensils
Utility clips
Valuable paper holders
Vests
Vinyl plastic specialties
Voice recorders
Wallets
Wands/scepters
Watches
Watch fobs
Water
Weather instruments
Whistles
Wind socks
Wine stuff
Wood specialties
Wristbands
Wrist rests
Yo-yos
Zipper pulls

Managing assets

Managing brand assets requires enlightened leadership and a long-term commitment to doing everything possible to build the brand. Although the mandate to build the brand must come from the top, the brand must ignite your employees first. This is just the beginning.

5 : managing assets

We are excited to use our new brand to better tell our story.

Joe Hart
CEO
Dale Carnegie

We knew that the moment we shared our new brand, it wasn't ours anymore. It was everyone's.

Michelle Bonterre
Chief Brand Officer
Dale Carnegie

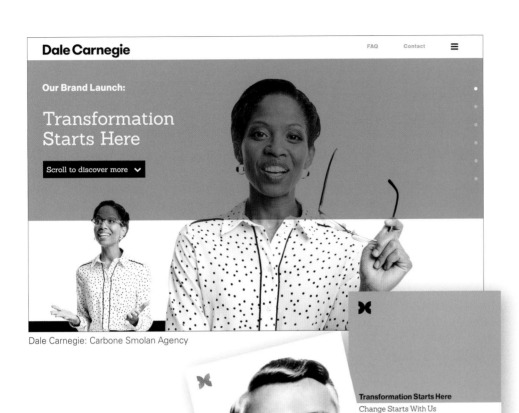

Dale Carnegie: Carbone Smolan Agency

Dale Carnegie's brand launch was carefully orchestrated—designed to engender excitement and build trust at their biannual international conference. Delegates began tweeting and texting as soon as the chief brand officer started to present the new visual identity system and monogram, built around the core unifying idea of transformation.

Large video monitors were placed throughout the convention center to create an immersive brand experience. Each delegate received a monogram pin and two brand-inspired booklets. Along with a global press release, a brand microsite was launched to jumpstart engagement.

Technology and social media enable a global community of stakeholders to participate, in real-time, play-by-play, in bringing the brand to life. There are no more internal launches.

Justin Peters
Executive Creative Director
Carbone Smolan Agency

Dale Carnegie is a global leadership training enterprise, founded on the principles chronicled in *How to Win Friends and Influence People*, one of the best-selling books of all time. Over 8 million people have attended their courses in ninety countries.

An Instagram of CEO Joe Hart and CBO Michelle Bonterre with a 3-D sculpture of Dale Carnegie's new monogram.

193

Changing brand assets Phase 5

Rare is the person in an organization who embraces change. Introducing a new name and identity to an existing organization or to merged entities is exponentially more difficult than creating a brand for a new company. The to-do list is extremely long, even in a small company. New brand identity implementation requires a vigilant strategic focus, advance planning, and obsession with detail.

Military mobilization skills come in handy, and boundless optimism helps. Typically, the director of marketing and public relations will oversee the change. In larger organizations, an individual may be retained to focus exclusively on implementation. The skills required are knowledge of branding, public relations, communications, identity design, production, and organizational management.

Who needs to know?
What do they need to know?
Why do they need to know?
Does the change affect them?
How are they going to find out?
When are they going to find out?

Key pre-launch questions

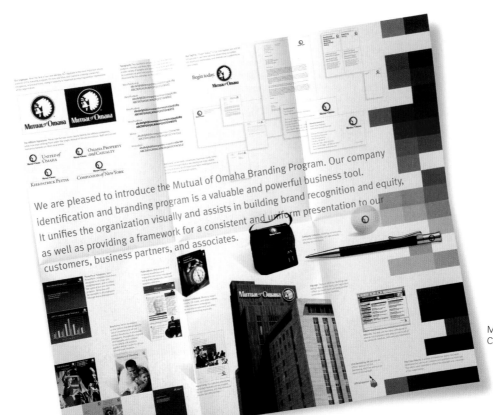

Mutual of Omaha:
Crosby Associates

194

Biggest challenges
Developed by Patricia Rice Baldridge

Time and money: planning enough advance time and an adequate budget

Deciding whether to go for a mega-launch or a phased-in launch

Internal buy-in and support

Keeping a strategic focus on all communications

Making the connection from old to new

Honoring one's heritage while celebrating the new

Identifying who is affected by the change

Helping people who have trouble with the change through a transition

Effectively communicating the essence of the brand within time and money constraints

Creating and maintaining message consistency

Reaching all audiences

Building excitement and understanding

Key beliefs

A strategic focus centers on the brand.

Brand identity can help to center a company on its mission.

A mega-launch means less chance for confusion.

Clarity about launch key messages is critical.

Go internal before you go external.

Once is never enough to communicate a new idea.

You need to sell a new name and build meaning.

Different audiences may require different messages.

Do whatever you can to keep the momentum going.

Recognize that an identity program is more than a new name or new logo.

Name change essentials

A sound reason for changing the name is the first and most critical step.

The change must have the potential to enhance, among others, the company's public perception, recognition, recruitment, customer relations, and partnerships.

Accept the fact that there will be resistance.

Keep the momentum going by creating an air of excitement.

Targeted messages are better but cost more.

Applications affected

Website and metatags

Stationery, business cards, forms

Email signatures

Signage

Advertising

Marketing materials

Uniforms, name tags

Social media

Voicemail, how you answer the phone

Hunter Christian School: Mezzanine.co

Launching Phase 5

Get ready. Get set. Launch. A launch represents a huge marketing opportunity. Smart organizations seize this chance to build brand awareness and synergy.

Different circumstances demand different launch strategies—from multimedia campaigns, company-wide meetings, and road tours, to a T-shirt for each employee. Some organizations execute massive visible change, including external signage and vehicles, virtually overnight, while others choose a phased approach.

Small organizations may not have the budget for a multimedia campaign, but can leverage social networks. Smart organizations create a sales call opportunity to present a new card, or send a blast email to each customer, colleague, and vendor. Others use existing marketing channels, such as monthly statements.

In nearly every launch, the most important audience is a company's employees. Regardless of the scope and budget, a launch requires a comprehensive communications plan. Rarely is the best launch strategy no strategy, which is the business-as-usual or un-launch.

As we continue to grow, we are updating the outward expression of our brand so it shows up bolder wherever we fly.

Sangita Woerner
VP, Marketing
Alaska Airlines

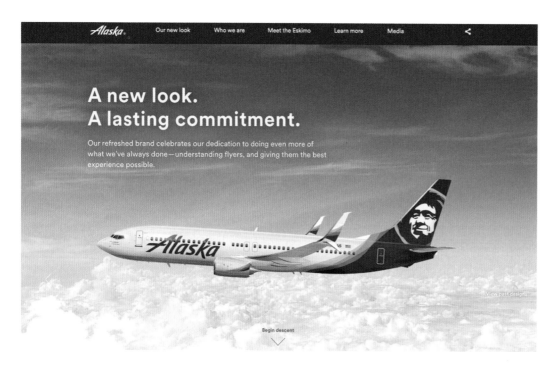

After a year of working with Alaska Airlines to develop a nationally visible and relevant brand, Hornall Anderson created a launch microsite to proudly introduce a broader audience to the new Alaska story. Always with a flyer's perspective in mind, the site takes visitors on a literal journey from the air to the ground, beginning with the brand's purest expression: the new plane flying proudly in the sky. The descent tells the story of the brand, from its accolades and love letters to the details of its unparalleled customer experience.

Alaska Airlines: Hornall Anderson

Strategic launch goals

Increase brand awareness and understanding among all stakeholders, including the general public.

Increase preference for the company, products, and services.

Build loyalty for the company.

Create an emotional connection with stakeholders.

Positively influence your constituents' choices and/or behavior.

Comprehensive plan elements

Goals and objectives of the new brand identity

Communications activities supporting brand implementation

Timeline for implementation and budget

Target audiences

Key messages

Communications strategies, including internal communications, social media, public relations, advertising, and direct marketing

Internal training strategy for employees

Standards and guidelines strategy

Methods

Organization-wide meetings

Social media

Press releases

Special events

Q & A hotline on website

Script of key messages

Print, radio, TV ads

Trade publications

Direct mail and blast email

Website launch

Internal launch basics

Make a moment. Create a buzz.

Communicate why this is important.

Reiterate what the brand stands for.

Tell employees why you did it.

Communicate what it means.

Talk about future goals and mission.

Review identity basics: meaning, sustainability.

Convey that this is a top-down initiative.

Make employees brand champions and ambassadors.

Show concrete examples of how employees can live the brand.

Give employees a sense of ownership.

Give something tangible, such as a T-shirt.

External launch basics

Timing is everything. Find the window.

Create consistent messages.

Target messages.

Create the right media mix.

Leverage public relations, marketing, and customer service.

Make sure your sales force knows the launch strategy.

Be customer-focused.

Schedule a lot of advance time.

Seize every opportunity to garner marketing synergy.

Tell them, tell them again, and then tell them again.

The unveiling of a new brand identity is an emotional opportunity to energize employees around a new sense of purpose.

Rodney Abbot
Creative Director
Lippincott

There are no internal launches anymore. From the moment you share something, it's out there in the world.

Justin Peters
Executive Creative Director
Carbone Smolan Agency

Building brand champions Phase 5

Employee engagement is one of the best invest-ments a company can make—whether you are a company of ten or ten thousand. Organizational development experts have long known that long-term success is directly influenced by the way employees share in their company's cul-ture—its values, stories, symbols, and heroes.

Before a new brand strategy is launched into the marketplace, it is essential that key stakeholders understand why the change is necessary, and how that change supports the organizations core purpose and vision.

Identify change agents. Empower staff to think creatively. Communicate. Communicate. Communicate more.

Advice from the American Alliance of Museums to organizations implementing large-scale change

It's not just values. It's the extensive sharing of them that makes a difference.

Terrence Deal and Allan Kennedy

Corporate Cultures: The Rites and Rituals of Corporate Life

At the foundation of Deloitte's brand are our organizational culture and values; this enables the brand to inform and shape our conversations and behaviors.

Alexander Hamilton

Brand Engagement Leader Deloitte

American Alliance of Museums

American Alliance of Museums and large-scale change

The American Alliance of Museums (AAM) successfully implemented multiple major organizational changes over several years. In advance of the 2012 rollout of a new membership program, a name, identity, and website, AAM created a calendar of tasks and events for the rollout. Briefings and webinars were conducted for key volunteer leaders and partners about planned changes. Staff and board members received talking points to help them explain the changes clearly and stay on message. Board members personally communicated the change to peers and hosted launch events in major cities. After the initial rollout, there were other key milestones to surprise and delight their members.

Our belief is that, if we get the culture right, most of the other stuff—like delivering great customer service or building a long-term enduring brand and business—will naturally happen on its own.

Tony Hsieh
CEO
Zappos

Zappos Core Values

Deliver WOW through service.

Embrace and drive change.

Create fun and a little weirdness.

Be adventurous, creative, and open-minded.

Pursue growth and learning.

Build open and honest relationships with communication.

Build a positive team and family spirit.

Do more with less.

Be passionate and determined.

Be humbled.

Zappos Culture Book

Each year, Tony Hsieh, CEO of Zappos, sends an email to all employees, partners, and vendors, asking them to write a few paragraphs about what the culture means to them. The submissions are unedited, except for typos, because one of the company's core values is to build "open and honest relationships with communication." The number one priority at Zappos is the company culture. Zappos's core values are embedded within every touchpoint, including in how the company hires, trains, and develops employees. The culture and the brand are viewed as "two sides of the same coin." Each year, Zappos publishes a full-color culture book filled with photos and what everyone wrote about what the culture means to them. It has become an annual tradition. The 2010 book was 304 pages and printed on recycled paper using soy inks.

Deloitte and eLearning

Deloitte has developed a new brand eLearning course designed to help drive consistency and engagement across a global network of more than 245,000 professionals. Unlike traditional eLearning, this course utilizes the latest technology and innovation in online learning to create a brand culture where practitioners are excited about the brand and feeling a sense of ownership. The modules use an assortment of interactive examples to illustrate the value of intangible properties such as reputation and trust, and how the various elements of brand work together to create distinction in a crowded market. The course will help cultivate a strong brand culture by shaping a network of champions with a deeper understanding of the power of brand.

Aramark and the road show

Public companies routinely use road shows to bring their messages directly to key investors and analysts. Road shows are also an effective tactic for initiatives. Aramark CEO Joe Neubauer traveled to seven cities to speak to 5,000 frontline managers to launch his company's new brand and to align employees with the vision of the company. "Employees carry the company's culture and character into the marketplace," said Bruce Berkowitz, director of advertising.

Aramark worked with a meeting planning company to produce a one-hour road show. The CEO reinforced key messages about the company's heritage and its leadership in the industry. His overarching message, "Employees are the heart of our success and convey our company's top-tier delivery of services," was supported by a new brandmark.

Managers were fully prepped on the new brand vision and strategy. They received an "Ambassador's Kit" that contained a company history, the new advertising campaign, a merchandise catalog, and a standards manual. The materials also included a manager's checklist and a media launch schedule with explicit instructions on how to handle and explain the launch, and how to implement the branding change.

Brand books Phase 5

Brand books, spirit books, and thought books inspire, educate, and build brand awareness. Brand strategy can't influence anyone if it stays in a conference room, in someone's head, or on page 3 of a marketing plan. The vision of a company and the meaning of a brand need a communications vehicle that is accessible, portable, and personal.

Timing is everything. Companies in the midst of organizational change need to convey "where the ship is going." Frequently, the brand identity process sparks a new clarity about the brand. Building awareness about how each employee can help build the brand is smart.

Our ability to keep our brand fresh and continue to surprise our audiences is key to who we are.

Theresa Fitzgerald
Vice President, Creative
Sesame Workshop

Sesame Street Brand Book: © Sesame Workshop

The purpose of this book is to ensure a consistently furry and funny Sesame Street experience no matter how or where in the world our audiences encounter us.

This book is not just for employees, but also coproducers, creative agencies, licensees, sponsors, and anyone else helping us create Sesame Street in all of its manifestations.

Together, we all contribute to building the Sesame Street brand on a daily basis.

Our VISION is to create a better world for us all.

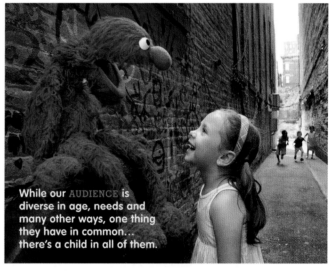

While our AUDIENCE is diverse in age, needs and many other ways, one thing they have in common... there's a child in all of them.

Our PROMISE is to educate preschoolers by using our proven recipe for success:

REAL
HEARTFELT
SIMPLE
FURRY
FUNNY

SESAME STREET
BRAND BOOK

OUR BRAND
ATTRIBUTES

14

real

Sesame Street is part of popular culture, always evolving to be relevant to kids' everyday lives. Its gritty and diverse landscape shows life's imperfections and challenges.

Guidelines Phase 5

Although intelligent guidelines for a rebrand help everyone stay on brand, they only get you halfway there. Organizations need to drive brand engagement. It's important to make it easy for people to adhere to new ways of communicating about the brand. Change is hard. You need to want to change.

Organizations need to be diligent about making sure that everyone understands why the change is necessary, and what benefits the change will bring. Guidelines have become more accessible, dynamic, and easier to produce. Now even the smallest nonprofit can provide streamlined standards, reproduction files, and electronic templates.

The beginning of change starts with the employees and the tools you give them.

Jackie Cutrone
Senior Director, Client Services
Monigle

We developed a brand engagement and asset management platform in the cloud to usher in the new era of the Brand Concierge. Imagine—a brand center that was on brand.

Gabriel Cohen
Chief Marketing Officer
BEAM by Monigle

Tailored Design & UX

Brand Guidelines

Asset Management

Office Template Generator

Brand Showcase

Dynamic Collateral

Workflow & Help Desk

Reporting & Analytics

Content Management

© 2017 BEAM by Monigle

Online brand centers

The web has made it easy to consolidate brand management in one place, giving employees and vendors user-friendly tools and resources.

In the cloud and on the ground

Frequently, a design firm provides a style guide and reproduction files that can be downloaded. Many organizations still publish the guidelines as a booklet and easy reference guide.

Media relations portals

Many corporations have downloadable logo and image files in the media relations section of their websites. These files are often accompanied by extensive legalese that outlines usage.

Marketing and sales toolkits

Companies that have independent distributors and dealerships need effective ways to control look and feel at the point of sale and achieve a distinctive and memorable retail presence through exterior signage, retail displays, and advertising.

Who needs access to guidelines?

Internal employees

Management
Marketing
Customer service
Communications
Design
Legal
Sales
IT
Web gurus
Human resources
PR
Product designers
Anyone creating a presentation

External creative partners

Branding firms
Design firms
Advertising agencies
Information architects
Technologists
Packaging design firms
Architects
Writers
Co-branding partners
SEO firms

Characteristics of the best guidelines

Are clear and easy to understand.

Have content that is current and easy to apply.

Provide accurate information.

Include "what the brand stands for."

Talk about the meaning of the identity.

Balance consistency with flexibility.

Are accessible to internal and external users.

Build brand awareness.

Consolidate all necessary files, templates, and guidelines.

Promise positive ROI contribution.

Provide a point person for questions.

Capture the spirit of the program.

Feature prototypes (best-in-class examples).

Online resources help build brands
Developed by Monigle

Engage stakeholders in the brand.

Communicate brand strategies and objectives.

Adjust to evolving brand practices.

Provide help and best practices as opposed to rules (tools, not rules).

Save users time.

Provide resources to participate in the brand-building process.

Consolidate disparate subjects into one online resource center.

Track user activity and ROI to help support future investments.

Reduce cost from strategy to implementation.

Build consistent implementation.

Reinforce the value of the brand site with instant updates.

Guidelines content Phase 5

Designing, specifying, publishing, and fabricating elements of a new brand identity system are all dependent on a set of intelligent standards and guidelines. Good, solid standards save time, money, and frustration. The size and nature of an organization affect the depth and breadth of the content and how marketing materials are conceived and produced in the future.

Legal and nomenclature guideline considerations are essential to protect brand equity and intellectual property.

The Nature Conservancy is a leading conservation organization working with governments, businesses, non-profits, and communities to solve some of the world's most pressing environmental challenges.

Using our logo with consistency and impact establishes and reinforces our brand leadership, confidence, and reliability.

*The Nature Conservancy
Visual Identity Guidelines*

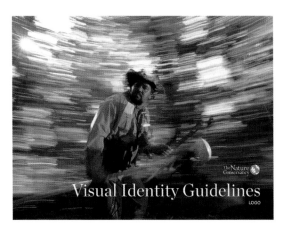

Guidelines content: an in-depth composite

Foreword

Our brand
Who we are
What we stand for
Our mission and values
Brand attributes
Message from CEO
How to use the guidelines

Brand identity elements

Brandmark
Logotype
Signature
Tagline
Name in text
Incorrect usage of elements

Nomenclature

Communicative vs. legal names
Corporate
Division
Business unit
Product and service trademarks

Color

Brand color system
Default color system
Supporting color system
Signature color options
Incorrect use of color

Signatures

Corporate signature
Signature variations
Incorrect signature usage
Subsidiary signatures
Product signature
Signature with tagline
Incorrect tagline treatment
Clear space around signature
Signature sizes
Email signatures

Typography

Typeface family
Supporting typefaces
Special display faces
Proprietary fonts

Image library

Photography
Illustration
Video
Data visualization

US business papers

Corporate letterhead
Typing template
Division letterhead
Personalized letterhead
Second sheet
#10 envelope
Monarch letterhead
Monarch envelope
Memo template
Business cards for corporate
Business cards for sales force
Notepads
News releases
Mailing labels
Window envelope
Large mailing envelope
Announcements
Invitations

International business papers

A-4 letterhead
A-4 personalized letterhead
A-4 business envelope
Business cards

Social networks

LinkedIn
Facebook
Twitter
Pinterest
Instagram
YouTube
Snapchat

Digital media

Website
Apps
Intranet
Extranet
Blogs
Style guides
Interactive
Content
Color
Typefaces
Imagery
Sound
Video
Animation

Forms

Form elements
Vertical and horizontal
Form grid
Purchase order
Invoice
Shipping

Marketing materials

Voice and tone
Imagery
Signature placement
Folder
Covers
Recommended grids
Brochure system, size variations
Mastheads
Product sheets
Direct mail
Newsletters
Posters
Postcards

Advertising

Advertising signatures
Tagline usage
Signature placement
Typography
Display
Television
Outdoor

Presentations and proposals

Vertical covers
Horizontal covers
Covers with windows
Interior grid
PowerPoint templates
PowerPoint imagery

Exhibits

Trade show booth
Banners
Point of purchase
Name tags

Signage

External signage
Internal signage
Color
Typography
Materials and finishes
Lighting considerations
Fabrication guidelines
Company flag

Vehicle identification

Vans
Cars
Buses
Planes
Trucks
Bikes

Packaging

Legal considerations
Package sizes
Package grids
Product signatures
Labeling system
Boxes
Bags
Cartons
Digital

Uniforms

Winter
Spring
Summer
Fall
Rain gear

Ephemera

Golf shirts
Baseball caps
Ties
Portfolios
Pens
Umbrellas
Mugs
Pins
Scarves
Golf balls
Memo cubes
Mouse pads
Customer store website

Reproduction files

Brandmark only
Signature variations
Full-color
One-color
Black
White

Miscellaneous

Whom to contact with questions
Frequently asked questions
Design inquiries
Clearance process
Legal information
Ordering information

In pocket

Color swatches on coated stock
Color swatches on uncoated stock

Online brand centers Phase 5

The web has transformed brand management, engaging stakeholders, consolidating brand assets, and establishing 24/7 access to user-friendly guidelines, tools, and templates. Scalable, modular sites are always current, and evolve as an organization grows.

Brand centers build engagement through sharing the brand vision, strategy, and attributes. Robust sites support strategic marketing, consistent communications, and quality execution.

Sites now encompass brand strategy, content development guidelines, and web resources, and may be used for online transactions.

Site monitoring tools and usage statistics validate ROI results. Creative partners and vendors are assigned passwords to access key messages, logos, image libraries, and intellectual property compliance. Access to certain sections may be limited to user groups.

A strong, visually cohesive brand helps communicate our company's vision, mission, and values.

Aniko DeLaney
Global Head of Corporate Marketing
BNY Mellon

BNY Mellon's Brand Center drives engagement with the legacy of innovation inspired by Alexander Hamilton, the company's founder.

Process: Online brand centers Developed by Monigle

> Initiate plan	> Build groundwork	> Launch project	> Prepare content	> Design + program
Determine goals	Build use cases	Conduct launch meeting	Determine author and status of content	Identify interface and navigation style
Identify brand management problems and issues	Review status of assets and standards	Develop: Site architecture map	Set editorial style guidelines	Develop and approve wireframes
Identify user groups and profiles	Determine content approval process	Project online workroom Timeline and launch plan User groups and user lists	Develop content update plan if needed	Develop and approve site interface
Identify stakeholders	Prioritize content and functionality	Access and security plans	Determine content file formatting and exchange	Initiate programming based on site map
Create project team and appoint leader	Research development options:	Determine IT requirements and hosting plan	requirements	Develop system functionality
Develop team roles, rules, and protocol	Internal and external Select site development	Identify brand assets and cataloging scheme	Secure final approval of content	
Identify budget process	resource	Define success metrics		
	Finalize budget and timeline			

206

Content guidelines

Write concisely. Less is more.

Outline carefully to create a logical order of information.

Know the culture and write accordingly.

Use commonly understood terminology; do not use unnecessary "brand speak."

Provide examples and illustrations.

Support site navigation.

Online brand center characteristics

Educational, user-friendly, and efficient

Accessible to internal and external users

Scalable and modular

Consolidate brand management in one place

Offer positive ROI contribution

Database-driven, not PDF-driven

New content and functions easy to add

Built-in transactional elements

Flexible in hosting and ongoing maintenance

The BNY Mellon Brand Center helps us drive our corporate strategy to deliver excellence, manage risk, and advance our strategic priorities.

Maria D'Errico
Global Head of Strategic
Marketing Services
BNY Mellon

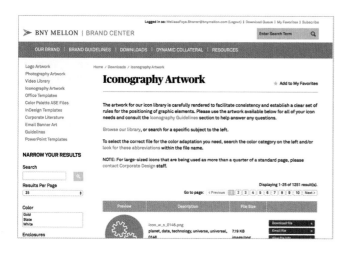

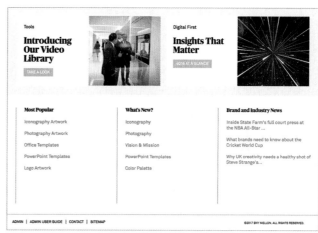

BNY Mellon: Monigle

> **Develop database**

Populate database with content and assets

Program links and required functions

Edit content and design by core team

> **Prototype + test**

Core team reviews beta site

Users test beta site

Make modifications as necessary

Approve site launch

> **Launch**

Finalize launch plan

Create communications and buzz

Promote site launch

Appoint brand champions

Conduct special training sessions

> **Monitor success**

Develop maintenance plan

Assign administrator

Assess usage trends and user reports

Identify content updates and process

Integrate technology and functional advances

Assign budget for management and upgrades

Define and measure impact

Communicate successes

Extraordinary work is done for extraordinary clients.

Milton Glaser
Designer

3 Best Practices

Part 3 showcases best practices. Local and global, public and private, these highly successful projects inspire and exemplify original, flexible, lasting solutions.

ACHC

Our family of companies build strong relationships with customers in continual pursuit of opportunities to enhance Iñupiat cultural and economic freedoms.

ACHC (ASRC Construction Holding Company) is the construction division of Arctic Slope Regional Corporation (ASRC), an Iñupiat-owned corporation created as a result of the Alaska Native Claims Settlement Act. ACHC provides oversight and support services for six companies that provide a broad range of construction services to a wide variety of customers in the private and government sectors.

Goals

Amplify competitive advantage.

Create a unified brand architecture.

Elevate public profile.

Honor ACHC cultural heritage.

Create an integrated system.

We have built a brand that fully supports the reasons for our existence. Our brand works as a foundation for our continued success while being a constant reminder of our core values and heritage.

Cheryl Qattaq Stine
President and CEO
ASRC Construction Holding
Company

Before	After
 ASRC Construction Holding Company, LLC.	 ASRC Construction Holding Company — THE ACHC FAMILY OF COMPANIES
 SKW/Eskimos, Inc. General Contractor	 ASRC SKW Eskimos — THE ACHC FAMILY OF COMPANIES
 ASRC Gulf States Constructors	 ASRC Gulf States Constructors — THE ACHC FAMILY OF COMPANIES
 ASRC Builders	 ASRC Builders — THE ACHC FAMILY OF COMPANIES
 ASRC Constructors Inc	 ASRC Constructors — THE ACHC FAMILY OF COMPANIES
ASRC Civil Construction, LLC	 ASRC Civil Construction — THE ACHC FAMILY OF COMPANIES
 arctic slope compliance technologies a subsidiary of Arctic Slope Regional Corporation	 ASRC Construction Technologies — THE ACHC FAMILY OF COMPANIES

Process and strategy: Sini Salminen, designer and brand consultant, guided ACHC upper management through a rebranding process. Comprehensive research was completed on the construction industry, company competencies, and company history along with a competitive audit. All of the existing subsidiary names and marketing and communications tools were analyzed. ACHC executives worked collaboratively to substantiate how Iñupiat values shape the way ACHC and its subsidiaries conduct business. There was unilateral agreement that the brand architecture needed to support and clearly communicate the fact that ACHC and the six subsidiaries work together as a unified team to provide unique efficiencies and value. It became clear that the final identity system had to communicate that each of the companies was part of something larger. A unified naming convention was developed to convey brand strength and support future growth through mergers and acquisitions. The ACHC Family of Companies was born, and became the platform for the creative process.

Creative solution: Salminen designed a simple and bold brandmark that forms a shield around a bowhead whale tail. The bowhead is regarded as the longest-living mammal and lives exclusively in the Arctic. In the Iñupiat culture, the bowhead whale is a powerful symbol of community,

cooperation, fairness, integrity, leadership, respect, and teamwork, which are the values of the ACHC Family of Companies. The white curve and lower shape represent the vast Arctic horizon. The brand architecture system positions the companies as one unified entity, and embraces cultural heritage. The parent company and subsidiaries each have one predominant designated color. The color palette was crafted to speak directly to the geographical location of the Iñupiat people, with color names such as Bowhead Gray, Baleen Black, Ice Blue, and Wetland Green. In addition to developing identity standards, Salminen designed collateral materials, signage, magazine ads, apparel, field gear, and seven websites.

Results: The new identity and brand architecture system has made it easier for existing clients and prospects to understand that each of the ACHC companies has a unique focus in the construction industry, and leverages the full technical, logistical, and personnel resources of the entire organization. To launch the brand internally, each employee was presented with a stylish coffee tumbler, a water bottle, and an invitation to experience the newly launched websites. An unanticipated benefit of the process was a proud workplace and renewed internal energy.

The strategic process was the core foundation and main driver that helped everyone involved make informed design decisions.

Sini Salminen
Designer and Brand Consultant

ACHC: Sini Salminen

ACLU

The American Civil Liberties Union (ACLU) works to defend the Bill of Rights, mounting court challenges to preserve racial justice, human rights, religious freedom, privacy, and free speech.

Founded in 1920, the ACLU is a nonprofit, nonpartisan organization with more than one million members and supporters. The national organization and its fifty state affiliates work in the courts, legislatures, and communities, handling six thousand court cases a year. The ACLU is supported by dues, contributions, and grants.

Goals

Create a unified image for the entire organization.

Develop an integrated, sustainable, and meaningful identity system.

Connect the organization to ideas and ideals.

Differentiate from other public advocacy groups.

Communicate stature and stability.

Facilitate consistent communications.

We have to be one.

Anthony Romero
Executive Director
ACLU

We wanted to help the ACLU look like the guardians of freedom.

Sylvia Harris
Information Design Strategist

Stand Up For Freedom
ACLU
AMERICAN CIVIL LIBERTIES UNION
of NORTHERN CALIFORNIA

Process and strategy: The ACLU set out to reach a broader constituency and build membership, and asked Fo Wilson Group to customize a team to build a unified, meaningful identity. The Fo Wilson Group, a design consultancy, was joined by Sylvia Harris, an information design strategist, and Michael Hirschhorn, an organizational dynamics expert. In the audit, the team found more than fifty logos. Every state affiliate had its own logo, website design, and architecture, with little connection to the national organization. Other advocacy organizations were studied, and Harris found that the "ACLU represents a set of principles, while most other advocacy groups represent a constituency." The team interviewed a wide range of stakeholders, including affiliates, communications staff, and members. The most frequently mentioned attribute that defined the ACLU was "principled," followed by "justice" and "guardian." A survey conducted in 2000 by Belden, Russonello & Stewart found that "over 8 out of 10 Americans (85 percent) had heard of the ACLU." The team realized that the ACLU identity needed to be recognized in a wide variety of arenas, from town halls to courtrooms and campuses.

Creative solution: The design directive was to capitalize on a highly recognizable acronym, and to connect ACLU principles and the spirit of freedom to the acronym. Fo Wilson Group designed a series of signatures with a contemporary logotype and expressive symbolism. Several options were tested for the modular system that used patriotic imagery. During the audit, the team found that the ACLU's original symbol from the 1930s was the Statue of Liberty, and it had been dropped in the 1980s. The Statue of Liberty tested the best, and although other advocacy groups used the symbol, the ACLU decided to return to its legacy and history. A unique photographic perspective of the statue's face was stylized, and a photographic signature was adopted to work in the digital environment. A range of applications demonstrated how the system worked, from website architecture to newsletters and membership cards. The flexible system needed to work for the national office, the affiliates, the foundations, and special projects.

Results: The ACLU's leadership group championed the identity initiative from the early planning through the analysis, decision making, and rollout. The identity team conducted a series of phone conference presentations to the affiliates. Educational programs for staff were conducted at the headquarters. The group was instrumental in getting forty-nine of the fifty affiliates to adopt the new identity system. The national organization paid to have new letterhead printed for the affiliates. Opto Design was retained to finalize the design system, produce all the preliminary applications, and develop an ACLU Identity Guidelines website. ACLU membership has since grown from 400,000 members to more than one million members.

We presented ACLU's visual history at the national and affiliate level: identity, imagery, printed donor materials, and the identities of other advocacy groups. We summarized our interview findings, other research, and our analysis. We ended the presentation with the new design directives.

Sylvia Harris
Information Design Strategist

The challenge was to develop an identity that could operate in multiple arenas and for multiple constituents simultaneously.

Fo Wilson
Designer and Educator

Although the ACLU had historically been strong in media relations, communications was a new function that was needed.

Emily Tynes
Communications Director
ACLU

With a complex national organizational model such as the ACLU, it is important to strategize thoughtfully how to gather input, test out ideas, and roll out new plans across the 50+ offices nationally.

Michael Hirschhorn
Organizational Dynamics Expert

National identity

Affiliate identity

Foundation identity

Action Against Hunger

We have led the global fight against world hunger, taking decisive action against the causes and effects of hunger, because the poor and malnourished are the victims of political and social turmoil, natural disasters, and inequality.

Action Against Hunger, a global humanitarian organization committed to ending world hunger, was founded in 1979. Working in nearly fifty countries, the organization helps malnourished children while providing communities with access to safe water and sustainable solutions to hunger. In 2015, more than 6,500 field staff assisted more than 14.9 million people.

Goals

Position the organization as global.

Clarify the organization's purpose.

Develop a clear, global brand architecture.

Create a memorable narrative.

Redesign the existing symbol, building on its equity.

If we are driving into a war zone in Mali and people can't read our logo, at least they should be able to recognize our symbol.

Field staff member
Action Against Hunger

Our new identity more clearly and powerfully explains who we are and what we stand for.

Action Against Hunger

Process and strategy: For almost forty years, Action Against Hunger has led the global fight against hunger. Founded in 1979 by a group of French activists, it has been known as ACF (Action Contre la Faim). As with many multicountry NGOs, it had a complicated mixture of local country names. Johnson Banks was retained to "find common ground," so that no matter where one would see ACF, it would look and sound the same.

Johnson Banks led many discussions and workshops about what needed to happen for the organization to represent itself as truly global: either everyone had to adopt the ACF name, or each country needed to adopt Action Against Hunger in its local language. Johnson Banks was looking for a rallying cry that could work in many languages, and realized there is a "for" and "against" in every language. In addition to being flexible, the new nomenclature and theme were more emotive, and clearly answered the question, "Why are we here?" *For* action *against* hunger.

Creative solution: For decades, the organization's identity was an illustrated plant and its root. Although the symbol had longevity and familiarity with employees, for newcomers and outsiders, it was confusing. Was it a symbol for a farming organization? Or, in some people's eyes, a marijuana leaf? After extensive discussions, and one false start, all agreed that a visual mark was imperative to glue the organization together; it needed to evolve from the old symbol in some way. Johnson Banks designed a new symbol by simply representing two key elements of the organization's work—food and water—and adapting their colors. Another way to bring the organization together was establishing one weight of one typeface (Futura Bold), along with a set of photographic and illustrative guidelines.

Results: Johnson Banks created a straightforward design toolkit. In the interim, a set of PDFs was distributed that will become part of a global hub of design assets. Clear rules will make it easier for local communications and fundraising teams to advance emergency appeals and initiatives. Action Against Hunger believes that its new identity more clearly and powerfully explains who it is and what it stands for. More effective and clear communications will enable the organization to have a bigger impact on the lives of vulnerable people, and bring us ever closer to a world without hunger.

FOR FOOD.
AGAINST HUNGER
AND MALNUTRITION.

FOR CLEAN WATER.
AGAINST KILLER DISEASES.

FOR CHILDREN THAT GROW
UP STRONG.
AGAINST LIVES CUT SHORT.

FOR CROPS THIS YEAR,
AND NEXT.
AGAINST DROUGHT
AND DISASTER.

FOR CHANGING MINDS.
AGAINST IGNORANCE
AND INDIFFERENCE.

FOR FREEDOM FROM HUNGER.
FOR EVERYONE. FOR GOOD.

FOR ACTION.
AGAINST HUNGER.

AKTION GEGEN DEN HUNGER

ACTION CONTRE LA FAIM

AZIONE CONTRO LA FAME

ACCIÓN CONTRA EL HAMBRE

Action Against Hunger: Johnson Banks

Adanu

We build schools in rural Ghana using education to transform children's lives—and entire villages—forever.

Adanu is a nongovernmental organization (NGO) that works alongside rural, underdeveloped communities in Ghana to create and establish sustainable solutions for education, and equal opportunities for all people regardless of gender, age, or economic status. Founded by Richard Yinkah in 1997 as Disaster Volunteers of Ghana (DIVOG), the organization has since served over fifty communities and hosted over 1,500 international volunteers, building schools, sanitation facilities, healthcare clinics, and more.

Goals

Advance awareness and increase support.

Represent the Ghanaian NGO in the US.

Rename the organization.

Develop a dynamic brand narrative.

Design a new visual identity system.

Adanu captures the essence of all our values: Ghana, community, collaboration, sustainability, inspiration, and empowerment.

Richard Yinkah
Founder and Executive Director
Adanu

As partners, we share the critical belief that an unwavering, collaborative spirit makes all the difference.

Shelly Morse
Board Chair
Adanu

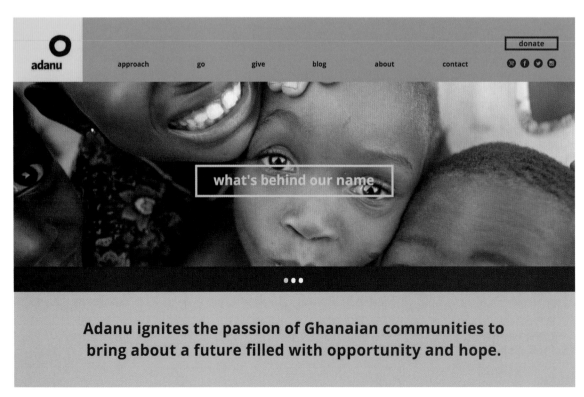

Adanu ignites the passion of Ghanaian communities to bring about a future filled with opportunity and hope.

Sun

Community

Village

Partnership

Process and strategy: Richard Yinkah founded DIVOG with the vision to empower rural, disadvantaged communities in Ghana through grassroots, Ghanaian solutions. The organization has since served over fifty communities and hosted over 1,500 international volunteers to build schools, sanitation facilities, and health care clinics throughout the Volta region. Matchstic was engaged to brand the "American Friends of DIVOG," a US fundraising structure. Rather than creating a whole new brand, Matchstic sought a simpler solution: rebrand DIVOG so that it makes sense in Ghana and in America. Matchstic wanted a name that would be bright, hopeful, and inspiring. During an all-day brainstorming session, the group was asked to translate a host of Ewe words into English in the hopes of finding this name. After many attempts, Matchstic asked the jackpot question, "What's the word for talent or gift?" The answer came with a smile, "Adanu. It means artistic, collaborative wisdom."

Creative solution: Adanu was easy to say in English and Ewe (the everyday language of the Volta region), and met the criteria of a sustainable naming strategy: meaningful, memorable, and an available URL. The brand needed to highlight DIVOG's unique approach to community development—one based on empowerment instead of charity, and sustainable partnerships instead of

fleeting relationships. For the visual language, Matchstic drew inspiration from the sun—as the ultimate symbol of optimism, and from West African Kente cloth and Adinkra symbols. The visual identity system uses solid black—a color that carries strong positive symbolism in the region—with a limited and bright color palette. The bold system of African-inspired imagery utilized Ghanaian colors, textures, and patterns. Symbols for community selection, community engagement, and community partnership were designed. Each shape within the system carries its own meaning and together they create a unique and unspoken language for the Adanu brand.

Results: In 2013, Adanu became an IRS registered 501(c)(3) nonprofit. Originally registered as American Friends of Divog, Inc., it is now doing business as Adanu. The new name, visual identity, and website have had a positive effect—both in Ghana and in the US, increasing recognition and attracting more inquiries and support. The Ghanaian name has made it easy to tell the NGO's story. The professionalism of the new communications tools has boosted morale and pride. By positioning Adanu shoulder to shoulder with other global nonprofits, even long-term partners have increased their support.

We wanted to create a unique and unspoken language for Adanu. An explosion of Ghanaian colors, textures, and patterns emerged.

Blake Howard
Creative Director
Matchstic

Adanu: Matchstic

Amazon.com

Amazon.com seeks to be the world's most customer-centric company, the place where people discover anything they want to buy online.

Originally an online bookstore, Amazon.com is positioned as the "world's largest online retailer," selling music, software, toys, tools, electronics, fashion, and housewares. Founded in 1994, the company has over 244 million customers and ships to over 100 countries.

Goals

Create a unique and proprietary identity.

Maintain the brand equity of the original identity.

Position Amazon.com as customer-focused and friendly.

Modify the core identity for global domains.

Why did you name your company Amazon?

Earth's biggest river. Earth's biggest selection.

Jeff Bezos
Founder and CEO
Amazon.com

As part of the Amazon.com brand identity design, Turner Duckworth created a single letter lock up with the smile, originally to be used online as a button. More than a decade later, Amazon is using this design on its gift cards.

Process and strategy: In 1999, Amazon.com retained Turner Duckworth to redesign its brand identity. Amazon.com's positioning as a customer-focused, friendly company was the core of its mission and values. The challenge was to create a unique and proprietary identity that maintained what Amazon.com believed were its brand equities: lowercase type in the logo and an orange swoosh underneath the name. Turner Duckworth immersed itself in the brand, spent a lot of time on the website, and examined competitor sites. The firm also analyzed what makes a logo effective or ineffective on the web. "Our goal was to infuse personality into the logo, and to create a compelling idea that would convey the brand message," said David Turner, head of design.

Creative solution: The design team developed distinct visual strategies at the first stage; each one emphasized a different aspect of the positioning brief. The final logo design was an evolutionary leap from the old logo. The central idea behind the new logo reflected the client's business strategy of selling more than just books. The design team connected the initial *a* of "amazon" to the *z*. This approach clearly communicated "Amazon.com

sells everything from A to Z." The graphic device that connects the *a* and the *z* also speaks to the brand positioning: customer focus and friendly service. This device forms a cheeky smile with a dimple that pushes up the *z*. The brown shipper box packaging was considered at every stage of the logo design. Turner Duckworth designed custom lettering for the wordmark and made the "amazon" more prominent than the ".com." The typography was designed to give the logo a friendlier and unique look. The design team also designed a full alphabet so that Amazon.com could update its international domains.

Results: Jeff Bezos, the CEO, founder, and visionary, was involved at every presentation and was the key decision maker. Amazon.com had determined that it would execute a "soft launch" of the new identity. The new brand identity was not announced to the press or highlighted on its website. Sensitive to the perceptions of customers and Wall Street analysts, the company felt it was important that Amazon.com did not appear to be a "different" company. Amazon.com will always be considered the e-commerce company that changed retailing forever.

Access to the key decision maker, and in particular to the visionary of a company, certainly makes our work easier. Not only does it accelerate the feedback, development, and approval processes, but it also allows us to ask questions of the visionary and hear unedited answers.

Joanne Chan
Head of Client Services
Turner Duckworth

When you have a leader with true vision and enthusiasm, it becomes contagious and inspires the team.

Jaleh Bisharat
Former VP of Marketing
Amazon.com

Amazon.com: Turner Duckworth

Ansible

We believe that complexity kills innovation. Ansible was created to give everyone in IT a simple way to automate the mundane tasks, so that they can focus on the more important work of innovation.

Ansible's simple, agentless, and powerful approach to automating IT workflows has made it one of the most popular open source software projects in the world, with over 2,250 contributors and thousands of downloads each day. Ansible technology is used in the largest IT organizations around the world to accelerate technology innovation. Based in Durham, North Carolina, Ansible is part of Red Hat, the world's leading provider of open source software solutions.

Goals

Galvanize and energize an open community.

Communicate the simplicity of the technology through the design.

Differentiate from a competitive crowd of legacy IT management software.

Establish a strong identity system that is easy to love and share.

Internal Core Beliefs

Simply clear

Simply fast

Simply complete

Simply efficient

Simply secure

ANSIBLE

At Ansible, we had to have a brand that communicated simplicity in an authentic way to an often skeptical audience (IT professionals). Ansible had to look like a breath of fresh air.

Todd Barr
GM
Ansible by Red Hat

The Ansible brand has become a badge that community users and customers are proud to share and be associated with. It's allowing us to grow organically and virally, through word-of-mouth.

Gretchen Miller
Head of Marketing
Ansible by Red Hat

Process and strategy: With roots in open source and a passionate community of users, Ansible had a solid platform for building a dynamic brand story, but its time had been spent on creating the technology—not the brand. New Kind was retained to conduct research with customers, partners, and employees to understand Ansible's strengths and opportunities. New Kind hosted a series of surveys and interviews, and took a detailed look at the competition. Preparing the brand for a clear new future evolved from studying the current community, customers, and company culture to better understand the possibilities for what it could become.

New Kind shared the learnings with the Ansible team, and worked together to synthesize the research into a unique story that would reflect the simple power of its product. Open source community members shared value that Ansible brought to their work, and helped the team discover that what differentiated Ansible was its powerful ability to hide the complexity of IT automation. The idea of sophisticated simplicity became the core of the Ansible story.

Creative solution: Working with the Ansible team, New Kind developed a brand messaging architecture and story, and began to imagine a visual identity for the brand that would strengthen the key story elements of simplicity. It was critical for the brand message to convey that everyone could use this powerful technology—not just a privileged few. A key strategy of the visual identity design was to engage and excite the community that was already contributing to the technology. The brand had to appeal to a passionate community that would hopefully display it on laptop stickers, T-shirts, and social media feeds in order to grow the community and the brand organically.

Results: Two years after the brand was introduced, Ansible's organic community and business growth exceeded expectations. Web traffic continued to grow well over 100 percent per year, and the business was growing even faster. In 2015, Ansible was acquired by Red Hat and continues to be a vibrant and growing technology in the Red Hat portfolio.

Ansible: New Kind

Beeline

Beeline believes in life on the bright side.
We aim to help people delight in the pleasure
of communications, and to always feel free
anytime and anywhere.

Beeline is the trademark of VEON (formerly VimpelCom), a global provider
of telecommunications services. Founded in 1992, VimpelCom was the first
Russian company to list its shares on the New York Stock Exchange. Beeline
offers voice, fixed broadband, data, and digital services for consumers and
businesses.

Goals

Stand out and raise the bar.

Set a new standard for
modern Russia.

Renew customer
understanding.

Become the market leader.

Build a sense of pride and
belonging.

play

live life

stand out

Process and strategy: In 2005, the Russian mobile communications market was approaching saturation, especially in Moscow. The principal players were competing for the leading position in the market and there was no clear point of differentiation between them. The competitive audit revealed that marketing and branding in the mobile communications sector was focused mostly on technology rather than people. Wolff Olins was engaged to create a new brand identity that would build an emotional bond with consumers in order to retain loyalty. The other prerequisite for the new brand was to provide an outward-looking, more modern face that would help the company prepare for regional and international expansion. The competitive audit also revealed that the market in general was cluttered and noisy. The opportunity for Wolff Olins was clear: create a brand that could stand out and cut through the noise. The brand team worked closely with Beeline's marketing team in Moscow to deliver a brand that was bold and that delivered maximum impact.

Creative solution: Inspired by the company's strategy, Wolff Olins developed a working platform to focus the work. "Beeline inspires me to live life to the fullest" was the idea used to drive all aspects of the creative work, both visually and tonally. The solution was not just a logo but a complete and coherent language that was flexible and universal, that captured the imagination of different audiences across Russia and that transcended cultural and social barriers. Visually, it was an invitation to see life with imagination, illustrated by the use of black and yellow stripes in an individual and ownable way. The new tagline, "Live on the bright side," informed the tone for the new brand's personality. Brightness, friendliness, simplicity, and positive emotions would be the new attributes of the revitalized brand. A new brand identity system, communications style guidelines, and an image library were created to get the company ready for the launch. Wolff Olins was also commissioned to create the launch campaign.

Results: The rebrand was a great success. At the end of 2005, revenue was up by 40 percent, market capitalization by 28 percent, and average revenue per user by 7 percent. Wolff Olins continues to work with Beeline as it grows into new regions and product areas. Since relaunching the brand, Beeline has been independently ranked the most valuable brand in Russia for three consecutive years, according to Interbrand Zintzmeyer & Lux in *Business Week*.

Beeline: Wolff Olins

Boston Consulting Group

In an increasingly complex world, we go deep to unlock insight and have the courage to act. We genuinely want to help our clients and each other succeed. We are shaping the future. Together.

The Boston Consulting Group (BCG) is an American worldwide management consulting firm and privately owned company with more than eighty offices in forty-eight countries. The firm advises clients in the private, public, and not-for-profit sectors around the world, including more than two-thirds of the Fortune 500.

We needed to transform our digital presence and do it in a way that elevates the brand well beyond what is expected in our sector.

Massimo Portincaso
Partner and Managing Director
Boston Consulting Group

BCG moves very fast and they are not afraid to try new things out. Our agile process was characterized by rapid prototyping and testing.

Paul Pierson
Managing Partner
CSA

© Paolo Pellegrin/Magnum Photos

Process and strategy: BCG wanted to transform its digital presence and have a more robust marketing engine to attract and recruit top talent. BCG's partner in charge of the brand and the partner in charge of global recruitment worked closely with the Carbone Smolan Agency (CSA). Their process was fluid and focused on a number of key initiatives, prototyping and testing throughout. With new technology companies competing for the top MBA students, management consultancies, like BCG, have to evolve to stay relevant. Global recruitment was the first priority. The agency began by conducting in-depth interviews to gain the best qualitative insight, surveyed more than 1,800 global consulting staff, and reviewed thousands of pages of BCG's research. An understanding of what was uniquely true about BCG was synthesized in a brief, focusing on three brand pillars and their supporting messages: building impact, connecting aspirations, and growing leaders.

Creative solution: To meet the challenge of "How do you get people interested in working at BCG?," CSA developed an integrated recruitment platform that included connection events, compelling stories, tools for introducing BCG, conversation starters, an advertising campaign, and an interactive case library. After CSA completed the recruitment microsite, they began to tackle the entire digital experience. In close collaboration with BCG, the firm led innovation workshops to bring other partners into the creative process.

CSA cocreated a suite of visual assets that could work across channels and devices, including motion tools and infographics. CSA partnered with Reza Ali, a digital media artist who uses algorithms and key codes to create parametric art, to distinguish practice areas on the website. Instead of using stock photography, BCG partnered with EyeEm, a global community of photographers, to source other thought-provoking images. They brought in photojournalist Paolo Pellegrin to capture moments in the global consultants' lives. CSA also designed social asset templates to make posting on social media easier, and introduced a simple navigational structure for BCG.com.

Results: The design transformation has touched all aspects of the brand. Firm recruitment has resulted in increased applications and offers accepted. Engagement on BCG.com has doubled, and CSA was able to reduce and simplify web content from 4,000 pages to 1,700 pages, a 68 percent reduction. In addition, social traffic and the numbers of contributors have both increased by 400 percent on redesigned microsites.

Algorithms and key codes were used to create parametric art.

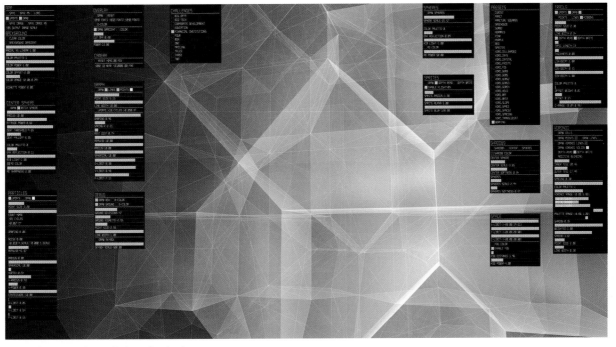

Boston Consulting Group: Carbone Smolan Agency

Boy Scouts of America

We believe in combining educational activities and lifelong values with fun. Our Sustainability Treehouse is a living education center immersing Scouts in the concept of sustainability.

The Boy Scouts of America (BSA) is the largest Scouting organization in the US and one of America's largest youth organizations, with more than 2.4 million youth participants and nearly one million adult volunteers. The BSA was founded in 1910 and, since then, more than 110 million Americans have participated in BSA programs at some time.

Goals

Design an exhibition program and experience.

Make learning an adventure.

Immerse Scouts in the concept of sustainability.

Deliver information in a surprising and unexpected way.

We wanted to create an experience that would inspire Scouts to be change agents.

Adam Brodsley
Creative Director
Volume

Fantastic!!! Period.

Absolutely fascinating exhibits. Thumbs up!

Lots of fun. And learned a lot. :)

Hilarious captions! Awesome!

Visitor feedback

Process and strategy: The Summit is a Scouting and adventure center for the millions of youth and adults involved in the Boy Scouts of America. Housed on 10,600 acres in West Virginia, it is a venue for the Jamboree, a high adventure summer camp, and a leadership center. The Scouts wanted an environmental education facility that would combine learning, conservation values, and fun. A towering, five-story treehouse with a 125-foot-high rooftop, rising above the forest, was designed by Mithun. Volume was engaged to design an immersive learning experience and hands-on exhibits about ecology and resource conservation. Volume assembled a multidisciplinary team that included exhibit designers, content developers, researchers, writers, videographers, and interactive exhibit builders. "How do you engage kids who just arrived at an adventure park to learn about sustainability?" was the challenge. Volume wanted to tell the sustainability story in a way that was authentic to the Scouts and to the site, deliver information in surprising and unexpected ways, and avoid outdated and formulaic exhibit solutions.

Creative solution: Emphasizing the role of natural systems in our lives, encouraging an understanding of the interconnectedness of things, and inspiring Scouts to be change agents were the exhibit design goals. Volume knew that a young and active audience needed an active learning experience, not preaching. The Recyclotron, for example, is activated when visitors pedal a stationary bike to trigger messages about how a sustainable building should function. A "rain chain" made of stainless steel camping cups transfers water from the roof to the cistern below. The cistern that cleans and purifies the water for the drinking fountain is next to an LED message board that displays how much was collected and consumed. All material decisions were made in accord with the Living Building Challenge sustainability standards. It was important to use low-tech, tactile solutions and repurposed materials. Although there is text to read, the tone is intentionally irreverent and words are mixed with icons.

Results: For more than a century, the Boy Scouts of America have been leaders in conservation education and environmental stewardship. They have always believed in combining educational activities and lifelong values with fun. The Sustainability Treehouse is a living education center that is authentic to the Scout's mission. "At each step, it captures the wonder of childhood adventure and challenges visitors to apply meaningful stewardship ideals in their own lives," said Mithun.

Boy Scouts of America/Trinity Works (client): Volume/Studio Terpeluk (exhibit design)
Mithun (design architect) + BNIM (architect of record)

Budweiser

We bottled up 140 years of America. And put it in your hands. The King of Beers—born in 1876. Brewed the hard way.

Budweiser is a filtered pale lager available in draft and packaged forms, produced by Anheuser-Busch, part of the multinational corporation Anheuser-Busch InBev. The brand was launched in 1876 by Carl Conrad & Co. of Saint Louis, and it has grown to become one of the highest-selling beers in the US, available in over eighty markets globally.

Goals

Embody one brand essence globally.

Regain relevance in the US.

Create a more modern, universal presentation.

Achieve global consistency, local relevance.

Our entire brand positioning is all around showing how much we care about the beer, that we're "Brewed the Hard Way."

Brian Perkins
Vice President of Marketing
Budweiser North America

228

Budweiser: Jones Knowles Ritchie

Process and strategy: As light beers gained relevance forty years ago, Budweiser had been managing a decline in the US for decades, while expanding globally. Different regions had different versions of Budweiser: different packaging, communications, and variants. Budweiser partnered with Jones Knowles Ritchie (JKR) to help the brand stand for the same thing globally and look and feel the same region to region. Another goal was to regain market share with younger drinkers in the US. Research had confirmed that while the perception of Budweiser was strong, it was nostalgic, so JKR's task was to make it modern yet universal. They believed that the craft of the product was not adequately reflected in the brand, and it was imperative to raise the perception of quality. JKR's creative director traveled to Saint Louis to visit the brewery, he met the brewmasters, and petted the Clydesdales. Most importantly, he spent the day with the Smithsonian-trained archivist who took him through every piece of packaging, ad, and communication ever created.

Creative solution: JKR began the process by focusing on the two core iconic elements: the Budweiser bowtie logo and the label. The Budweiser bowtie was dramatically simplified and reduced to one color so it could function digitally. Every typographic element of the iconic packaging (over fourteen custom type specimens) was redrawn and crafted. In addition, all illustrative elements like the grains, hops, and the AB seal were redrawn by hand. Finally, a custom sans serif font was designed for use in advertising, inspired by the nineteenth-century American industrial type used on the original Budweiser bottle. Multiple rounds of qualitative and quantitative testing in six global markets reinforced the new strategy and visual language. After updating the packaging, JKR created a visual identity system that stripped everything down to its essence: the color red, the product, and strong messaging displayed in the new custom typeface. The visual identity system was created in the local language of each of the brand's markets worldwide, communicating the brand's "Brewed the Hard Way" message.

Results: The redesigned visual identity system and packaging unified the brand across the globe. The simplified design language has allowed for dynamic brand activations, regaining relevance with young consumers, and re-establishing the brand as the King of Beers. The new design has also increased Budweiser's ranking on the 100 Best Global Brands list. The "America" can and campaign succeeded in Budweiser gaining relevance in its most mature market, garnering 1.3 billion impressions worldwide—more than the last two Superbowl commercials combined.

We redesigned Budweiser because it deserved to be redesigned. It is an artifact of our culture— it deserves to be great.

Tosh Hall
Global Executive Creative Director
Jones Knowles Ritchie

Cerner

We are committed to anticipating the needs of the healthcare industry and developing innovative technologies that help create a healthier tomorrow, today.

Cerner Corporation is a health information technology company that provides solutions, services, devices, and hardware to support the clinical, financial, and operational needs of healthcare organizations. Cerner solutions are licensed at more than 25,000 facilities in over thirty-five countries. The Kansas City-based company has more than 25,000 Cerner associates worldwide. Cerner is publicly traded (NASDAQ: CERN), and its 2015 revenue was $4.4 billion.

Goals

Create relevancy for healthcare consumers.

Advance the understanding of the company's vision and mission.

Strengthen brand perception.

Create efficiencies of scale across marketing campaigns and events.

Develop of toolkit of messaging and creative assets.

Cerner Corporation / 2015 Annual Report

We've been through the digitization of health care. Now we're going to make being a patient a new experience.

Neal Patterson
Chairman of the Board
CEO and Cofounder
Cerner Corporation

Our commitment to the brand is at the heart of our actions. It informs our decisions and influences our responses.

Melissa Hendricks
Vice President, Marketing Strategy
Cerner Corporation

As a global brand, we worked with our teams around the world to create a theme that resonated across borders.

Sarah Bond
Director, Brand and Digital Experience
Cerner Corporation

Process and strategy: From its beginning, Cerner envisioned itself as a company that would transform healthcare. For more than thirty-five years, Cerner has been a pioneer in electronic health records, and its target market has been administrators, doctors, nurses, and other healthcare professionals. As the healthcare industry shifts from a fee-for-service model to one where providers are paid based on patient outcomes, the role of the individual in managing their own health care will become increasingly important.

Connecting with consumers will drive the next stage of Cerner's growth. As the company increases its focus on the consumer market, Cerner's brand team needed to develop a new communications approach and messaging. Historically, although the team has launched between five and seven campaigns a year, it was decided that a single consistent core strategy would have more impact and be critical as the company enters the consumer market.

Creative solution: Cerner's brand team led an initiative and involved members from its in-house creative agency, internal communications, and global marketing to drive the initial brainstorming and explore possible themes that would be able to extend across the globe, and used across campaigns and all marketing channels. Key to the

brainstorming was developing a theme that enhanced the brand's approachability for consumer audiences. The theme, "Creating Healthier Stories," was launched with the company's annual report in 2015 and was incorporated across events and messaging. The addition of a toolkit with creative assets and messaging resources created more bandwidth for the in-house creative agency to focus on new projects rather than creating assets for numerous themes. A strong central idea has improved the strength of the Cerner brand by reducing the number of different messages experienced by customers and employees.

Results: "Creating Healthier Stories" was quickly embraced across the company. Employees have shared their own #healthierstories on social media, and submitted photos that show how the work they do creates healthier stories. The theme has been adopted across the global marketing community, to customer events around the world, from Spain to Saudi Arabia. It has been used at the company's premier client event, Cerner Health Conference, which draws more than 15,000 attendees. It was also used as the theme for the company's internal executive training event with more than seven hundred executives across the company.

City of Melbourne

Melbourne is a bold, inspirational, and sustainable city—a place that inspires experimentation, innovation, and creativity, and fosters leaders of ideas and courage.

Melbourne is the capital of the Australian state of Victoria and the second most populous city in Australia. Melbourne rates highly in education, entertainment, health care, research and development, tourism, and sport, making it the world's most livable city—for the sixth year in a row in 2016, according to the Economist Intelligence Unit. The City of Melbourne Council supports the city's world-class offerings and represents it nationally and internationally.

Goals

Develop a cohesive brand strategy and identity system.

Identify and articulate a core brand idea.

Instill a sense of pride.

Establish insights into the needs of a global audience.

Improve cost-effectiveness of managing the brand.

City of Melbourne Council Goals

A city for people

A creative city

Economic prosperity

A knowledge city

An eco-city

A connected city

Lead by example

Manage our resources well

CITY OF MELBOURNE

Process and strategy: In 2009, the City of Melbourne asked Landor to develop a cohesive brand strategy and new identity system. Landor conducted a thorough audit of the City of Melbourne's existing, varied identities, and its long-term sustainability and strategic plans. The audit assessed public opinion and interviewed stakeholders who included local government officials, business owners, and community representatives. In addition, communications, behavior, brand architecture, and other world-class cities were examined. The new identity also needed to overcome political complexities, improve the cost-effectiveness of managing the brand, and unite a disparate range of governing bodies and an ever-growing portfolio of initiatives, programs, services, events, and activities.

The challenge was to identify an accurate view of the city's deepest, truest distinctions. Unique stories, habits, promises, and aspirations, when unearthed, can be consolidated into symbols, signals, and values. The diversity of Melbourne became the unifying idea that would allow Melbourne to flex, grow, and evolve along with a growing and changing population and connect dynamically with future opportunities.

Creative solution: At the heart of the new design, Landor designed a bold "M" that was as multifaceted as the city itself: creative, cultural, and sustainable. A degree of flexibility was built into the identity system, leaving room for initiative and creative interpretation, and embracing the idea of modulation and adaptation. A system of color, typography, imagery, and tone of voice was applied to a series of templates. A range of applications guidelines included advertisements, sponsorships, events, co-branding partnerships, signage, and 3-D environments. Comprehensive guidelines were developed to help manage the rollout of the new identity.

Results: Melbourne's new identity has helped create positive, distinguishing associations for the workforce, business and civic leaders, global business partners, tourists, and residents. It was adopted by a city council that believed a distinctive identity could provide an immediate visual trigger to a set of emotions or ideas that put a city in the best possible light. The system has instilled pride and a sense of place, and has helped spark economic growth through tourism and business investment.

We wanted to create an identity that reflected the creative and diverse culture that sits at the heart of the City of Melbourne.

Mike Staniford
Executive Creative Director
Landor

City of Melbourne: Landor

Coca-Cola

Coca-Cola brings joy. It's happiness in a bottle. Let's find the truth and celebrate it.

The Coca-Cola Company is the world's largest beverage company and one of the world's most valuable brands. People in more than two hundred countries enjoy more than five hundred still and sparkling beverage brands at a rate of 1.9 billion servings a day.

Principles of iconic brands
Developed by Turner Duckworth

Confidence to be simple

Honesty (no overpromising)

In tune with the current culture

Highly considered use of icons

Attention to details

Goals

Make Coca-Cola feel happy, fresh, and honest.

Visually leverage the trademark's iconic, enduring values.

Drive compelling, cohesive 360° brand experiences.

Evoke meaningful and memorable consumer connections.

Reestablish Coca-Cola's reputation as a design leader.

This strategy inspired a multidimensional design language that amplifies Coca-Cola equities across all consumer touchpoints.

Vince Voron

Head of Design
Coca-Cola North America

234

Process and strategy: Coca-Cola is the most valuable and recognized brand in the world. Its trademark and contour bottle design are ubiquitous cultural icons. In late 2005, Coca-Cola North America engaged Turner Duckworth with the design goal of making the brand feel happy, fresh, and honest. The process began with analyzing Coca-Cola's heritage and visual assets, and demonstrating how leadership brands use design and visual identity to achieve a competitive advantage. There was agreement that Coca-Cola's identity had become cluttered, uninspiring, and static. Given the rapid pace of change in today's consumer society, the team felt that Coca-Cola's identity needed to be dynamic and constantly relevant to the culture. Turner Duckworth identified five principles of iconic brands to guide the design thinking against the brand idea "Coke brings joy."

Creative solution: Turner Duckworth focused on Coca-Cola's iconic elements that no other brand can own: the white Spencerian script on a red background, the trademark contour bottle, and the dynamic ribbon. Turner Duckworth showed what the design of "Coke brings joy" looks like and feels like across multiple touchpoints, from cups to trucks to environments. Turner Duckworth examined the entire visual identity toolbox: trademarks, icons, color, scale, symbols, patterns, forms, typography, and photography. At various stages of the process, designs were sent into research to verify that they were aligned with company strategy. The new bold and simple design strategy leveraged the trademark's enduring and emotional appeal. The design has the simplicity, confidence, and flexibility to work in different environments and media. It was designed to be in tune with the culture. The value of design leadership was discussed with key decision makers. The new design guidelines were developed and posted online for suppliers, creative partners, and design centers around the world.

Results: The revitalized visual identity made the brand relevant to a new generation, reconnected with people who grew up with the brand, and increased sales. Turner Duckworth and the Coca-Cola Company received a number of global awards including the coveted Design Grand Prix at the Cannes Lions International Festival of Creativity and the Gold Lion for its aluminum bottle. The design strategy gave Coca-Cola a new leadership position that has expanded across other key brands. Furthermore, it has helped the company attract creative talent from organizations like Nike and Apple.

The secret to making work like this happen is passion, persuasion, and perseverance.

David Turner
Principal
Turner Duckworth

Coca-Cola: Turner Duckworth

Cocktails Against Cancer

We go beyond the usual check writing to fight this disease the best way we know how: bringing friends and family together for a night of unity, spirit, love, and, that's right, cocktails.

Cocktails Against Cancer is a nonprofit organization that holds annual cocktail parties to raise donations that support programs with an immediate impact on the lives of people battling cancer in the Philadelphia region. Cocktails Against Cancer is a registered 501(c)(3) and was founded in 2008.

Goals

Attract support and engagement.

Drive ticket sales, donations, and sponsorship.

Create an annual campaign.

Design a memorable unifying image.

We want to give back to the community organizations that have had an immediate impact on quality of life for cancer patients.

Sharon Sulecki
Founder
Cocktails Against Cancer

Cocktails against Cancer™

The founder, age 2, and her mom

County Fair in 2015

Jukebox Boogie in 2016

236

Process and strategy: Cocktails Against Cancer began as a humble house party in 2008 when the founder's mother was diagnosed with cancer for the fourth time, this time at stage four. Sharon Sulecki wanted an active way to express solidarity with her mother's fight, and decided to use her hostess superpowers to throw a fabulous cocktail party and ask her guests to give. Since her mother's passing in 2010, the annual event has paid tribute by continuing to support programs that have an impact on those currently in the fight.

Sulecki, with a background in marketing, recognized and valued the power of design. She invited designer Kathy Mueller to join the first Board of Directors, established in 2014. Mueller was tasked with using design to keep loyal supporters engaged and expand the audience beyond the network of the founder. After five years of steady growth, themes for the cocktail parties were introduced as a way to keep the event fresh and continuously engage supporters.

Creative solution: Each year, the event takes on a different theme and a new promotional campaign is launched. The project includes event naming, an identity design, a poster, a flyer, a landing page, social media, a press kit, and day-of decorative elements like photobooth props. Every touchpoint is redesigned to reflect the theme, creating an immersive experience for the audience. Even the logo is modified to reflect the theme and social media profiles undergo a complete theme takeover.

With previous themes of Retro Carnival, '80s Prom, and County Fair, guests most recently attended Jukebox Boogie in poodle skirts and letterman sweaters—ready for a swell night out and primed to give.

Results: Thanks to guests and sponsors, Cocktails Against Cancer has raised close to $100,000 over the years. Funds raised go to organizations with programs that have an immediate impact on the lives of people battling cancer in the Philadelphia region, such as Philadelphia Ronald McDonald House Camp and Cancer Support Community of Greater Philadelphia.

Facebook reach and engagement metrics spiked when we delighted our audience with animated GIFs.

Kathy Mueller
Kathy Mueller Design

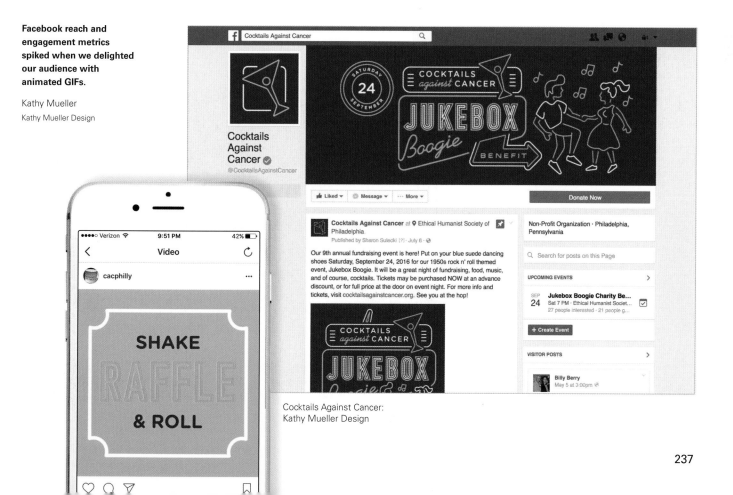

Cocktails Against Cancer:
Kathy Mueller Design

Coors Light

Our beer is lagered, filtered, and packaged at the edge of freezing, as crisp and refreshing as the Rockies themselves. Our mountains make us who we are.

Coors Brewing Company was founded in 1873 by Adolph Coors, who chose the Clear Creek Valley in Golden, Colorado, for his new brewery because of the pure water in the nearby Rocky Mountain springs. Coors Light was introduced in 1978 and is now brewed throughout the US. Coors Light is the second-best-selling beer in the US, where it is made and sold by MillerCoors, which is owned by Molson Coors, the third largest brewer in the world.

Goals

Build on the brand's heritage.

Evoke stronger emotional connections.

Refresh the brand experience.

Deliver a consistent experience for a lifestyle brand.

Through the evolution of our campaign and the creation of a visually iconic brand world, we established Coors Light as a lifestyle brand positioned for sustainable growth.

Elina Vives
Senior Marketing Director
Miller Coors

Process and strategy: Coors Light is a brand with a genuine sense of place and a pioneering spirit. Since Coors Light was introduced in 1978, the brand had enjoyed broad relevance across ages, genders, and ethnicities. Since the Coors Light brand story had lost some of its richness and dimension, the brand team approached Turner Duckworth in 2014 to revitalize the brand's visual identity. The design firm conducted research in the company archives, and interviewed beer distributors and salespeople. The creative process began by mapping out the dimensions of the Coors Light story to express the same pioneering spirit that, in 1978, led Coors to craft a cold-filtered, clean, crisp beer, "looking to the mountain and the power of cold."

Creative solution: Turner Duckworth started with the design of Coors Light packaging, and then developed the wider visual identity for the brand. Taking inspiration from Ansel Adams's images of America's mountains, the design firm developed a grittier, granite-edged photographic aesthetic, lit with blue and overlaid with Coors' iconic red script. To bring a graphic dimension to the brand, Turner Duckworth created a provenance mark, at the center of which is a graphic Coors Light mountain. Creating a new brand language meant building on the iconic elements in the package redesign. Essential brand activation applications included trucks, signage, tap handles, bar interiors, and on-premise tools. The 72andSunny team brought the brand strategy to life by developing the "Climb On" campaign. The goal was to build a stronger brand purpose—insightful, inviting, optimistic, and determined—to appeal to Coors Light target consumers—the men and women who believe that "life is a journey and not a destination." The final step was to make an asset of the brand's nickname, "The Silver Bullet," and to build brand equity.

Results: Turner Duckworth developed guidelines to onboard new agency members to understand what the brand stood for and how to apply the visual identity principles, since Coors Light marketing includes everything from glassware to pop-up bars to apparel and stadium signage. Since the campaign launch in January 2016, Coors Light has seen a steady increase in drinker penetration, especially with women beer drinkers and Hispanic drinkers.

We wanted to give Coors the confidence to be simple and a design in tune with the current culture.

Bruce Duckworth
Principal
Turner Duckworth

Coors Light: Turner Duckworth

Cooper Hewitt, Smithsonian Design Museum

The only museum in the United States devoted exclusively to historical and contemporary design, Cooper Hewitt is the steward of one of the most diverse and comprehensive design collections.

Founded in 1897 by Sarah and Eleanor Hewitt, granddaughters of industrialist Peter Cooper, Cooper Hewitt, Smithsonian Design Museum advances the public understanding of design through interactive exhibitions, programming, and online learning resources. The permanent collection includes more than 210,000 design objects, telling the story of design's paramount importance in improving our world.

COOPER HEWITT

Goals

Redefine and transform the visitor experience.

Advance public understanding of design.

Reach a broader national and global audience.

Position the museum as the educational authority on design.

Redesign the visual brand, website, and exhibit and signage graphics.

We want to shape how people think about the power of design and ultimately, its capability to solve real world problems.

Caroline Baumann
Director
Cooper Hewitt

Cooper Hewitt's new identity is straightforward with no play on visual or theoretical complexity. Function is its primary goal.

Eddie Opara
Partner
Pentagram

Process and strategy: Advancing the public understanding of design is Cooper Hewitt's mission. In 2011, the museum embarked on a three-year collaborative process to rethink the visitor experience, attract a broader audience, and create an immersive learning experience that would bring the design process to life. Integral to the need to increase exhibition space by 60 percent, and to restore the landmark Andrew Carnegie Mansion, was an overarching goal to bring the museum into the twenty-first century. More than thirteen leading design firms would begin work with the Board of Trustees, the director, and all staff to envision a new future. While the museum was closed for three years, it continued to curate traveling exhibitions to reinforce its position as the preeminent museum and educational authority for the study of design. Pentagram began the identity process by working on the name. By replacing "National" with "Smithsonian" and eliminating the hyphen in Cooper-Hewitt, the identity would be strengthened and simplified.

Creative solution: The new name, visual identity system, and website needed to be launched before the museum reopened. Pentagram designed a bold new wordmark and brand architecture system for all physical and digital communications. A new collaborator, the type foundry collective Village, was engaged to develop a proprietary Cooper Hewitt typeface

family inspired by the wordmark. Pentagram also began to address wayfinding. The signage and environmental graphics program needed to creatively address historical landmark constraints.

Cooper Hewitt wanted to develop a unique visitor innovation that would emphasize play and make the design process come alive. Local Projects working with Diller Scofidio + Renfro envisioned an interactive tool, "the Pen." Visitors use the tool to collect any museum object or to design and draw. Visitors receive the Pen with their admission ticket, which contains a dedicated URL to access their present and future curated collection. To convert the concept into a robust piece of consumer hardware, Cooper Hewitt worked with Bloomberg Philanthropies and a global team of technologists and experts.

Results: Cooper Hewitt's new interactive and immersive learning experiences have been the result of a collaborative, international design process, exemplifying how designers solve real-world problems. Cooper Hewitt's transformation has begun to engage new and broader audiences—students, teachers, families, young children, designers, and the general public. Their digitized collection is online for everyone to enjoy. As of early 2017, more than twenty-five thousand people have downloaded Cooper Hewitt, the free-of-charge, open source typeface for unrestricted public use.

What if we give visitors of all ages the tools to become designers for a day?

Jake Barton
Founder and Principal
Local Projects

Cooper Hewitt: Pentagram; The Pen: Local Projects + Diller Scofidio + Renfro

Credit Suisse

We are built on a strong 160-year Swiss heritage of entrepreneurial spirit and innovation. We strive to anticipate clients' needs and to offer them tailored solutions and insights.

Credit Suisse is one of the world's leading financial services providers. As an integrated bank, Credit Suisse offers clients its combined expertise in the areas of private banking, investment banking, and asset management. Founded in 1856, it has a global reach, with operations in over fifty countries and 48,000 employees from over 150 different nations.

Goals

Unify the global voice and brand.

Energize our brand expressions.

Make communications more client-centric.

Grow our client base.

Build an integrated system and streamline efficiency.

We needed to look like a global player. The vibrancy of our new system helps us stand out in an ever more crowded marketplace.

Ramona Boston
Global Head of Marketing and Communications
Credit Suisse

Content management needed to be more client-focused, effective, and streamlined—so that the Credit Suisse brand was contributing to the success of the business.

Leslie Smolan
Cofounder
Carbone Smolan Agency

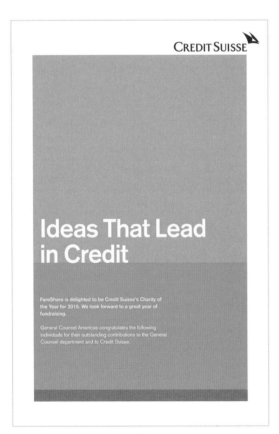

Process and strategy: Credit Suisse engaged Carbone Smolan Agency (CSA) to enhance the bank's image and to develop a client-focused approach to content management. CSA worked closely with the chief marketing and talent officer, and the global head of branding and marketing. The bank wanted to streamline how component communications work together across divisions and regions, and demonstrate the global bank's attentiveness and inventiveness across marketing channels. The design-driven agency conducted an in-depth audit of all communications by content and audience, and developed a master matrix organized by brand awareness, capabilities, products and programs, thought leadership, events, and sponsorship. In addition, the various divisions and global regions were analyzed to further understand what content was needed by whom and for what purpose. While the extensive audit was being conducted, CSA began to rethink a global recruiting campaign.

Creative solution: Designing a wide range of functional tools from online communications to high net worth events, CSA began to demonstrate the impact of simplicity, color, images, and typography. A video for global recruiting, *The Future at Work*, has no spoken words, just music—to appeal to a new generation of multilingual bankers. A unique photographic style was conceptualized to be personally relevant to Credit Suisse's audiences and uses simple graphic compositions with pops of color from a new corporate color palette. Subjects ranging from clients and lifestyle, to clients and business, to business sectors, global regions, investment solutions, and philanthropy, as well as metaphorical ideas and concepts such as achievement, networks, and innovation were organized into categories and a content architecture. The image library includes over 1,200 images, infographics, and icons, all designed to make them more differentiated in the global financial marketplace.

Results: By developing a system of foundational elements for the Credit Suisse brand, the global marketing team is able to deploy a robust system of marketing tools to put the brand in action. There is more confidence in the brand system, and during eighty-four global training workshops in thirteen worldwide locations, employees embraced the refresh as "vibrant, dynamic, and global." The Future at Work recruiting video garnered a 72 percent positive response in testing. *The Financialist*, a daily online newsletter, increased high net worth customer engagement by 54 percent and social media penetration by 22 percent.

Credit Suisse: Carbone Smolan Agency

Deloitte

What makes us truly different is not how big we are, where we are, or what services we offer. What really defines us is our drive to make an impact that matters in the world. We are only as good as the good we do.

Deloitte has more than 244,400 professionals in 150 countries providing audit, tax, consulting, financial advisory, risk advisory, and related services to public and private clients spanning multiple industries. Deloitte refers to one or more of Deloitte Touche Tohmatsu Limited, a UK private company limited by guarantee ("Deloitte Global"), its network of member firms, and their related entities. Aggregate revenues for fiscal year 2016 were US$36.8 billion.

Deloitte.

Goals

Bring the brand to life.

Engage all Deloitte professionals in building the company's reputation.

Expand on the success of Brand Space, providing both rules and tools.

Develop an evolving brand center to deliver consistency and efficiencies.

Provide a consistent, intuitive user experience.

Our purpose—to make an impact that matters—has given Deloitte people a common anchor in talking about our organization.

Michele Parmelee
Managing Principal, Global Talent,
Brand & Communications
Deloitte

Process and strategy: In 2016, Deloitte launched a refreshed brand identity—its first since 2003. The goal was to create a single brand architecture and identity system so that regardless of where a client is geographically, what business they interact with, or what device they use to reach Deloitte professionals, they have a consistent and meaningful experience.

To support the activation of this brand refresh, Deloitte brand team members, in collaboration with Monigle, began the process of defining requirements for Brand Space, a global brand center site. Aligning with the new brand vision and building even more engagement for brand advocacy was paramount. In addition, the new Brand Space site needed to match the energy of the brand refresh—advanced capabilities and better tools would be required. The process began with focus groups to gain insights, and wireframe exercises to explore interface possibilities. Requirements were defined and informed by industry best practices and features. The final site update plan launched the four-month development process.

Creative solution: Brand Space anticipates everything that Deloitte professionals and external users need to provide a consistent brand experience whether in print, on their desktops, or on

their mobile devices. Beyond visual elements, the brand center demonstrates how to guide the tone of all communications and ensure that Deloitte's confident, clear, and human personality is authentically expressed.

New functional capabilities such as responsive site design, digital guidelines and tools, training materials, and best practice libraries were implemented to improve the user experience. A robust content management functionality allows Deloitte site administrative staff to update all elements of the site and track usage and return on investment calculations. Regular surveys and usage tracking analytics lead to regular site updates. Additionally, the SaaS model provides updates on a regular basis to keep site functionality current.

Results: In the first six months after Brand Space was relaunched in mid-2016, activity on the site was up twenty-five fold. The site has been extremely well-received by the global Deloitte community, with an increase of about 70,000 new active users. References and downloads of brand support are also up significantly. And users can access a robust series of brand training videos to further engage in raising the Deloitte brand to the next level.

Deloitte's brand center has evolved to meet current brand activation needs, and provide the ability to move from brand cops to brand concierges.

Mike Reinhardt
Associate
Monigle

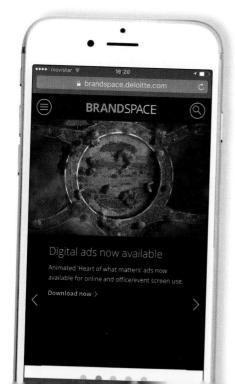

Deloitte Brand Space: Monigle

Fern by Haworth

Our design puts people at the center, so they can sit better, work better, and feel better in today's changing workplace.

Haworth designs and manufactures adaptable workspaces, including raised floors, movable walls, office furniture, and seating. Founded in 1948, Haworth is a family-owned and privately held company serving markets in more than 120 countries through a global network of 650 dealers. Haworth employs over six thousand people worldwide, conducts business in thirty languages, and is headquartered in Holland, Michigan.

HAWORTH®

Our customers influence the objects we design. Fern started with the person, and we maintained that focus throughout development.

Michael Welsh
Seating Design Manager
Haworth Design Studio

Fern embodies Haworth's foundation of research, innovation, and collaborative culture—leveraging cross-functional teams driven by a well-defined strategy.

Mabel Casey
VP Global Marketing +
Sales Support
Haworth

Process and strategy: Drawing from resources and knowledge around the world, Haworth collaborates with ergonomic research and development partners to identify, develop, and launch new and breakthrough innovations. For more than a decade, Haworth and the Human Performance Institute at Western Michigan University have gathered more than five billion pressure mapping data points to understand the physical relationship between a person and a seating surface. The Haworth Design Studio collaborated with ITO Design, a German firm, to design the next generation seating experience. In search of new levels of performance, balancing motion, flexibility, and support, the design team looked to nature for inspiration. They wanted a chair that was less machine and more human, embracing and integrating a high level of engineering and science. The team designed, sculpted, and built a number of functional prototypes. The chairs were tested with customers in the US and abroad. The favored prototype featured a suspension innovation, which responds to the user's body, allowing for a new movement with flexibility and great support.

Creative solution: New engineering innovations were named and trademarked—making it easy to talk about and protect proprietary brand assets. The task chair became Fern, the injection-molded back structure became Fronds, the centered structure became Stem, and the new system was named Wave Suspension. Prior to the official brand launch at the industry's leading trade show, Haworth conducted a robust training program to connect the benefits of comfortable seating with employee engagement in the workplace—good ergonomic seating enables concentration and minimizes discomfort.

Results: After five years of research and development, Fern was introduced at Haworth's showroom at the 2016 NeoCon trade show, along with other Haworth workplace innovations. Designer Patricia Urquiola was engaged to design a showroom that would illuminate the design-build story by showing various phases of production and the R&D process. A towering terrarium, filled with paper fronds, was neon-lit and added visual interest to the memorable and meaningful name.

The trade show hosted 50,000 attendees, including design professionals, business leaders, facility managers, ergonomists, and others who influence chair purchases for work environments. Fern received Best of Year and HiP Awards (Honoring Industry People and Product) from *Interior Design* magazine in the category of Workplace: Seating, Task. Fern was also endorsed by United States Ergonomics.

Design should provide an experience that's more human and natural. Fern embodies a life-enriching design that helps people live better.

Kyle Fleet
Industrial Designer
Haworth Design Studio

247

Fred Hutch

From the founding of Fred Hutch almost forty years ago, cures have started here, and we have shared them with the world. Our mission is the elimination of cancer and related diseases as causes of human suffering and death.

The Fred Hutchinson Cancer Research Center, also known as Fred Hutch, was founded in 1972 in Seattle. Its interdisciplinary teams of world-renowned scientists and humanitarians work together to prevent, diagnose, and treat cancer, HIV/AIDS, and other diseases. Fred Hutch scientists have received major awards for their research and discoveries, including three who have been honored with the Nobel Prize in physiology and medicine.

Goals

Bring the brand to life and convey its spirit.

Articulate what Fred Hutch stands for.

Reimagine the center's brand.

Advance understanding of Fred Hutch's work.

Link scientific research and lives changed.

We've been researching how we can best serve our digital audience—and how that can best align with the work we're doing to better define Fred Hutch in the non-virtual world.

This isn't an advertising campaign. It's an expression of our life-saving research, passion, hope, and collaborative spirit that makes Fred Hutch such an important and special place.

Jennifer Sizemore
VP, Communications & Marketing
Fred Hutch

Before Fred Hutch could tell its story to the world, we had to find common ground within its own walls.

Michael Connors
VP, Creative
Hornall Anderson

Process and strategy: The Fred Hutchinson Cancer Research Center is renowned as a leading force in the fight against cancer and one of the most prominent research organizations in the world. But the reality was that most people didn't understand the breadth of its work or the link between its scientific research and the lives it changes—world-changing breakthroughs like bone marrow transplantation and HPV vaccine development.

Hornall Anderson, a Seattle-based global brand and design agency, partnered with the team at Fred Hutch to reimagine the brand. They convened a series of campus-wide conversations that began with the importance of the very idea of brand itself, and used that shared understanding as a launching point for deep and honest conversation about the work and people of Fred Hutch. The teams wanted to identify "one true thing": that essence of the organization, what it stands for, and the spirit of the place in a common language. During one of the campus-wide meetings, a Fred Hutch staff member stood up and said, "Cures Start Here"—the truth of this simple statement reverberated throughout the stories.

Creative solution: A third-party survey was conducted to gain insight into how people talk about the organization, and "Fred Hutch" was the communicative name the majority of stakeholders

use. The creative exploration began with a new visual identity system. The logo needed to communicate that Fred Hutch does the scientific research and development that leads to cures. One of the researchers had mentioned that looking for cancer is looking for a moment of change—when cells begin to behave differently than they should. This was the key that made it all click together. The logo appears as if you were observing a cell culture through a microscope. The joiner between the two stems of the H became the catalyst moment that ultimately brought the mark to its final state. The website process began with clear imperatives to better showcase researchers, science, and discoveries and Fred Hutch's most important stories by patients, survivors, and caregivers.

Results: The new Fred Hutch brand came to life in a powerful and targeted launch effort designed to drive awareness and engagement. From a new website, built by the Fred Hutch team around human-scale stories of people impacted by the work of Fred Hutch, to emotional radio ads featuring those stories, the link between research and outcomes is made emphatically across touchpoints. Advertising and print campaigns continue to speak to Fred Hutch's mission in a way that brings complex science to a human scale.

Fred Hutch: Hornall Anderson

Global Handwashing Day

We encourage children to be agents of change in their homes, schools, and communities around the world. Clean hands save lives—more than any single vaccine or medical intervention.

Global Handwashing Day (October 15) was created by the Global Public-Private Partnership for Handwashing (PPPHW) to motivate and mobilize millions of people around the world to wash their hands with soap. PPPHW is a coalition of international handwashing stakeholders established in 2001.

Goals

Raise awareness of the benefits of handwashing with soap.

Foster a global culture of handwashing with soap.

Develop a unique visual identity without text.

Appeal to adults and children around the world.

Create guidelines for future stakeholders.

The challenge is to transform handwashing with soap into an ingrained habit that can be performed in homes, schools, and communities worldwide. Washing hands with a quality soap, like Safeguard, can prevent diseases like diarrhea and respiratory infections, which take the lives of millions of children each year.

Aziz Jindani
Marketing Director
Safeguard

In branding and design, one doesn't often have the opportunity to create work that can help save lives. This was a program that provided design satisfaction and was heartwarming as well.

Richard Westendorf
Executive Creative Director
Landor

Process and strategy: Handwashing with soap is among the most effective and inexpensive ways to prevent diarrheal diseases and pneumonia, which together are responsible for the majority of child deaths around the world. Global Handwashing Day was established in 2008 by PPPHW to motivate people around the world to adopt handwashing with soap. Once October 15 was designated as Global Handwashing Day, PPPHW decided that a unique and ownable visual identity was needed for the global campaign. The identity had to translate easily across multiple cultures and languages to communicate its powerful, lifesaving message. Procter & Gamble (part of PPPHW's international coalition of stakeholders) and its Safeguard brand team asked Landor to create an identity for an annual campaign that would help transform handwashing with soap from an abstract good idea into an automatic behavior performed in homes, schools, and communities worldwide. The firm began its process by auditing other successful behavior-changing global campaigns to establish design criteria.

Creative solution: In response to the brief from Safeguard, the flagship soap brand of Procter & Gamble, six Landor offices around the world collaborated to create an iconic, memorable identity that would encourage the adoption of a lifesaving behavior. The identity had to be appealing and easily understood by adults and children in different cultures worldwide. It needed to be pictorial and not dependent on language, and to work in a range of applications, media, and scales. Landor designed three friendly and appealing characters holding hands to communicate that when water and hands are brought together with soap, health is the result—and health is worth smiling about. Landor developed identity guidelines, sample applications, and environmental standards that could be used by event planners and future stakeholders in their myriad efforts to build awareness across various communication channels. The firm also created multiple promotional materials for the inaugural event that included a planners guide for local teams in sixty countries, figurines, and cause bracelets.

Results: Global Handwashing Day has become the centerpiece of a global campaign that has motivated over 200 million people in over one hundred countries. 2016 marked its eighth year. It has become a powerful platform for advocacy by policymakers and has inspired concrete public commitment to actions that will spur public change and shift behavior. The memorable and upbeat identity has worked effectively across initiatives and media platforms across cultures and countries.

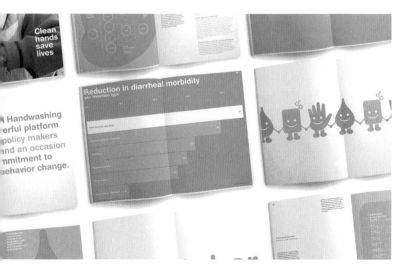

Global Handwashing Day: Landor

IBM 100 Icons of Progress

IBM's 100 Icons of Progress demonstrate our faith in science, our pursuit of knowledge, and our belief that together we make the world work better.

IBM is a globally integrated enterprise that helps its clients succeed in delivering business value by becoming more innovative, efficient, and competitive through the use of business insight and information technology solutions. IBM has more than 380,000 employees.

Goals

Mark IBM's yearlong centennial program.

Celebrate innovations, ideas, and people.

Capture patterns of progress.

Look forward and seed the future.

Tap into institutional memory.

We asked ourselves: "Why just one identity? Why not one hundred marks to celebrate one hundred innovations and achievements?"

Jon Iwata
SVP, Marketing and Communications
IBM

The icons tell IBM's story in an unprecedented and highly visual way, underscoring the company's prolific impact on the world.

Curt Schreiber
Principal
VSA Partners

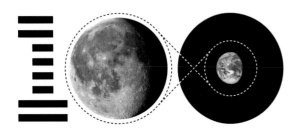

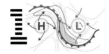

We never imagined how powerful and engaging the stories were to our clients, our workforce, and other forward thinkers around the globe.

Terry Yoo
Director, Brand Expression
IBM

Process and strategy: In 2009, IBM reached out to its partner agencies and asked them to explore and conceptualize an identity for IBM's 2011 centennial celebration. After three months of vigorous experimentation and ideation, IBM's top marketing, communications, and brand teams gathered alongside the agency teams to look at hundreds of sketches, and to form a vision for the centennial identity. Ideas were deconstructed and discussed while new designs were generated. A rough collaged sketch that integrated Paul Rand's landmark 1972 8-bar logo with a Selectric typewriter sparked an epiphany: Why only one? What if we had a system of one hundred marks and the moments they celebrate? What if we paid homage to the ideas and innovations that have shaped who we are? It would be called IBM 100 Icons of Progress. A dedicated, thirty-member team was formed to oversee a cadre of developers, designers, writers, content managers, producers, editors, and subject matter experts.

Creative solution: Each icon needed to be a unique vessel for meaning and storytelling. The content process began with a call for submissions to IBMers around the world: "We want to know about the innovations, projects, and partnerships—past and present—that had led to transformative change in local and regional markets, helping to make the world work better." While hundreds of submissions were being reviewed, VSA Partners led an exploration process to develop a cohesive and flexible design and content system. Each icon needed to function as a visually arresting prompt for a powerful idea, and was based on the number one hundred. An exhaustive internal and external review process of 860 stories was edited to one hundred iconic moments. A team of writers, editors, and content managers conducted additional research and crafted the voice and tone of each story. Designers drew inspiration from the IBM archives, third-party materials, and both contemporary and historical art and culture. The design team created thousands of iterations in order to best capture the iconic story behind each mark.

Results: The Icons of Progress were launched in early 2011 on IBM100.com and multiple other channels throughout the year. The stories ignited conversations in 186 countries about the many ways that IBM has transformed business, science, and society, from helping to put the first man on the moon to developing the bar code and the personal computer. For IBM, the value of its centennial lies not in merely celebrating past accomplishments, but in recognizing fundamental patterns of progress as a means to look forward and seed the future.

IBM 100 Icons of Progress: VSA Partners

IBM Watson

IBM Watson embodies humanity's quest for knowledge, answers, and discoveries. By unleashing the power of human intellect and wisdom, Watson symbolizes our hope for and belief in a brighter future.

IBM is a globally integrated enterprise dedicated to the application of intelligence, reason, and science to advance business, society, and the human condition. IBM has more than 375,000 employees.

Goals

Teach a new, complex technology concept.

Make IBM relevant to a broad audience.

Capture the world's imagination.

Watson has been a catalyst to bring our very complex company together, with a common purpose, point of view, and business objectives. It continues to be a great source of pride for our employees, impacting our culture, and making it easier for everyone to communicate what we do.

Noah Syken

Manager, Business Analytics and Optimization Leadership Marketing IBM

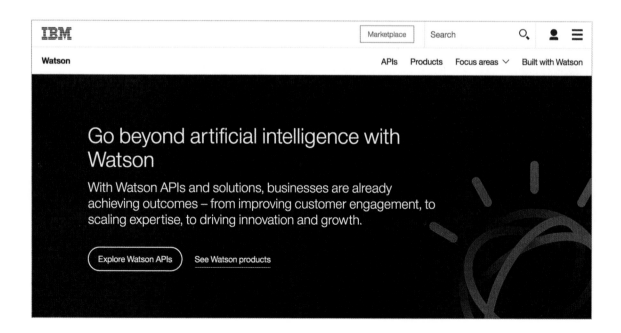

Process and strategy: For a number of years, IBM scientists worked on a highly advanced computing system that could understand human language. The research team believed that this system would be able to answer complex questions with enough precision, confidence, and speed to compete on *Jeopardy!*, an American TV quiz show. Since 80 percent of all the world's data is unstructured—natural language, images, video and more—and therefore impossible for traditional computing systems to understand, IBM believed that this scientific advancement had the potential to transform many industries and solve some of the world's most critical problems. IBM challenged its agency, Ogilvy & Mather Worldwide, to stage the event, to create the visual representation of the technology, and to communicate to a global audience about the far-reaching relevance and value of this complex computing system. While the research scientists worked on the leap in technology, the Ogilvy creative team pondered these questions: What should it look like? How human should it be? How will it work on TV? What should we call it? VSA, a partner agency, suggested Watson, in honor of IBM's visionary president, Thomas J. Watson.

Creative solution: The design process demonstrated what happens when science meets art. The challenge was to achieve the right balance between human emotional characteristics and digital data. After designing hundreds of visual concepts, the Ogilvy creative team realized that the avatar needed to visually connect to IBM Smarter Planet. Watson was clearly a part of the IBM agenda to contribute to a world that is instrumented, interconnected, and intelligent. The creative breakthrough was to develop an answer panel visible to the TV audience that would somehow reveal Watson's thinking process and confidence level. Digital artist Joshua Davis developed a series of animated patterns that were based on data generated by Watson while playing the game. While the public face was being developed, the agency explained the science behind the technological capability, and began to educate the world about the possibilities of this technology. A video series was developed that documented Watson's journey through the eyes of the IBM researchers led by principal investigator David Ferrucci.

Results: Although IBM Watson outperformed its human opponents in its first public test on *Jeopardy!* in February 2011, IBM viewed the real test as applying the technology across different industries to deliver outcomes that were never before possible, beginning with health care. IBM Watson attracted global media coverage, garnering over a billion impressions. A whole new division was subsequently formed to apply this technology, but the profound value was to the IBM culture, inspiring IBM employees around the world with a new sense of purpose and pride.

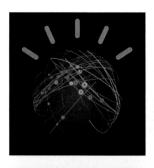
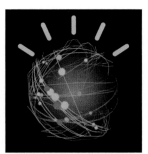

The avatar was programmed to reflect Watson's thinking process.

IBM: Ogilvy & Mather Worldwide

Jawwy from STC

Jawwy is a new digital mobile experience for Saudi's digital generation. It is a personalized mobile service that allows you to build, manage, and share your plan.

Jawwy is a personal mobile service, owned by the Saudi Telecom Group (STC Group). Headquartered in Riyadh, Saudi Arabia, STC Group is the largest telecommunications company in the Middle East and North Africa (MENA) based on market capitalization, and offers landline, mobile, internet services, and computer networks.

Goals

Cocreate a brand with the consumer at the core.

Transform mobile buying, usage, and care experience.

Redefine the customer service journey.

Gain insight into Saudi millennials.

Name a new service and create a bold, visual identity.

Research and insight, strategic rigor, and inspired design are all essential ingredients for brand creation and implementation.

Ash Banerjee
Former Chief Brand Officer
Jawwy from STC

The challenge was to create an identity that not only reflected something radically new but remained simple and true to the region, its people, the product, and the new company.

Mark Scragg
Partner, Design
Lippincott

Process and strategy: With roughly 65 percent of its population between the ages of 15 and 34, Saudi Arabia has a passionate mobile audience and the highest rates of Twitter and YouTube penetration in the world. The gulf between what mobile consumers wanted and what carriers delivered spanned major issues from legacy technology to cultural priorities and generational differences. The STC Group and its new business unit, Sapphire, partnered with Lippincott and a number of other agencies to transform every dimension of the mobile buying, usage, and care experience for this digitally native generation of Saudis—and for the first time in the region, to adopt the power of cocreation. Working with Studio D Radiodurans, the client team launched an exhaustive ethnographic study, surfacing key findings of how the digital revolution, powered by social media, is influencing culture within the country. Along with the study, the team relied on highly engaged consumer panels to explore key elements of the brand strategy, name, functional design, and user experience.

Creative solution: In collaboration with the client team, Lippincott developed an experience-driven brand strategy and positioning to serve as the foundation for the service. A radical redefinition of the entire mobile service customer journey was the real opportunity—starting with how consumers wish to buy, pay, use, and communicate with their mobile provider.

Lippincott took an Arabic-first approach to develop a contemporary and relevant brand name. After extensive testing, Jawwy emerged as the winner, outscoring the next most favored name 2:1. Jawwy is contemporary Saudi colloquial for "my atmosphere," "my space," or "my vibe"—a fitting name for Saudi Arabia's new, personalizable digital mobile service. "From STC" was added to tie it back to the parent company and provide the necessary regulatory transparency.

The wordmark comprises Arabic letterforms stacked vertically. The shadda accent is left off to mirror messaging text. Its simple geometric shapes became the foundation of the visual system, allowing flexibility and functionality across print and digital applications. The vibrant color palette is a big departure from the predictable feel of the competition.

Results: The youthful and optimistic brand connects through digital and social. Jawwy's pricing is transparent and the service completely customizable, enabling users to configure or change their plans and share credits in seconds, all from their devices. Instead of faceless call centers, customers enjoy a self-care online community for faster support. Jawwy's launch represents a historic MENA first: a cocreated brand with the consumer at its core, transforming how consumers use and experience mobile service.

Brand Guidelines

Jawwy: Lippincott

Laughing Cow

Whether it's called La Vache qui rit in France, Die Lachende Kuh in Germany, or Con bo cuoi in Vietnam, Laughing Cow always brings smiles and eating pleasure to consumers.

Laughing Cow is one of the Bel Group's global brands that include Babybel, Kiri, Leerdammer, and Boursin. With the single-serving portion, Bel invented a new way to eat cheese 150 years ago. An international business led by family members for five generations, Bel Group has 12,000 employees, and its brands are distributed in 130 countries.

Goals

Continue the tradition of innovation and creativity.

Bring contemporary art to the broadest audience.

Epitomize the Lab'Bel, the artistic laboratory of the Bel Group.

Mark the brand's 2021 100th anniversary.

For a few coins, you can rise from the status of mere viewer of works displayed in museums and galleries to that of proprietor of an original artwork. Now art exhibition and art criticism take place at home on the kitchen table.

Michael Staab
Curator
Lab'Bel

These collaborations continue the special rapport that has always existed between Laughing Cow and the artists who have used this modern icon as a source of inspiration for nearly a century.

Laurent Fiévet
Director
Lab'Bel

2014 Collector's Edition Box by Hans-Peter Feldmann
©GroupeBel-Hans-Peter Feldmann 2014

Process and strategy: In 1921, Leon Bel, the son of the founder of Bel Group, formerly Fromageries Bel, trademarked the Laughing Cow. This patent was the very first branded cheese product registered in France. In 1923, a famous illustrator, Benjamin Rabier, created a drawing of a laughing cow that contains most of the characteristics that make the brand so recognizable to this day: humor, the color red, the earrings, and the mischievous eyes.

In 2010, Lab'Bel was created to be the artistic laboratory of the Bel Group. Lab'Bel was born out of a keen desire to engage the parent company in a broad policy of support for contemporary art. Lab'Bel works with visual artists and actors from the world of contemporary art that combine humor, impertinence, and the unconventional, and has begun to build a unique position in the world of French cultural patronage.

Creative solution: Between now and the brand's 100th anniversary in 2021, Lab'Bel has planned a series of collaborations with major contemporary artists, each of whom will design a collector's edition box. Each box is made available to

thousands of consumers and collectors at the standard retail price in select stores in France and Germany. This unusual venture is a way of making art more accessible to a broader public, and offers the public a choice: to eat the content or to collect them.

In 2014, the Bel Group initiated its first collector's edition box series by German conceptual artist Hans-Peter Feldmann. Thomas Bayrle, a pioneer of Pop Art in Europe who has used the Laughing Cow logo in his work since 1967, created the second collector's box. Jonathan Monk, a British conceptual artist, created the third in the series.

Results: During the 2016 international art fair in Paris (FIAC), Lab'Bel unveiled Jonathan Monk's collector's edition box in a space designed in collaboration with the artist to resemble a mini-supermarket. By bringing contemporary art to the broadest audience possible in a way that's original, offbeat, and frequently irreverent, the collector's edition box project epitomizes the philosophy of Lab'Bel, and continues to blur the boundaries between consumers, collectors, and art lovers.

2015 Collector's Edition Box by Thomas Bayrle
©GroupeBel-Thomas Bayrle 2015

2016 Collector's Edition Box by Jonathan Monk
©GroupeBel-Jonathan Monk 2016

LinkedIn China

We connect the world's professionals to make you productive and successful. When you join, you get access to people, jobs, news, and insights that help you initiate professional opportunities, business deals, and new ventures.

LinkedIn is a business-oriented social networking service and public company. Founded in 2002 and launched in 2003, it is mainly used for professional networking. LinkedIn is the world's largest professional network, with more than 460 million members in 200 countries and territories around the globe. It is available in twenty-four languages. In 2016, Microsoft acquired LinkedIn.

Goals

Establish a simple, easy-to-read, and memorable Chinese name that maintains a phonetic link with LinkedIn.

Ensure that the name is linguistically appealing and can be trademarked.

Build on existing global brand equity and meaning, while exploring China-specific positioning and attributes.

Integrate the Chinese brand name into the brand signature.

Coordinate research and implementation.

Often, a company's most important marketing decision in China is localizing its name.

Angela Doland
AdAge

Process and strategy: Professional social network LinkedIn wanted to expand in China. As the world's largest professional network, with 225 million members in over two hundred countries, LinkedIn already had over four million registered users in China. In order to boost its member base in China, LinkedIn wanted to establish a Chinese name and identity for the Chinese audience. In 2012, LinkedIn appointed Labbrand to create the Chinese verbal identity and integration strategy. LinkedIn's Chinese brand name needed to be simple, easy to read, and memorable. It needed to reflect the qualities of LinkedIn's users.

Labbrand conducted three rounds of name creation along with linguistic checks in Mandarin and five major Chinese dialects to ensure the name was suitable for consumers. In China, since brands often run into potential problems with trademarking their Chinese brand name, Labbrand conducted Smart Legal Check to ensure that the brand name was available for trademark.

Creative solution: With a comprehensive understanding of the Chinese market, Labbrand explored various creative directions for LinkedIn's brand name. The brand's original English name is approachable and accessible, describing a platform that connects and includes everyone, while Chinese consumers are highly aspirational and driven. LinkedIn's brand identity needed to maintain consistency with its global brand as well as resonate in the Chinese context. During focus group discussions with target consumers, it was found that the most appealing was 领英 [lǐng yīng], which was both phonetically similar to the original name and aspirational due to the connotations of leadership and elite.

Labbrand also worked with LinkedIn on the integration strategy for its Chinese name into the brand signature/lock-up, to realize a powerful and consistent brand identity in China.

Results: Since the launch in 2014, LinkedIn China has attracted more than twenty million members. The Chinese brand name paved the way for LinkedIn to further innovate locally. It has partnered with leading technology platforms in China such as Tencent's WeChat and Alibaba's Ant Financial, as well as the Shanghai government to build its brand and its business.

A Chinese name should reflect brand attributes. LinkedIn China's new name, 领英 [lǐng yīng], emphasizes leadership and elite connotations to resonate with the target audience in China.

Amanda Liu
Creative Director
Labbrand

LinkedIn China: Labbrand

Mack Trucks

Mack Trucks stands for durability, courage, and toughness and has become an iconic brand synonymous with trucking itself. We make the machines that make men legendary.

Founded in 1900, Mack Trucks is one of North America's largest public manufacturers of heavy-duty trucks, engines, and transmissions. Mack trucks are sold and serviced in more than forty-five countries worldwide. Mack is part of the Volvo Group, one of the world's leading manufacturers of trucks, buses, construction equipment, and marine and industrial engines.

Goals

Revive what Mack Trucks stands for in a rapidly changing, global market.

Restore and unlock the brand's unique emotional purpose.

Rally the Mack Trucks organization and partners around an authentic and aspirational brand.

Amplify the best of Mack Trucks' legacy to pave the way for future growth.

The Mack rebrand was all about authenticity and insights. Our goal was to build the brand from the ground up and present a real, emotionally charged story at every turn.

Design Team
VSA Partners

262

Process and strategy: Mack Trucks wanted to send a strong message to its key stakeholders about the significant changes in the organization, its products, and customer support solutions. Leadership wanted to regain the emotional core of the Mack Trucks brand, drive customer loyalty, and increase new relationships and truck sales. They embarked on a brand revitalization process with VSA Partners, who examined all aspects of the brand, balancing the perspectives of various stakeholders.

VSA engaged with global executives and brand historians, along with conducting a thorough competitive market analysis and field research with dealers, sales teams, fleet owners, drivers, customers, and Mack employees. Key was VSA looking internally, externally, and at marketing conditions—an end-to-end view. From there, VSA developed a new, differentiated strategic position, authentic purpose, and emotional persona centered around the importance of the relationship between man and machine.

Creative solution: VSA crafted a differentiated strategic position for Mack Trucks to reignite the brand. A new global tagline, Born Ready, captures Mack's unshakable, bareknuckle spirit and speaks to a legacy of customer-centricity. The brand work included the development of a new identity based on the iconic Mack hood ornament, patented in 1932. VSA also developed brand videos, a collateral system, packaging, and a comprehensive set of identity and retail guidelines. The 360° messaging framework addressed a new customer segmentation, and was supplemented by an advertising campaign, a new signage system, and a completely overhauled Mack website.

Results: Launched to the leadership team and dealers at their biggest trade show in Las Vegas, the initiative has been lauded by management as instrumental in helping grow desired market share. It was met by rave reviews among the trucking community as illustrating key brand values, history, and culture. VSA's work with Mack Trucks represents the most comprehensive and strategic brand evolution in the company's history.

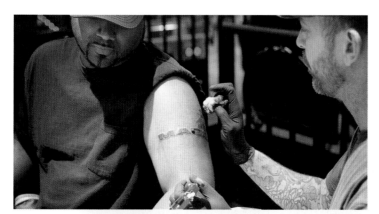

Mack Trucks: VSA Partners

Mastercard

For fifty years, Mastercard has been transforming how the world pays and gets paid, by making transactions faster, easier, and more convenient and secure.

Mastercard is a leading global payments and technology company that connects consumers, businesses, merchants, issuers, and governments around the world. Mastercard Worldwide has been a publicly traded company since 2006 (NYSE: MA). The corporation has more than 10,000 employees. Prior to its initial public offering, Mastercard Worldwide was a cooperative owned by the more than 25,000 financial institutions that issued its branded cards.

Goals

Optimize identity for digital.

Highlight Mastercard's connectivity and seamlessness.

Build on heritage and brand equity.

Simplify system and set standards for future products and services.

Position Mastercard as a technology company.

Today, it is all about connected consumers, and digital is at the heart of enabling practically everything they do in all spheres of their lives.

Raja Rajamannar
Chief Marketing & Communications Officer
Mastercard

Process and strategy: Digital technology is a growing segment of Mastercard's business, and the global company wanted to position its brand as a forward-thinking, people-centered technology company. The brand mark was last designed in 1996, and the iconic red and yellow intersecting circles are one of the world's most recognized brands. To date, over 2.3 billion cards have been issued with an existing Mastercard brand mark, and millions of merchants display the Mastercard acceptance mark. Raja Rajamannar, Chief Marketing and Communications Officer, and the Mastercard leadership team worked closely with Pentagram. The design goal was to convey simplicity and modernity, while preserving the company's heritage and enormous brand equity. The new mark needed to work seamlessly across all digital platforms, retail channels, and connected devices.

Creative solution: To create the new symbol, the design team isolated the brand's elements to their purest form. From the very beginning, in 1968, Mastercard's brandmark has relied on extraordinarily simple elements: two interlocking circles in red and yellow. The overlapping forms effortlessly express the idea of connection, while the basic circular shapes suggest inclusiveness and accessibility, key to Mastercard's brand message of "priceless possibilities." The new brand mark preserves and builds on this iconic

foundation, providing a crisper look that has flexible configurations more suited for digital applications. In the new identity, the word Mastercard is placed outside the interlocking circles and can easily be used horizontally or vertically. In view of the evolution of digital payments, the capital letter C in Mastercard has been lowercased to reduce the emphasis on the card itself.

The new logo represents both Mastercard the company and the full suite of Mastercard products and services, creating a single brand system for the entire organization as well as its existing and future products. It replaces a 2006 version of the logo that was meant to distinguish the brand's corporate image from the consumer-facing image.

Results: In global market research for the mark, Mastercard found that 81 percent of consumers spontaneously recognized the new symbol without the inclusion of the Mastercard brand name. The new brand mark will be used across every touchpoint of the Mastercard brand, from the cards carried by consumers, to signage at Mastercard headquarters, to the digital payment system on smartphones. Brand mark guidelines have been posted on the Mastercard website, and multiple configurations and versions of the mark are available to those who agree to the Mastercard Artwork Download Agreement.

Through decades of exposure, the interlocking circles have become so recognizable that they can be reduced to their essence and still communicate Mastercard, at scales large and small, analog and digital, and ultimately, even without words.

Michael Bierut
Partner
Pentagram

Mastercard's new symbol returns the brand to its fundamental roots.

Luke Hayman
Partner
Pentagram

Mastercard: Pentagram

Mozilla

We're a global community of technologists, thinkers, and builders working together to keep the internet healthy, open and accessible, on behalf of every individual who values the internet as a global public resource.

Mozilla is nonprofit organization first formed in 1998 by a group of open-source advocates within Netscape. Supported by a global community of volunteer contributors, Mozilla creates programs, technologies, and products that benefit the health of the internet. Firefox, the open-source web browser developed by Mozilla, is used by more than 100 million people daily, demonstrating the organization's values in action.

Goals

Increase brand recognition using open source principles.

Reinforce core purpose and not-for-profit status.

Be known as the champions of a healthy internet.

Create a visual and verbal toolkit.

Differentiate Mozilla from its core product, Firefox.

Our brand identity—our logo, our voice, our design—is an important signal of what we believe in and what we do. We've designed the language of the internet into our brand identity.

Tim Murray
Creative Director
Mozilla

This open source process has been a great way to collect insights from a very engaged online community. No one will be able to say, "You didn't ask me."

Michael Johnson
Founder
Johnson Banks

Paint: ©Olesya22, iStockphoto   Iron filings: ©Windell H. Oskay, Flickr   Abstract light curves, Pexels

Process and strategy: Mozilla had long been associated only with their most famous product, Firefox, a free web browser used daily by more than 100 million people around the world. Mozilla's not-for-profit status simply hadn't registered with their key constituencies, and they wanted to be better known and better understood. Mozilla retained Johnson Banks to visually rebrand the organization. Through numerous discussions, scenarios, workshops, and research, Johnson Banks sought to illuminate a clear strategic sweet spot to create a platform for the visual brand. Mozilla's core purpose became clear: "We're uniquely able to build products, technologies, and programs that keep the internet growing and healthy, with individuals informed and in control of their online lives."

The design process used open source principles, encouraging Mozilla's global network to comment on the work in progress on the Mozilla Open Design blog, known as "branding without walls." From the original strategy and narrative stages, through first design concepts and development, there have been numerous posts and thousands of blog comments, even from interested designers outside Mozilla's global network.

Creative solution: Johnson Banks developed an idea that built part of the code of an internet URL into Mozilla's name to represent how people and knowledge are linked in an increasingly connected world. This meaning resonated with both core and external audiences, and was chosen as the final strategy, after an in-depth exploration and discussion of other concepts. Typotheque, in the Netherlands, designed a new font, which was used in the wordmark and accompanying content.

The internet pioneer needed a system that would make it easier to know that something is from Mozilla. The dynamic system simplifies and unifies a multitude of Mozilla activities from programs to events, and can integrate various core messages. Color flows into the new logo and changes with context. Ever-changing imagery represents the unlimited bounty of the online ecosystem. Mozilla will engage new artists, coders, and developers to make imagery that will be available to all under Creative Commons. Zilla, the new font, is now free and open to all.

Results: The process used to rebrand Mozilla was authentic to who they are, what they do, and what they stand for. The process itself acted as a catalyst to conversations across the world with numerous audiences, and resulted in increased brand recognition by technologists, thinkers, and builders. As a not-for-profit organization, Mozilla has boldly and publicly reaffirmed that it is uniquely able to build products, technologies, and programs that keep the internet growing and healthy, with individuals informed and in control of their online lives.

> **It will now be easier to know that something is from Mozilla and understand how their global initiatives connect and reinforce one another.**
>
> Tim Murray
> Creative Director
> Mozilla

zilla:
a contemporary
slab serif font
that directly echoes
the new **moz://a** logo

abcdefghi
jklmnopqr
stuvwxyz

0123456789 0123456789
#%$£€¥://@&\>,.;?!_

moz://a
we stand for
the internet

moz://a
all hands

moz://a
emerging
technologies

moz://a
deutschland

Mozilla: Johnson Banks

Mural Arts Philadelphia

We believe that art ignites change. We are the nation's largest public art program and unite individuals and communities to transform public spaces and individual lives.

The City of Philadelphia Mural Arts Program was first established in 1984 by Jane Golden as part of the Anti Graffiti Network's effort to eradicate the city's graffiti crisis. Mural Arts engages communities in fifty to one hundred public art projects each year, and maintains its more than 3,500 murals through a restoration initiative. Art Education, Restorative Justice, and Porch Light core programs yield unique, project-based learning opportunities for thousands of youth and adults.

Goals

Reposition Mural Arts on the national and global stage.

Simplify the brand story.

Showcase the organization's impact.

Engage diverse artists and communities.

Inspire investment in the organization.

We want to build bridges of connection and understanding in our communities, and stimulate dialogue about critical issues.

Jane Golden
Founder and Executive Director
City of Philadelphia Mural Arts
Program

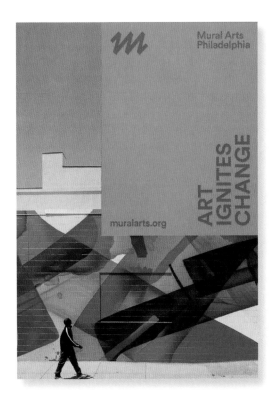

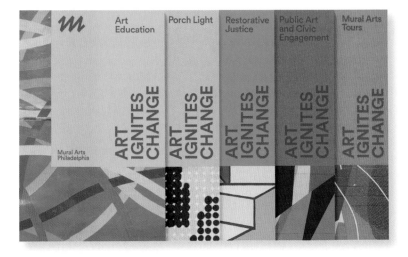

Process and strategy: Over the last thirty years, the City of Philadelphia Mural Arts Program has evolved from a small city agency into the nation's largest public art program and a global model for community development. More than 3,500 murals have transformed neighborhoods across the city.

The program's collaborative process has yielded a multitude of interagency programs in art education, restorative justice, and behavioral health. Communicating that Mural Arts is more than paint on the walls and showcasing the far-reaching impact on individuals and communities were the ongoing challenges.

J2 Design was engaged to rebrand and reposition the organization, and began the process with in-depth interviews of staff, the Board, city partner agencies, and stakeholders. The firm led workshops to elicit insights into the most meaningful outcomes of Mural Arts work. J2 audited all existing communications to identify key issues and areas for improvement. As a way to strengthen communications, the program's communicative name was simplified to Mural Arts Philadelphia.

Creative solution: "Art ignites change" was the core brand idea that would inspire the creative process. Since the organization creates art with others to transform places, individuals, communities, and institutions, J2 designed an active *M*

that is repurposed, reinterpreted, and reimagined. The variations of the *M* represent Mural Arts—a visionary organization that continues to shift, adapt, and lead since its founding by Jane Golden.

An integrated communications system was designed that includes a family of key messages, typefaces, templates, and new narratives. The primary shift in the messaging was from the murals themselves to the impact of the work. Presenting quantitative results and impact was an equal driver with the visual design of the identity system to communicate the return on investment that Mural Arts brings to its supporters and the people of the city. The new brand was launched during Philadelphia's Mural Arts Month at a DesignPhiladelphia keynote event and supported by a redesigned website by Bluecadet, banners across the city, and updated collateral.

Results: Mural Arts continues to benefit from the surge of public attention via social media, public events, and media coverage. While the identity system allows the communications team to efficiently deliver their message with limited resources, the design process and new brand identity have sparked a renewed sense of enthusiasm from the staff, board of directors, fans, and supporters of Mural Arts Philadelphia and a fresh promise of great work ahead.

> **Mural Arts is reinventing how the public engages with art. We need to reinforce that "Mural Arts" is a lot more than just painted walls.**
>
> Brian Jacobson
> Cofounder
> J2 Design

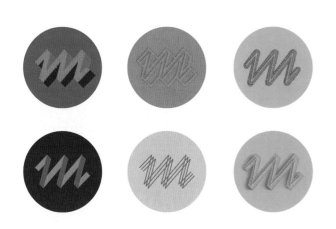

Mural Arts Philadelphia: J2 Design

NIZUC Resort & Spa

A Mexican spirit. A Mayan soul. Located in a secluded enclave, we want to redefine luxury and put a new destination on the map.

NIZUC is an ultra-luxury resort property located on Mexico's Yucatán Peninsula. It is a twenty-nine-acre resort with 274 suites and private villas, six restaurants, three bars, two beaches, two tennis courts, and a 30,000-square-foot spa. It opened in March 2014.

Goals

Create a luxury lifestyle brand with a soul.

Distinguish NIZUC from other world-class luxury destinations.

Attract the world's best architectural, culinary, spa, and hotel partners.

Create a launch campaign that translated to bookings.

For us at NIZUC, brand was essential. It was created from scratch yet has quickly established itself and stands out against our competitors in the luxury market.

Darrick Eman
Director of Sales & Marketing
NIZUC Resort & Spa

Design was at the heart of our process. We envisioned a place before there was a place. We defined a NIZUC lifestyle and guests came.

Leslie Smolan
Cofounder and Creative Director
Carbone Smolan Agency

Process and strategy: Prior to any architectural design or construction, Carbone Smolan Agency (CSA) was engaged to create a unique brand platform for an ultra-luxury resort in Mexico's Yucatán Peninsula. CSA designed a brand book that expressed the developer's vision and brand promise. Inspired by the site's Mayan heritage and the natural forms of the environment, the agency created the foundation for the brand.

They built a story around the key messages of a serene experience, unspoiled nature, warm personalized service, and sophisticated design. These ideas drove a custom photography shoot, the products of which were leveraged to attract the hotel operator, a world-class architectural team, and premium travel industry partners. The brand aspired to connect people to the experience of the resort, and evoke images of NIZUC's endless ocean horizon and the authentically Mexican aesthetic. Establishing a brand platform and a branding-first approach worked from an investment perspective, as well as a marketing perspective.

Creative solution: An elegant and primitive logo was designed as part of a rich portfolio of brand elements. The modern iconic glyph lent itself to creating beautiful patterns and facilitated the design of objects of desire, from amulets to wraps. The on-property experience was communicated through narratives and onsite photography, and formed the core of a robust advertising, social media, and direct marketing campaign. CSA balanced brand-driven print media placements with sales-driven digital marketing to launch an integrated media campaign aimed at the US luxury market. The digital advertising, which featured in-banner video, drove people to a newly designed and highly immersive website, designed to translate interest in the brand to online bookings.

Results: Direct marketing initiatives garnered the support of travel professionals, while the social media campaign created word-of-mouth endorsements from a range of fans. *Conde Nast Traveler*, *Fodor's*, and *Travel + Leisure* all named NIZUC Resort & Spa one of the world's best new hotels in 2014. The launch advertising campaign delivered over seventy million impressions, reaching over thirteen million people. The social media campaign increased Instagram followers by 558 percent, with numbers still climbing. This multi-pronged strategy translated to bottom line success—the hotel was "in the black" for the first year of operation and 100 percent booked for its first holiday season in 2014.

NIZUC Resort & Spa: Carbone Smolan Agency

NO MORE

Together we can end domestic violence and sexual assault. NO MORE aspires to radically increase the awareness of domestic violence and sexual assault in our society and activate change under one brand and one symbol.

NO MORE was founded in 2011 to raise awareness, galvanize change, and remove the stigma associated with domestic violence and sexual abuse. NO MORE's mission is to change social norms, improve public policies, and generate more resources for research and prevention.

Goals

Increase visibility and conversation around domestic violence and sexual assault.

Remove shame, silence, and stigma surrounding these issues.

Increase the understanding that domestic violence and sexual assault affects everyone—directly or indirectly.

Improve public policies and increase resources.

Create a universal, immediately recognizable symbol.

NO MÁS
JUNTOS PODEMOS PONER FIN A LA VIOLENCIA DOMÉSTICA Y AL ABUSO SEXUAL

With NO MORE, we are spotlighting a pervasive yet hidden problem in order to increase visibility, start a dialogue, and help change social norms. Simply put, domestic violence and sexual assault are all around us and people we know and love are being victimized every day. It's time to take action—it's time to say NO MORE.

Executive Committee
The NO MORE Project

NO MORE's symbol is both aspirational and conceptual. It represents a vanishing point, because we envision a time when this problem no longer exists in our culture.

Christine Mau
NO MORE Board Member

Photo: SR 2 Motor Sports

Process and strategy: NO MORE was created by fifty individuals from the private and public sectors who were frustrated by the fact that even though domestic violence and sexual assault (DV/SA) are devastatingly pervasive—impacting rich, poor, young, old, male, and female from every race, region, and religion—the problem is not a priority in this country. These issues are underfunded, with shame and stigma still surrounding them.

To address this, Anne Glauber, Virginia Witt, Maile Zambuto, and Jane Randel led an effort to increase visibility and better connect the public to these issues. The question: How could we support survivors, show perpetrators that their crimes won't be tolerated, and demonstrate broad concern to public officials? First they reached out to every major US DV/SA organization to share this bold strategy that would help individuals, organizations, and national brands take action. Then they held numerous exploratory meetings to build consensus and strategic alliances. Ultimately, all agreed that a universal symbol, widely visible across platforms, could galvanize support, generate funding, and increase awareness.

Creative solution: The founders started by organizing think tanks made up of leading branding and marketing experts who had never considered these issues before. These creative visioning sessions produced what ultimately became "NO MORE"—a symbol that expresses the universal and collective emotion and imperative. Like the peace sign, the red AIDS ribbon, or the pink breast cancer ribbon, the NO MORE symbol will be used by the public, influencers, and DV/SA organizations to move these issues higher on the public's agenda. As such, it has to work across platforms—from a Twitter page on a mobile device to a T-shirt. A three-year launch plan called for celebrities, influencers, and everyday people to wear the symbol to express their commitment and inspire action. National brands and strategic alliances will demonstrate their support through a variety of co-branding platforms.

Results: In 2013, NO MORE launched its first public service announcement campaign, which was created by the Joyful Heart Foundation and Rachel Howald at Young & Rubicam. In 2014, the National Football League began airing NO MORE PSAs during football broadcasts, and twenty-three current and former players participated in the "NFL Players Say NO MORE" PSAs. In 2015, the NFL donated Super Bowl airtime for the first time to elevate domestic violence and sexual assault for more than 100 million viewers with the NO MORE Super Bowl PSA. In 2016, the "Text Talk" ad campaign for Super Bowl L was launched. NO MORE PSAs have generated more than four billion media impressions, secured nearly $100 million in donated air time, and reached every one of the 210 media markets in the United States. UK Says NO MORE was launched in 2015.

NO MORE: Sterling Brands

Ohio & Erie Canalway

As a National Heritage Area, we are a place to experience trails, trains and scenic byways, canal towns and ethnic neighborhoods, parks, working rivers and great lakes, industrial landscapes and green valleys.

The Ohio & Erie Canalway is one of forty-nine National Heritage Areas that preserves and shares important aspects of America's heritage. More than 2.5 million visitors annually have explored the eighty-six-mile Towpath Trail that runs through the heart of the Canalway. Whether birding, hiking, bicycling, or traveling by horseback, rail, or byway, visitors experience the cultural, historic, recreational, and natural resources of northeastern Ohio.

Goals

Name and brand the region.

Develop a comprehensive wayfinding, orientation, and interpretive system.

Share the rich interpretive stories and exhibits with visitors.

Attract local and regional investment and growth.

Raise regional and national awareness.

We started out on a journey to join together all the stakeholders in a unified effort to recognize the incredible potential of the Canalway, and lay the foundation for turning it into a major visitor destination.

Tim Donovan
Executive Director
Canalway Partners

Process and strategy: In the nineteenth century, the canal system in Northeastern Ohio contributed to regional and national prosperity. Although the region was rich in cultural, recreational, and natural resources, it needed to stimulate economic growth, encourage high-tech investment, and build green development, tourism, and community support. Forty-eight communities participated in developing a heritage management plan in 2001. Subsequently, the sixteen-member steering committee retained Cloud Gehshan (CG) to name and brand the region, and to design a comprehensive branding, marketing, wayfinding signage, and interpretive display system.

In order to understand the user and visitor experience, CG began with a photographic audit of all routes and venues. Through interviews and forums, the firm solicited a broad range of ideas from the forty-eight communities. Renaming the 110-mile Ohio and Erie Canal National Heritage Corridor became a priority—the name needed to be easy to say and remember, and effective on signage and all other media.

Creative solution: The name Ohio & Erie Canalway was chosen because it was short, concise, and could be differentiated from other venues. When the word "canal" was joined with "way," it signified that the canal was part of a larger idea, as well as a passageway. CG designed a visual identity that was authentic and effective in signage and on the website and other digital media. The wayfinding and signage system needed to be user-friendly and help residents and visitors navigate the communities, lakes, buildings, gardens, and events. CG partnered with Dommert Phillips to create an interpretive plan to illuminate O&E's rich historical themes and stories.

A guidelines manual provided comprehensive standards for the logo and its application to a wide range of print, clothing, retail, and promotional items. It also contained complete signage fabrication standards and specifications that included entrance markers, vehicular direction and pathfinder signs, trailhead and pedestrian orientation signage, visitor information kiosks, a range of interpretive tools, mile markers, hiking and biking signs, building identification, and banner programs.

Results: Since the new name was introduced, several million more people have enjoyed the wide array of tours, trails, water sports, entertainment venues, and museums. The vision that the Ohio & Erie Canalway Association began building is steadily coming to fruition. Working with limited resources to coordinate all forms of outreach, positioning the entire region as a vital and exciting place for people to live, work, and visit is now in its second phase of development and investment.

When a collection of cities and towns markets itself as a region, the result is greater than the sum of its parts.

Dan Rice
President & CEO
Ohio and Erie Canal Coalition

It's about transforming the industrial backyards of the past into the cultural and recreational front yards of the future.

Jerome Cloud
Principal
Cloud Gehshan

Ohio and Erie Canalway: Cloud Gehshan

Peru

From its cities and towns to the Amazon River basin and the Andes Mountains, Peru is a multicultural nation in the midst of evolution, change, and transformation.

Located in western South America, Peru has a population of 31.7 million. The country's main industries include agriculture, fishing, mining, and manufacturing. Commonly spoken languages include Spanish and Quechua, among others.

Goals

Transmit a clear brand promise.

Increase investments, tourism, and exports.

Increase demand for products and services.

Create a brand identity system.

A recent survey gives the Peru brand a 94 percent approval rating among Peruvian citizens. Some already consider it a favorite motif for a skin-deep tattoo!

Isabella Falco
Head
Brand Perú

The hand-drawn graphic highlights the human or artisanal qualities through a series of lines that can be seen in Inca and pre-Incan cultures as well.

Gustavo Koniszczer
Managing Director
FutureBrand Spanish Latin America

Private and public institutions are eager to represent the Peru country brand's spirit, and other countries are studying the brand and its instant local success with its most important audience, Peru's citizens.

Julia Viñas
Executive Director
FutureBrand Lima

Peru: FutureBrand

276

Process and strategy: A task force initiated by Promperu (Peru's exports and tourism promotion commission), the Ministry of Foreign Affairs, and Proinversión (the private investment promotion agency) was tasked with building the nation's brand and communicating a differentiated brand promise. FutureBrand was engaged to provide positioning, brand strategy, and design services for the country with the long-term goal of building tourism, exports, and investments. The research process included multidisciplinary global, national, and local perspectives from a broad team of experts. Tours of archeological districts, tourism sites, museums, and various manufacturing areas included interviews with different stakeholder groups. FutureBrand developed various positioning platforms that were evaluated in eight Peruvian regions and seven cities in prioritized external markets.

The strategic platforms led to positioning the Peru brand based on three pillars: multifaceted, specialized, and captivating, reflecting the country's uniqueness from a cultural and natural standpoint. A team of brand ambassadors from tourism, exports, and investments agreed that Peru's big idea was evolution, change, and transformation.

Creative solution: Peru is the birthplace of South American civilization, with both natural and man-made wonders, from the magic citadel of Machu Picchu to the Amazon rainforest. The juxtaposition of indigenous cultures such as Inca, Nazca, Moche, and Mochica with Spanish cultures inspired the FutureBrand team to design an iconic spiral form that emanates from the letterform *P*, reflecting evolution and transformation. The icon, like a fingerprint, communicates that "there is a Peru for each individual." The design team also developed a proprietary image style to capture the wonders of the country. The iconic color is red, with a default to white. TypeTogether created a proprietary font family to complement the brand identity system. FutureBrand created guidelines that are clearly explained in a brand book.

Results: Peru's new image was launched nationally in March 2011 by means of an advertising campaign created by Young & Rubicam. Today the new identity is visible throughout the country. Tourists are greeted with it in airports and train stations, and citizens of all ages and means wear Peru brand T-shirts. The campaign has engendered a widespread sentiment: "I am proud to be Peruvian." Working together, the public and private sectors continue to build tourism and exports and position Peru in the global marketplace.

The brand was displayed in the first-ever Peru Day on Times Square and Wall Street in New York.

Philadelphia Museum of Art

We are Philadelphia's art museum. A place for creative play. A world-renowned collection. A surprise around every corner where visitors see the world—and themselves—anew through the beauty and expressive power of the arts.

One of the hundred most visited museums in the world, the Philadelphia Museum of Art has a world-renowned collection of more than 240,000 works. The museum administers several sites, including the Rodin Museum, which holds the largest public Rodin collection outside Paris; the Ruth and Raymond G. Perelman Building; and two historic colonial-era houses. Its Greek Revival–style main building is one of Philadelphia's great landmarks.

Goals

Reignite the museum's core purpose.

Increase participation and visitation.

Engage new audiences.

Be more visible and accessible.

Design a dynamic visual identity system.

We want the museum to be welcoming to all, creative, and imbued with a sense of surprise and delight.

Timothy Rub

George D. Widener
Director and CEO
Philadelphia Museum of Art

Our new brand strategy amplifies the museum's voice in the local, regional, national, and international cultural community, and connects us with new audiences.

Jennifer Francis

Executive Director of Marketing and Communications
Philadelphia Museum of Art

Process and strategy: The Philadelphia Museum of Art is one of the great US museums, with a collection that is respected by art lovers all over the world. In 2012, under the leadership of the new CEO and CMO, brand positioning and competitive research were conducted. Visitor numbers were flat. Local residents perceived the museum as elitist and inaccessible. Historically, marketing had focused on the blockbuster shows, and not the collections.

Jane Wentworth Associates, a London-based strategic consultancy specializing in the cultural sector, was engaged to help make the museum more relevant to a younger and more diverse audience. A series of workshops with staff and key stakeholders were conducted to establish how the museum could tell a more compelling story and deliver on its strategic objectives. Starting with a vision to become "Philadelphia's place for creative play," the new brand strategy would put visitors at the heart of every decision, inviting them to see the world anew by entering the world of the artist and making art an integral part of their lives.

Creative solution: Pentagram was engaged to design a flexible identity system that was dynamic and inclusive. The popular local name for the museum had always been simply "the art museum." The new identity puts "art" at the center and highlights the breadth of the collection through an imaginative library of visual assets. Dramatically differentiated from other local and global cultural institutions, the digital animations of the word "Art" underscore the creative play strategy. The new identity was launched during the same week as the announcement of a major expansion of the museum by celebrated architect Frank Gehry.

Results: Reigniting the museum's vision and purpose, identifying strategic priorities, and creating a new visual identity has been a catalyst for change, impacting both staff engagement and museum attendance. The brand strategy has been used as a guide to transforming the museum's internal culture, encouraging more experimentation and collaboration, and creating a clear and confident verbal identity. Change was led from the top by the senior management team and at a departmental level by a museum-wide group of Brand Champions, whose role is to implement the brand strategy across all activities. The museum's attendance numbers continue to exceed growth projections.

The brand strategy process has given the museum staff the confidence to reach out to the city and share their superb collection with a much wider and more diverse audience.

Jane Wentworth
Jane Wentworth Associates

This first-rate museum needed an identity that would lead the public to one of the best and broadest collections of art in the US.

Paula Scher
Partner
Pentagram

Philadelphia Museum of Art: Pentagram

Pitney Bowes

At Pitney Bowes, we deliver accuracy and precision across the connected and borderless world of commerce to help our clients create meaningful impact.

Pitney Bowes is a global technology company powering billions of physical and digital transactions. Clients around the world, including 90 percent of the Fortune 500, rely on products, solutions, and services from Pitney Bowes in the areas of customer information management, location intelligence, customer engagement, shipping, mailing, and global ecommerce.

Goals

Redefine the business category and brand strategy.

Create pull from buyers and partners.

Modernize the visual identity and refresh the tone of voice.

Rally employees around the new brand.

Demonstrate clearly how the brand delivers on its promise.

We wanted our new brand strategy and identity not only to reflect who we are today but where we are going in the future.

Marc Lautenbach
President and CEO
Pitney Bowes

The new brand strategy will clarify our role in the changing world commerce and make us more relevant to a wider audience around the world.

Abby Kohnstamm
EVP and Chief Marketing Officer
Pitney Bowes

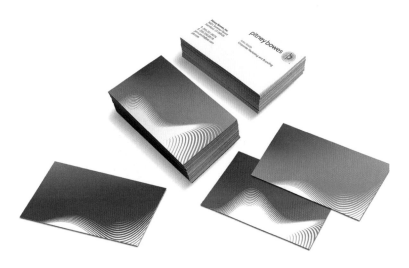

Pitney Bowes: FutureBrand

Process and strategy: When the PNC Financial Services Group (PNC) acquired National City Corporation (NCC), an unprecedented level of conversion activity was required to manufacture and install over 26,000 new signs at 1,640 branches, facilities, and 1,524 ATMs in over nine states. A multi-team task force was formed with PNC Realty Services and National City's facilities management team members. PNC engaged Monigle to provide expertise and assist in managing the day-to-day tactical project rollout. The project demanded strict adherence to the defined conversion schedule, the highest quality of product and installation standards, and control of the project's costs. An overarching goal was adherence to PNC's core values: first, to maintain customer relationships with PNC and NCC customers and second, to hold true to PNC's "green" values. The project started with a sixteen-week supplier evaluation to examine production and installation capabilities. Monigle's project management software, *SignChart*, housed specifications and tracked milestones and metrics critical to managing multiple contractors through the complex conversion process.

Creative solution: Although PNC's standard family of signs had been previously established, improvements were made to increase energy efficiency and branding needs. Once facility design recommendations were approved by the sign conversion team, all of the sign recommendation packages were personally delivered to the individual retail market managers for their final review.

After the branding was approved, sign packages for leased sites were sent by the PNC Leasing Group to landlords for review and approval. Some high-visibility sites underwent complex variance process hearings with zoning and architectural review boards. Beyond the direct savings achieved from lower-cost manufacturing and installation, ongoing expenses were reduced through the analysis and implementation of a new LED illuminated package of signs. Power consumption of an average wall sign was reduced by 62 percent without sacrificing quality and required less effort to maintain. Fifty percent of the suppliers who were awarded business had strong relationships with the bank, and minority suppliers represented almost 25 percent of the workforce, which had a positive impact on the diversity of PNC's supplier portfolio.

Results: The entire conversion took seventy-six weeks from kickoff to completion. A check system verified that all markets in each phase were pleased with the sign conversion results. PNC and NCC employees utilized an internal news network to talk about the quality and speed of the project, which coincided with the phased rollout of branding. The strategic sourcing team's multimedia presentations focused on the savings and diversity impact. The sign conversion team received numerous accolades from executive management regarding how well the sign conversion project was planned, communicated, and executed.

Our goal was to improve the branding and visibility at every National City location, while meeting tight timeframes and managing costs.

Kurt Monigle
Principal
Monigle

PNC Bank: Monigle

Quartz

We are a guide to the new global economy for people excited by change. Our coverage centers around a collection of "obsessions"—the trends, phenomena, and seismic shifts that are shaping the world.

Quartz is a digitally native news outlet for business people in the new global economy. Quartz is owned by Atlantic Media. Designed for mobile and built for social distribution with no paywalls or registration walls, Quartz can be accessed at qz.com, and via email, social media, and its native app.

Goals

Name a disruptive news outlet and retain credibility and gravitas.

Appropriately differentiate the first digitally native global news publication.

Create the foundation for a brand that could thrive across cultures and nationalities.

Support a strategy focused on social sharing and consumption on mobile devices.

Facilitate consensus and clarity around product definition and direction.

QUARTZ

We got a name that defined what we could be, but just as importantly, it served from the first day to remind us what we were not.

Zach Seward
SVP of Product & Executive Editor
Quartz

David Bradley asked for something that was 'breakthrough creative.' It was a freeing set of instructions.

Howard Fish
Fish Partners

Quartz: Fish Partners

Process and strategy: Atlantic Media had a strong track record of turning legacy print brands into digital successes, and they wanted to apply what they had learned to a new, digital-first global media product. Fish Partners were brought in by Justin Smith (then president of Atlantic Media) to direct the naming process in parallel with the formation of the new core team. Fish began by conducting research and interviews with Atlantic Media's leadership and key stakeholders. Fish then worked with the new core team to clarify a shared definition of the product and its aspirations. Fish built consensus around specific metrics and imperatives for what the name needed to accomplish. Fish reviewed tens of thousands of prospective words and phrases, tested candidates against those metrics and imperatives, and finally narrowed down to a shortlist and a recommendation for name and URL.

Creative solution: The name needed to be fast, smart, and differentiable from existing global business news products; it needed to suggest disruption and digital focus, and work around the world. As a name, Quartz is short, visually and linguistically unique (bookended by the two rarest letters in the English language), semantically rich, and clearly different from existing publications. The word suggested a digital quality without lapsing into potentially transient neologisms. The mineral has appealing associations: it generates electrical current under stress, plays an important part facilitating tectonic shifts, is known everywhere on earth, and has no implied country of origin. The URL, qz.com, was extremely practical and immediately communicated the publication's digital focus.

Results: Within two years, Quartz reached five million monthly unique visitors, and within four years, twenty million. Advertising revenues have set new records in each quarter since launch. Quartz has since successfully launched Quartz India, Quartz Africa, a mobile app, Atlas (a chart-building platform), multiple newsletters, and a global conference business.

Interior Design: Desai Chia Architecture

(RED)

(RED) embraces brands and empowers the consumer to choose products that raise money for the Global Fund to help eliminate AIDS in Africa.

(RED) is a global licensed brand created in 2006 to raise money and awareness of AIDS in Africa. (RED) works with partners to create and market exclusive (RED) products; a portion of the profits goes directly to the Global Fund to invest in HIV and AIDS programs.

Goals

Harness the power of the world's greatest companies to eliminate AIDS in Africa.

Develop a new business and brand model.

Develop a source of sustainable private sector income for the Global Fund.

Make it easy for consumers to participate.

Inspire partner companies to participate.

(RED) was born from friendship and anger, ambition and heart, and the sheer will to make the impossible possible.

www.joinRED.com

(RED)™

286

Process and strategy: Harnessing the private sector and partnering with successful global brands to eliminate AIDS in Africa was the big idea conceived by Bono and Bobby Shriver. Bono calls it "conscious consumerism." Their new business model had three overarching principles: deliver a source of sustainable private sector income to the Global Fund, the acknowledged leader and expert in financing the fight against AIDS; provide consumers with a choice that made giving effortless at no extra cost; and generate profits and a sense of purpose for partner companies. Brand partners pay a licensing fee for use of the (RED) brand, which they then use to manage and market their (RED) products. The fee does not infringe on the amount of money sent to the Global Fund. Wolff Olins was engaged to work with Bobby Shriver and his team to paint a vision of the new brand and develop a strategy to attract founding partners, and to create a unique brand expression that allows (RED) to interface with iconic brands in a way that allows them to be themselves, but also to be (RED).

Creative solution: Wolff Olins built the brand around the idea that (RED) inspires, connects, and gives consumers power. The design team needed to create a brand architecture that showcases the participating brand and, at the same time, links that brand to the power of (RED). The identity system needed to be immediately recognizable and work across media, in marketing and on product. Although making the products the color red was not a requirement, many of the participating businesses extended the idea of (RED) to the product. Apple created red iPod Shuffles and iPod Nanos. In the UK, there was a (RED) American Express card that gave money to the Global Fund each time a consumer made a purchase. All bear the (product/brand) (RED) lockup.

Results: Within weeks of the US launch, the (RED) brand registered 30 percent unaided awareness. (RED) is now a real phenomenon, with over four million fans on Facebook. Since its launch in 2006, (RED) has raised more than $465 million for the Global Fund, and has impacted more than ninety million lives.

Two-thirds of people affected with AIDS in Africa are women and children.

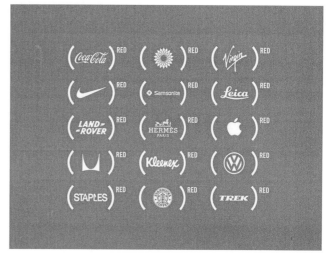

(RED): Wolff Olins

RideKC Streetcar

Kansas City's RideKC Streetcar is free to ride as it travels the two miles through the heart of downtown, leading the way for a new regional transit experience.

The Kansas City Streetcar Authority (KCSA) is a not-for-profit organization that manages, operates, and maintains the RideKC Streetcar. KCSA also supports system branding, marketing, public communications, and community engagement. It works closely with the City of Kansas City, Missouri, and the downtown Transportation Development District (TDD).

Goals

Name and brand a unified regional transit system, beginning with the new streetcar.

Unify the region around the expanded transportation brands.

Spark renewed interest and pride in public transit.

Be immediately recognizable, intuitive, cohesive, and unique to Kansas City.

Establish transit brand standards.

Our new branding allows us to move forward with regional collaboration, keeping the focus on the downtown streetcar line as a catalyst for economic development and improved linkage of downtown neighborhoods and job centers.

Tom Gerend
Executive Director
KCSA

Civic design projects are lessons in design diplomacy. The methodical unification of transit stakeholders from five independent systems and two states around shared civic pride was the impetus for this co-branding success.

Megan Stephens
Managing Principal
Willoughby Design

Process and strategy: The construction of the new Kansas City streetcar starter line was voter approved to enhance the urban experience and serve as a catalyst for sustained economic development downtown. At the same time, the Regional Transit Coordinating Council (RTCC), spanning two states and four major metropolitan areas with 2.34 million people, was formed to oversee the creation of an umbrella brand that would unite all of the independent transit operations and give regional riders one source for information.

The regional transit system and the streetcar naming and brand design projects were two different RFPs from two different client groups. Willoughby Design responded to both RFPs because they believed it was important for the new Kansas City regional transportation brand to include the new streetcar. They won both, and the two-plus year process began on parallel paths.

Willoughby conducted a global audit of regional transit best practices, notably the LA Metro, RATP in Paris, Transport for London, and GVB in Amsterdam. They learned that all of the best systems are holistically designed to be easy to understand and use.

Creative solution: Following an intensive research and design exploration process, Willoughby presented the final recommendation for the streetcar identity. The name, RideKC Streetcar, is intuitive, simple, and unique, giving Kansas City a place among the best transit systems in the world. The brand gives the universal rail symbol a Kansas City twist with an open, friendly feel and a timeless color palette.

Designed to boldly lead the way for the proposed regional branding, the functional name Streetcar pairs with the regional name RideKC to become RideKC Streetcar. Willoughby designed a family of transit icons and a branded kit of parts that works across the entire communications system including vehicle design (streetcar, bus, Metro Area express), shelters, wayfinding signage, digital, collateral, and safety/promotional campaigns.

Results: RideKC Streetcar has had some of the highest ridership, per mile, of any system in the country, and sales tax receipts have grown 58 percent along the corridor. It surpassed its one-millionth ride in the first five months—with twice the projected ridership. The cars are so crowded that the KCSA is already proposing the purchase of two more vehicles and possible route expansion.

KC Streetcar was exactly what's needed for Kansas City to remain in the big leagues. You have to be bold.

Sly James
Mayor
Kansas City, Missouri

RideKC: Willoughby Design

Santos Brasil

Santos Brasil is dedicated to a sustainable growth model, which combines high-level financial and operating performance with environmental preservation and social responsibility.

Santos Brasil, a public company with 3,500 employees, is one of the major port operator and logistics service providers in South America. It throughputs approximately 25 percent of the containers in Brazil. Its container terminals are located in strategic ports on the Brazilian coast.

Goals

Position Santos Brasil as a global market leader.

Communicate responsible leadership.

Increase employee esprit de corps.

Build synergy between business units.

Build brand awareness.

Our new brand has given us strength to demonstrate to the world and to ourselves that we are a global company.

Antonio C.D. Sepúlveda
CEO
Santos Brasil

 SANTOS BRASIL
TECON SANTOS

 SANTOS BRASIL
TECON IMBITUBA

 SANTOS BRASIL
TECON VILA DO CONDE

 SANTOS BRASIL
LOGÍSTICA

 SANTOS BRASIL
TERMINAL DE VEÍCULOS

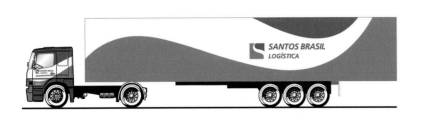

Process and strategy: Initially, Santos Brasil engaged Cauduro Associates to change the name of its public company. The process began with the senior management team reaffirming its vision for the future: to be the best port infrastructure and integrated logistics service company in the markets in which it operates. Santos Brasil wanted to be perceived as friendly and socially and environmentally responsible. The company wanted to be positioned as global, because its terminals had the operational efficiency of the world's leading port terminals. Research studies revealed that there was overall low awareness and brand visibility within the investment community. Cauduro's analysis and insights determined that the name Santos Brasil appealed to audiences around the world. Santos, the largest port in Brasil, is relevant to the industry category, as well as a concrete expression of the company's concern about its communities and commitment to sustainable development. The total brand would be built around the idea of responsible leadership.

Creative solution: Cauduro began by creating a monolithic brand architecture that would become the framework for positioning the public company as a market leader. Both the logistics and container management companies would be organized under the Santos Brasil master brand. Naming was streamlined and unified across business units, so that future acquisitions would be facilitated. The new Santos Brasil symbol was designed to synthesize economic and symbolic value. The *S* design is a translation of Santos port geography. The colors came from a logical choice: blue for the sea and green for nature. A master plan was developed to make the new brand identity system very visible in all the port terminals and on investment and internal communications.

Results: Santos Brasil's new brand symbolizes its commitment to business excellence and continuous improvement and to generating value for shareholders, clients, suppliers, employees, local communities, and society. It has engendered pride in the workforce, creating a sense of unity between the business units. Brand awareness has increased in the investment community and in the country as well. In 2011, Santos Brasil was listed as the market leader in its category. The new brand identity is visible on every piece of equipment and can be seen across all of its port terminals and facilities.

Santos Brasil is an open, progressive, and socially responsible corporation that is utilizing its new brand to shift perceptions and build awareness as a responsible industry leader.

Marco A. Rezende
Director
Cauduro Associates

Santos Brasil: Cauduro Associates

Shinola Detroit

We are an American company dedicated to making quality products and meaningful jobs. We are dedicated to the preservation of craft, and the beauty of industry. There's not just history in Detroit, there is a future. It's why we are here.

Shinola is a luxury lifestyle brand based in Detroit, and dedicated to producing products that create jobs, including watches, bicycles, leather goods, jewelry, audio products, and journals of the highest quality. Bedrock Manufacturing and Ronda AG own the company. Shinola has over six hundred employees and twenty-two stores and is also sold in over three hundred luxury retail shops worldwide.

Goals

Create world-class manufacturing jobs.

Build a global luxury lifestyle brand, through quality of craft and pride of work.

Have a positive impact on the city where the company is based, Detroit.

Redefine American luxury.

Use authentic storytelling to drive desire and brand affinity.

The face of luxury is changing. It's much less about logos, and people are looking for those stories behind their brands.

Bridget Russo
CMO
Shinola

SHINOLA
DETROIT

Process and strategy: Shinola was envisioned by Tom Kartsotis, a cofounder of the Fossil Watches and accessories brand, and is part of Dallas-based Bedrock Manufacturing, a private equity and venture capital firm. Kartsotis's intention was to establish a true, American design brand that would reignite world-class manufacturing capabilities, starting with Detroit. Research confirmed that consumers were willing to pay a premium for Detroit-made products. The name, Shinola, was purchased. The shoe polish brand, Shinola, was founded in 1877, and out of business by 1960 and reimagined in 2012. The immortal phrase "You don't know shit from Shinola" was widely popular during World War II.

To kick-start the actual watchmaking, Shinola partnered with Ronda AG, a Swiss manufacturer of watch movements. The company's headquarters and watch factory are housed in the College for Creative Studies.

The Shinola brand is powerful because it isn't selling a fictitious lifestyle, rather it stands for making real progress for real communities.

Anthony Sperduti
Partners & Spade

Creative solution: Shinola's founders worked with Partners & Spade to launch the brand in 2013. The firm was retained to develop a messaging strategy, brand book, and website design, as well as all advertising needs. The work began after the name, and the logo was designed by Shinola's in-house creative team. Partners & Spade also directed both brand and product photography, and worked with photographers like Bruce Weber to produce campaigns that would appeal to Shinola's growing female audience.

Results: The brand has become a symbol of Detroit's revival and American manufacturing potential. Shinola had $80 million in total orders in the first eighteen months after its launch. Shinola products are sold online, at flagship stores in twenty-one American cities (there is also a store in London), and upscale retailers across the globe. Shinola continues to expand its offerings, forming new partnerships that include leather goods, bicycles, journals, jewelry, turntables, and headphones. Since the company's founding in 2011, it has grown to over six hundred employees.

Izzy Pullen

Shinola: Partners & Spade

293

Smithsonian National Air and Space Museum

The most popular museum in the US is filled with fascinating artifacts and stories: the Apollo 11 command module *Columbia*, the *Spirit of St. Louis*, the Space Shuttle *Discovery*, and the fastest jet airplane in the world.

In 1976, the National Air and Space Museum in Washington, DC opened to the public as a gift to the nation during the United States' bicentennial year. Since then, more than 320 million visitors have seen the milestones of modern aviation and spaceflight firsthand. The museum is the largest of the Smithsonian's nineteen museums, and its Center for Earth and Planetary Studies is one of the institution's nine research centers.

Goals

Create a digital ecosystem.

Reimagine the visitor experience.

Celebrate the museum's fortieth anniversary.

Surface stories connected to the collection.

Revitalize the website and app.

By experiencing more detailed displays and digital technology, visitors will walk away with a deeper understanding of how spaceflight and aviation have affected their lives.

Gen. J.R. "Jack" Dailey
The John and Adrienne Mars Director
National Air and Space Museum

Process and strategy: The National Air and Space Museum hosts more than eight million visitors a year, and has thousands of the most iconic objects in air and space history. How do you excite and educate a new generation of visitors who weren't alive when these objects made history? How do you help visitors engage with the objects, both onsite in Boeing Milestones of Flight Hall, and before their actual visit? Bluecadet, a digital experience firm, was retained to conceptualize a new memorable experience, and to develop a digital ecosystem that would allow for a range of dynamic content that could change quickly and be maintained across platforms and departments.

Bluecadet worked closely with a cross-disciplinary, cross-departmental group of curators, space and aviation experts, and teams from digital, marketing, and exhibitions. The discovery phase included staff interviews across departments, content audits of current platforms, and a review of analytics.

Creative solution: Bluecadet's architects, strategists, and UX designers proposed a number of approaches during a quick concept phase. The museum approved a 200-square-foot interactive wall experience, and Go Flight, an app and web digital experience designed to allow visitors to quickly access stories and related content about the objects near them or access a predefined tour based on their interest and location. For the app's in-gallery experience, Bluecadet developed a "near me" feed that refreshes as you explore the museum—when you're standing in front of the Bell X-1 and want to see it being air-dropped from a B-52. Through motion, and a playful interface, the interactive wall rewards serendipitous exploration. Visitors can even favorite objects, sync them to the app or website, and take their own personalized tour.

The suite of interconnected digital products and strategies, including a new website, tie into the existing content management system (CMS). The same CMS that drives the website and the mobile applications delivers content to the wall.

Results: The museum opened its newly renovated Boeing Milestones of Flight Hall to the public during its fortieth anniversary celebration event, and thousands of visitors experienced the huge interactive touchscreen on opening day. The digital ecosystem strategy was launched in concert, facilitating better workflow and content management. In the first two months, the wall was touched over a million times. Half a million of those touches were different objects, in 200,000 categories. The new website has had over three million page views.

> **The experience begins when the visitor enters and explores the museum, and continues to drive exploration long after visitors head home.**
>
> Josh Goldblum
> CEO
> Bluecadet

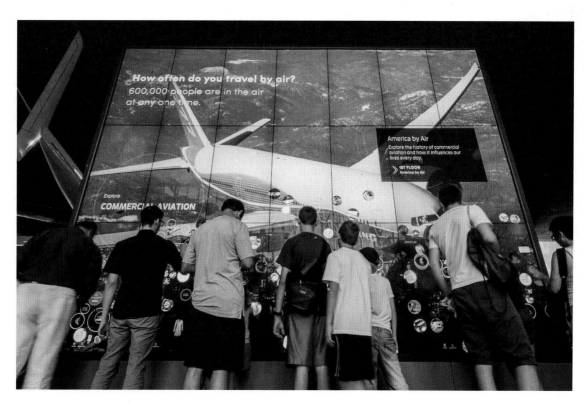

Smithsonian National Air and Space Museum: Bluecadet

SocialSecurity.gov

We are with you through life's journey. See how Social Security is there for you throughout every stage of your life—securing today and tomorrow.

The United States Social Security Administration (SSA) is an independent agency of the United States federal government that administers Social Security, a social insurance program consisting of retirement, disability, and survivors' benefits. The agency, created in 1935 by President Franklin D. Roosevelt, was the first program of its kind created by the federal government, designed to help Americans during the latter years of life or those with disabilities.

Goals

Help people understand and plan for retirement, Medicare, and disability benefits.

Create a user-friendly interface and a positive experience.

Provide a secure online hub and a way for people to file online.

Revitalize retirement planning tools.

Provide the public with their choice of service channel.

my Social Security

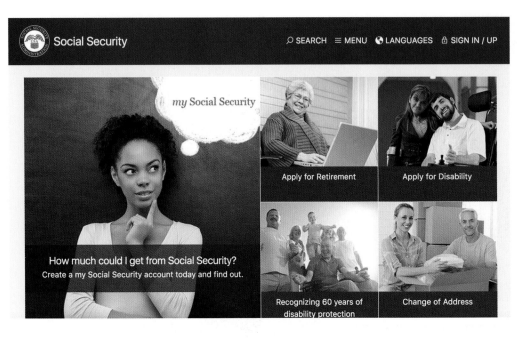

SocialSecurity.gov facts

215 million visitors a year to SocialSecurity.gov *(Fiscal year 2015)*.

Approximately 60 million people receive monthly Social Security benefits.

Nearly 44 million of beneficiaries are retired workers or their dependents.

88 million transactions through *my* Social Security (September 2016).

Process and strategy: The Social Security Administration (SSA) has provided online applications for retirement, disability, and spousal benefits since the early 2000s. The key benefit of both the online application and the *my* Social Security portal is offering a convenient alternative to individuals who wish to conduct business online 24/7, without having to visit a local office. Additionally, this allows agency employees more time to process complex workloads in the office that cannot be done online, and more time to serve people who do not have internet access, or just prefer to speak to a person.

The key goals were, and continue to be, to provide the public with their choice of service channel, and to make the online experience user-friendly, secure, seamless, and efficient.

Creative solution: Due to the baby boomer generation reaching retirement age, the agency was on the cusp of a large increase in claims, the agency redesigned the online claims application, "iClaim." Accompanied with a publicity campaign when launched early in FY 2009, online claims jumped 32 percent that year. In 2012, a new website and the *my* Social Security service were launched, adding new services, for beneficiaries and non-beneficiaries (age 18 and older).

The challenge of making these improvements was large, given the variety and complexity of users' needs, the hundreds of millions of transactions and people that use the tools, applications, and other information resources. Prior to each change, SSA conducted public usability testing, focus groups, and customer interviews in local offices. For *my* Social Security, they also bench marked websites of financial institutions, healthcare organizations, private sector companies, and other government agencies. Customer satisfaction for the online application is consistently at or near the top of the ForeSee customer satisfaction index, and regularly scores higher than the best performing private sector sites.

Results: The percentage of claims submitted online has increased from under 10 percent of all claims in the early 2000s, to over 50 percent of all retirement and disability claims, and over 70 percent of Medicare-only claims in the past few years. *My* Social Security has also shown its success through the fact that more than 27 million people have registered to use the service, and since its inception in 2012, almost 260 million transactions have been conducted. In FY 2013, the first full year in production, users conducted 32.5 million transactions. In FY 2016 transactions were up over 140 percent, to 88 million through September 2016.

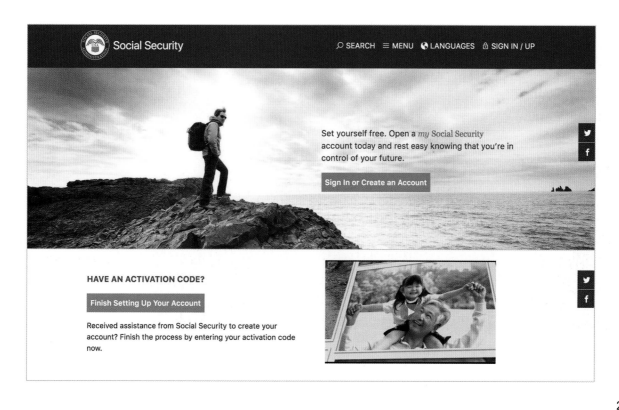

Southwest Airlines

We like to think of ourselves as a customer service company that happens to fly airplanes. Without a heart, our planes are just machines.

Southwest Airlines Co. is a major US airline and the world's largest low-cost carrier, headquartered in Dallas, Texas. Southwest has more than 45,000 employees and serves more than 100 million customers annually. The airline was established by Herb Kelleher in 1967.

Goals

Create a new, impactful look.

Express the hallmarks of Southwest's culture.

Unite a fragmented system.

Attract millennials and business travelers.

The heart emblazoned on our aircraft symbolizes our commitment that we'll remain true to our core values as we set our sights on the future.

Gary Kelly
Chairman, President, CEO
Southwest Airlines

We already know who we are. The job was to keep the elements of Southwest that our employees and customers love, and to make them a bold, modern expression of our future.

Kevin Krone
President and CMO
Southwest Airlines

Southwest®

Even on the belly of the plane, the heart is a symbolic reminder that Southwest puts its heart into every flight.

Stephen Keller, Southwest Airlines

Process and strategy: Even with a very human reputation and more than forty consecutive years of profitability, Southwest was ready to rethink and refresh its look, and unite a fragmented visual system. Southwest wanted to express the hallmarks of its culture—humanity and a personal touch—in ways that would resonate more clearly in an increasingly jaded market.

Lippincott's goals were to distill the airline's success and to help Southwest connect with two highly desirable segments: millennials and business travelers.

Achieving a successful design solution required aligning the company's vision with its tremendous history. Lippincott conducted an investigation of assets, barriers, and benchmarks. Southwest had long stood for freedom. Findings pointed to a powerful accompaniment: from the start, Southwest has treated every passenger equally—they democratized air travel. From this came the insight to focus on what has always made Southwest great—its emphasis on people first.

Creative solution: Lippincott identified the heart as Southwest's most potent symbolic asset. They chose to use the heart to make a bigger statement—for the heart to become a truly iconic symbol. The heart—thoughtfully utilized at moments of connection—is the identity's emotional punctuation. In the customer experience, it signifies what makes the brand unique: a personal touch. Surrounding it is a redesign of Southwest's livery, in flight materials, airports, and website. From planes to peanut packaging, the refresh is modern and true to Southwest's DNA—confident, authentic, and full of personality.

Results: In 2014, Southwest announced the humble and bold heart as its brand symbol, crystallizing its business philosophy and showing the world that what started Southwest is exactly what will lead them into future—treating people more like people. Southwest was built on the idea that people come first; now they're showing the world that a little heart goes a long way. More than ever, travelers know they're flying with people who care—no matter where they sit.

As we developed the identity, it wasn't just about the new livery or the logo, but about developing the total, integrated brand expression of Southwest.

Rodney Abbot
Senior Partner, Design
Lippincott

Southwest Airlines: Lippincott

Spectrum Health System

Our employees, physicians, and volunteers share a common mission: to improve the health of the communities we serve. Our history began with the desire to ease human suffering.

Spectrum Health is one of Michigan's largest and most comprehensive health systems, with 25,000 employees, 3,100 physicians, and 2,300 active volunteers. The Spectrum Health system includes a major medical center, 12 regional community hospitals including a dedicated children's hospital, a multi-specialty medical group, and a nationally recognized health plan.

We knew that health care would be going through tremendous changes. We wanted to make sure that our public expression was clear and succinct. We needed to inspire confidence in what we were doing.

Richard C. Breon
President and CEO
Spectrum Health System

Throughout rapid growth and expansion, Spectrum Health has consistently used brand as an organizational catalyst and management strategy.

Bart Crosby
Principal
Crosby Associates

Process and strategy: Spectrum Health was formed in 1997 by the merger of two competing Grand Rapids hospitals, followed by the acquisition of nine additional hospitals and over 190 service sites. Historically, names of entities were retained or altered slightly as they joined Spectrum Health. Medical professionals and people in the community continued to refer to entities by their old, familiar names. Like many rapidly growing organizations, Spectrum quickly outgrew its original visual identity and nomenclature structure. Management recognized the need for a sophisticated and consistent system of identity and nomenclature to define and describe the organization, and to serve it through future decades of expansion. In 2008, Crosby Associates began working with the organization to develop a new visual identity and an integrated branding program. The process began with establishing a hierarchy of branded entities from administrative and organizational units, to departments and divisions, to centers and institutes. Standards were also established for naming new acquisitions and alliances.

Creative solution: Crosby designed a dynamic symbol for the master brand that connotes energy and forward movement, and represents Spectrum Health's many components, services, and locations. Along with a positioning strategy, the firm developed a comprehensive system for sub-brands, typography, color, and formatting. Standards were developed for every structure and item that represented the health system, including signage, vehicles, stationery, print and electronic communications, gifts and gear, food service, uniforms, and Microsoft Word-based templates for all system documents. Standards were then incorporated into a password-protected website that can be accessed by all internal communications teams and external vendors. All of these standards are now integrated into the system's official policies and procedures manual. After completing the standards, Crosby continued to provide ongoing brand consultation and supervision of the work of outside design firms and vendors.

Results: Spectrum Health's brand has contributed to its ability to attract top quality physicians and other health care professionals, and to be a leading choice for health care services providers in search of a merger partner. The visual identity and nomenclature standards facilitate a smooth integration of acquired organizations. On five occasions between 2010 and 2016, Spectrum Health was named one of the nation's top 15 health systems—and in the top five among the largest health systems—by Truven Health Analytics™. Spectrum Health continues to be the region's largest health care provider and West Michigan's largest employer.

> One of the results of a well-executed program is internal pride—people within the organization understanding who they are working for, understanding the values of the organization, and understanding that "brand" is all of the things that each of them do everyday.
>
> Nancy A. Tait
> Senior Director, Development
> Spectrum Health System

Spectrum Health System: Crosby Associates

Starbucks

Our mission is to inspire and nurture the human spirit—one person, one cup, and one neighborhood at a time. Every Starbucks store is part of a community, and we take our responsibility to be good neighbors seriously.

Starbucks is the world's largest roaster and retailer of specialty coffee. The company operates in more than 24,000 locations in over seventy different countries and has over 190,000 employees. The first Starbucks store was opened in 1971.

Goals

Celebrate the fortieth anniversary.

Envision a future broader than coffee.

Refresh the customer experience.

Revitalize the visual expression.

Implement a new global strategy.

The Starbucks brand continues to embrace our heritage in ways that are true to our core values and that also ensure that we stay relevant and poised for future growth.

Howard Schultz
CEO and Chairman
Starbucks

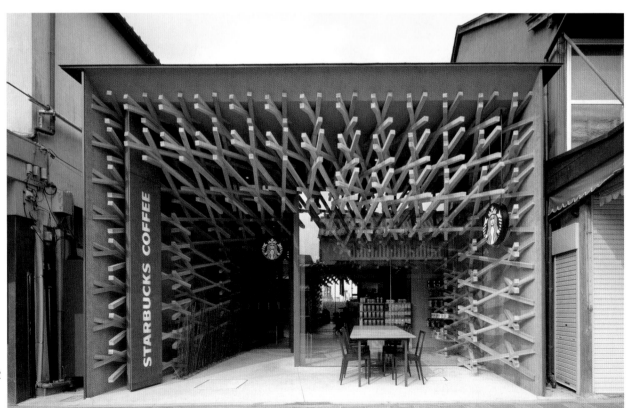

Photograph: Masao Nishikawa

Process and strategy: With a fortieth anniversary fast approaching in 2011, Starbucks wanted to use the milestone as an opportunity to clarify its future vision and refresh its customer experience and visual expression. In early 2010, the Starbucks Global Creative Studio conducted a comprehensive brand, marketing, and strategy assessment, and began to identify the quintessential elements of the brand across touchpoints. Starbucks determined through extensive strategic planning that its brand needed the flexibility to explore product innovation, become globally and regionally relevant, and develop an evolved customer experience. Starbucks decided to free the Siren from the logo and enable customers to make a more personal connection with the brand. The internal creative group explored hundreds of graphic alternatives for the Siren symbol, as well as size and relationship alternatives for use with the Starbucks (Coffee) name, before arriving at the simple, clean mark.

The Starbucks Global Creative Studio engaged Lippincott to help refine brand elements, and to bring a cross-cultural perspective to building an integrated, multi-platform system. Lippincott's extensive global branding and implementation experience would be valuable during the planning phase, and in building consensus within the global corporation.

Creative solution: Starbucks wanted the visual identity system to say as much about its future as it did about its past, building on forty years of trust. Lippincott examined how the positioning strategy would work across marketing, retail environments, and packaging, examining the hierarchy of elements from the look and feel to the color, typography and use of patterns, photography, and illustration. Throughout the process, Lippincott partnered with the internal creative group to refine and define brand elements and character attributes, develop implementation guidelines, and help build consensus among internal stakeholders. The Siren is liberated from her ring and the identity is free of words, with a vibrant green introduced to signal the bright future ahead.

Results: On Tuesday, March 8, 2011, Starbucks marked its fortieth-year celebration. Starbucks began to roll out the new program to its 16,500 stores around the world, starting with Chairman Howard Schultz's video asking customers from around the world to join in conversation about the Siren. This next evolution of the brand has given Starbucks the freedom and flexibility to explore innovations and new channels of distribution that will keep the company in step with current customers while building strong connections with new customers.

For forty years the Siren has been at the center of our passion for coffee. And now she's an icon representing not only our heritage, but also the future of the Starbucks brand.

Jeffrey Fields
Vice President, Global Creative Studio
Starbucks

We worked closely with the Starbucks Global Creative Studio to revitalize the brand of one of the most unique retail experiences in the world.

Connie Birdsall
Creative Director
Lippincott

Sydney Opera House

Our vision for the Sydney Opera House recognized that creativity and the arts could help inspire and support Australia's search to figure out who we were as a country and who we wanted to become.

With its iconic sails, the Sydney Opera House has long been Australia's most visited destination and one of the world's most recognizable buildings. The Unesco World Heritage site is a place of immense pride for Australians, and for the 8.2 million people who visit annually, one of wonder and awe. It is a multi-venue performance art center and hosts more than two thousand performances a year.

Goals

Bring to life the vision that drove the center's creation.

Position the performing arts center for its next horizon of growth.

Unify all experiences, offerings, communications.

Build brand equity.

Communicate that the magic happens inside.

Shifting perspectives

We're open to new ideas, new people, and new experiences.

To daydreamers and free thinkers, to old friends, fresh faces, and those who find comfort in the unknown.

So if you see things differently, if you're willing to consider more than one point of view, if you're open to challenge, to change, to who you can become— we're open to you.

Although our building looks breathtaking from the harbor, the real magic happens inside.

Process and strategy: The Sydney Opera House and Interbrand Australia partnered to revitalize a brand that could prepare and preserve itself for the next generation. The project commenced with an extensive discovery phase, which included over 50 hours of immersion, over 30 on-site intercepts, over 20 hours of social listening, over 100 hours of desk research, 120 individual interviews, and numerous workshops. It became clear that the brand needed to inspire conversation around performance, art, and culture.

Shifting Perspectives, the new core brand idea, encourages the brand to offer thoughtful comparisons. Make provocative statements. Pose what-if's, ask why-not's, and come at everyday messages from creative and surprising angles. It welcomes the visitor in, all inclusive and warm, before inviting them to try something new, think again, and get involved with performing arts culture.

Creative solution: Shifting Perspectives informed a refined approach to language, and a more evocative approach to communications and visual design. Interbrand designed a proprietary sculptural typeface, that embodies the form and movement of the building itself. It was developed using engineering software to ensure it had the structural integrity necessary to be replicated in physical form with cast letters or 3-D printing.

The brand's primary colors of shell and black are inspired by the stark exterior of the building. The brand's secondary color palette celebrates the vibrancy and energy found inside the Sydney Opera House. Bright and diverse, the palette allows communications linked to specific performances to take on the color and mood of the performance itself. Jørn Utzon, the architect, had visions of a building filled with color.

Since the brand idea was inspired by the different sights experienced as one moves around the building, it was imperative that the brand captured a sense of movement and shifting light in a motion toolbox. Interbrand worked with animation specialists Collider to create a suite of animated elements that allow the brand to come to life in film, digital, and signage.

Results: Having drawn directly from Utzon's vision and creative principles, as well as the opera house's iconic architecture, the brand conveys a sense of permanence. Yet at the same time, it has revolutionized the way the performing arts center approaches not only communications and customers, but also itself. With its ability to foster a welcoming and collaborative company culture, drive community conversation, and visually represent a decade of renewal, the brand has become as bold and inspiring as the building it represents.

Sydney Opera House: Interbrand Australia

Unstuck

We combine online learning, personalized digital tools, and tips and know-how to help you understand what's holding you back and how to move forward.

Unstuck is an app, online learning platform, and content site that equips people to take on challenges and move forward in their lives. Unstuck is an in-the-moment digital coach that's ready any time they're feeling stuck. The app helps people see and solve situations through provocative questions, targeted tips, and action-oriented tools.

Goals

Lead a new category of personal growth and technology products.

Design a new brand from the ground up—and thoughtfully evolve it as it expands.

Combine psychology, human behavior, and design.

Establish Unstuck's online learning platform as a unique experience in the personal development space.

We believe there is more than one right way to move forward, which makes Unstuck different from traditional self-help solutions. Our app, Life Courses, and content use gentle provocation to help people discover the right path for them.

Nancy Hawley
Vice President + GM
Unstuck

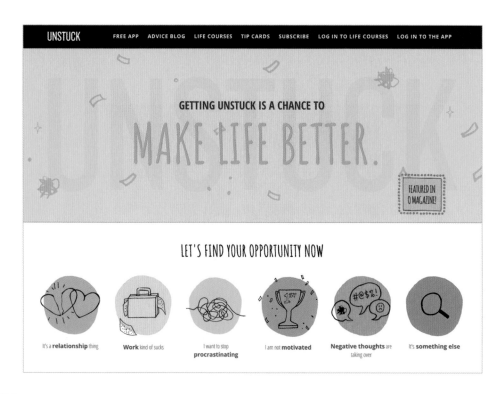

Process and strategy: The idea for Unstuck came from SYPartners, a transformation company that has long helped individuals, leaders, teams, and organizations become the best versions of themselves. Having worked with leaders at companies such as IBM, Starbucks, Facebook, and GE, SYPartners wanted to bring its methods to an individual audience. With the introduction of the Apple iPad, the company finally felt it had found the right medium to create a tactile, engaging, and (most importantly) human-centered system that could serve as the first Unstuck offering.

A core team of people with skills across strategy, product design, project management, and product development used three key design principles to guide the creation of the brand: It had to be smart but accessible, it had to inspire action, and it had to be empathetic and aspirational. The team also took inspiration from gaming and did extensive research into traditional therapeutic techniques. Trial and error and user testing helped the team stay on track and in tune with the user base throughout development, and has continued to inform the expansion of the product assortment.

Creative solution: There are three distinct but seamless sections to the app's flow: figuring out how you're stuck, learning how to get unstuck, and taking action. Each is infused with candor, wit, information, and a sense of fun, all of which mask the complex technical underpinnings that make the app effective.

From the user's perspective, section one consists of several multiple-choice questions asked in an engaging, gamelike way. On the back-end, an algorithm based on human behavior patterns dictates the choices presented to each person, depending on his or her previous answers. Similarly, the prescriptions in section two (how to get unstuck) spring from a simple yet encompassing idea that stuck moments result from a gap in seeing, believing, thinking, or acting. And in the third section—the tools that help you take action—both the process and the summary screen give the user continual payoff via thought-provoking exercises and presentation. The final takeaway for any user: Personalized insight that is actionable in real life.

Results: Unstuck launched in December 2011, and a small team handled everything, from marketing, public relations, customer service, and social media to technical bug fixes. Unstuck received coverage from a number of outlets, including the New Yorker, Oprah.com, TechCrunch, Lifehacker, and Fast Company. Ultimately, iTunes user reviews determined success, and with a 4.5-star rating, the download rate continued to grow. Unstuck has since expanded its offerings to a web app version of the tools, an online learning platform called Life Courses, and a growing editorial program.

> We didn't want Unstuck to be too clinical (boring) or too whimsical (insensitive). We wanted it to feel like a good friend or coach—someone who is genuinely trying to work through your issue with you.

Audrey Liu
Creative Director
Unstuck

Unstuck: SYPartners

Vueling

Vueling is straightforward and fast forward. It's not just about low price; it's about being down to earth and one step ahead—in everything we do.

Vueling Airlines SA serves over one hundred destinations in Africa, Asia, and Europe, and is currently the second-largest airline in Spain. The company was founded in 2002 and is headquartered in Barcelona, Spain.

Goals

Envision and name a new brand.

Create a category-bending, envelope-pushing, new generation airline.

Design an integrated visual, verbal, and behavioral identity.

Delight the customer.

Vueling has become what we designed it to be: a new generation airline combining low prices, high style, and good service.

Juan Pablo Ramírez
Brand Strategist
Saffron Brand Consultants

vueling

Vueling: Saffron Brand Consultants

Process and strategy: Vueling began as an idea for the first budget airline that would compete nationally in Spain and southern Europe from a hub in Barcelona. Public opinion of the low-cost airline category was characterized by disappointment, mistrust, and mixed feelings. Conceived jointly by founder Carlos Muñoz and Saffron Brand Consultants, the challenge was to reinvent the category and prove that cheap flights didn't have to mean lower standards of service, comfort, and style. Saffron began by creating the name. In Spain, Spanglish is hip. In Spanish, *vuela* means to fly, ergo, Vueling. The URL was available—vital for a service that sells mostly online. Saffron proceeded to design a new experience for customers: direct, simple, unexpected, and down-to-earth with low prices and great service. All brand expressions would embody *espíritu* Vueling, doing things the Vueling way. Online transactions would be as easy as one, two, three. New planes, not old, would fly from major, not secondary, airports.

Creative solution: Saffron created the name and an entire identity system—not only visual and verbal but also behavioral—from nose to tail, from staff-customer contact to online interface to music and menu planning. Straightforward and fast forward, *espíritu* Vueling inspired all customer touchpoints to feel fresh, cosmopolitan, and cool. Voice was first. Saffron engineered a cultural shift from formal to informal. All brand communications speak informally by using *tú*, not *usted*. Airbus even had to rewrite the onboard signage for Vueling's planes. From the beginning, Saffron and Vueling management agreed that as a service brand, the people are paramount. The identity work informed the airline's HR policies, and has been reinforced subsequently by leading many employee training sessions. After the core brand engagement was complete, Saffron continued to keep *espíritu* Vueling alive through training, and working on the brand committee.

Results: At launch, Vueling achieved the highest capitalization to date by a new airline in Europe. It reached its full-year revenue target of twenty-one million euros within the first six months. In less than a year, Vueling had carried more than 1.2 million passengers on twenty-two routes between fourteen cities. In 2008, Vueling announced it would merge with Clickair, another low-cost airline that is 80 percent owned by flag carrier Iberia. The decision to name the merged company Vueling was supported by surveys that confirmed the superior strength of the brand among customers and employees.

Bibliography

Aaker, David A., and Erich Joachimsthaler. *Brand Leadership.* New York: The Free Press, 2000.

Aaker, David. *Brand Portfolio Strategy.* New York: The Free Press, 2004.

Adams, Sean. *The Designer's Dictionary of Color.* New York: Abrams, 2017.

Adamson, Allen P. *BrandDigital: Simple Ways Top Brands Succeed in the Digital World.* New York: Palgrave Macmillan, 2008.

Adamson, Allen P. *BrandSimple: How the Best Brands Keep It Simple and Succeed.* New York: Palgrave Macmillan, 2006.

Advertising Metrics, www.marketingterms.com.

Airey, David. *Logo Design Love: A Guide to Creating Iconic Brand Identities.* Berkeley: New Riders Press, 2009.

Beckwith, Harry. *Selling the Invisible: A Field Guide to Modern Marketing.* New York: Warner Books, 1997.

Bierut, Michael. *How To.* New York: Harper Design, 2015.

Birsel, Ayse. *Design the Life You Love: A Step-by-Step Guide to Building a Meaningful Future.* New York: Ten Speed Press, 2015.

Blake, George Burroughs, and Nancy Blake-Bohne. *Crafting the Perfect Name: The Art and Science of Naming a Company or Product.* Chicago: Probus Publishing Company, 1991.

Bruce-Mitford, Miranda. *The Illustrated Book of Signs & Symbols.* New York: DK Publishing, Inc., 1996.

Brunner, Robert, and Stewart Emery. *Do You Matter? How Great Design Will Make People Love Your Company.* Upper Saddle River, NJ: Pearson Education, 2009.

Buell, Barbara. "Can a Global Brand Speak Different Languages?" *Stanford Business,* August 2000.

Business Attitudes to Design. www.design-council.org.uk.

Calver, Giles. *What Is Packaging Design?* Switzerland: RotoVision, 2004.

Carlzon, Jan. *Moments of Truth.* New York: Harper Collins, 1987.

Carter, Rob, Ben Day, and Philip Meggs. *Typographic Design: Form and Communication.* New York: John Wiley & Sons, Inc., 1993.

Chermayeff, Ivan, Tom Geismar, and Steff Geissbuhler. *Trademarks Designed by Chermayeff & Geismar.* Basel, Switzerland: Lars Muller Publishers, 2000.

"Crowned at Last: A Survey of Consumer Power." *The Economist,* April 2, 2005.

DeNeve, Rose. *The Designer's Guide to Creating Corporate I.D. Systems.* Cincinnati: North Light Books, 1992.

"A Discussion with Chris Hacker," *Enlightened Brand Journal,* www.enlightenedbrand.com.

Doctoroff, Tom. "What Chinese Want"—Thoughtful China. YouTube video, 16:44. Posted June 19, 2012. http://www.youtube.com/watch?v=2TiMRFydnsM.

Duffy, Joe. *Brand Apart.* New York: One Club Publishing, 2005.

Eiber, Rick, ed. *World Trademarks: 100 Years,* Volumes I and II. New York: Graphis US, Inc., 1996.

Ellwood, Iain. *The Essential Brand Book.* London: Kogan Page Limited, 2002.

Friedman, Thomas L. *Hot, Flat, and Crowded: Why We Need a Green Revolution—and How It Can Renew America.* New York: Farrar, Straus and Giroux, 2008.

Gallardo, Luis. *Brands and Rousers: The Holistic System to Foster High-Performing Businesses, Brands, and Careers.* London: LID Publishing Ltd., 2012.

Geismar, Tom, Sagi Haviv, and Ivan Chermayeff. *Identify: Basic Principles of Identity Design in the Iconic Trademarks of Chermayeff & Geismar.* New York, NY: Print Publishing, 2011.

Gilmore, James H. *Look: A Practical Guide for Improving Your Observational Skills.* Austin, Texas: Greenleaf Book Group Press, 2016.

Gilmore, James H., and B. Joseph Pine II. *Authenticity: What Consumers Really Want.* Boston: Harvard Business School Press, 2007.

Giudice, Maria, and Christopher Ireland. *Rise of the DEO: Leadership by Design.* San Francisco: New Riders, 2014.

Gladwell, Malcolm. *The Tipping Point: How Little Things Can Make a Big Difference.* New York: Little, Brown and Company, 2000.

Glaser, Milton. *Art Is Work.* Woodstock, NY: The Overlook Press, 2000.

Gobe, Marc. *Emotional Branding, The New Paradigm for Connecting Brands to People.* New York: Allworth Press, 2001.

Godin, Seth. *Purple Cow: Transform Your Business by Being Remarkable.* New York: Portfolio, 2003.

Godin, Seth. *Tribes: We Need You to Lead Us.* New York: Portfolio, 2008.

Grams, Chris. *The Ad-Free Brand: Secrets to Building Successful Brands in a Digital World.* Indianapolis: Que, 2011.

Grant, John. *The New Marketing Manifesto: The 12 Rules for Building Successful Brands in the 21st Century.* London: Texere Publishing Limited, 2000.

Hawken, Paul. *Blessed Unrest: How the Largest Social Movement in History Is Restoring Grace, Justice, and Beauty to the World.* New York: Penguin Books, 2007.

Heath, Chip, and Dan Heath. *Made to Stick: Why Some Ideas Survive and Others Die.* New York: Random House, 2007.

Heller, Steven. *Paul Rand.* London: Phaidon Press Limited, 1999.

Hill, Sam, and Chris Lederer. *The Infinite Asset: Managing Brands to Build New Value.* Boston: Harvard Business School Press, 2001.

Hine, Thomas. *The Total Package: The Evolution and Secret Meanings of Boxes, Bottles, Cans, and Tubes.* Boston: Little, Brown and Company, 1995.

Holtzschue, Linda. *Understanding Color: An Introduction for Designers.* New York: John Wiley & Sons, Inc., 2002.

Isaacson, Walter. *Steve Jobs.* Simon & Schuster. New York: 2011

Joachimsthaler, Erich, David A. Aaker, John Quelch, David Kenny, Vijay Vishwanath, and Mark Jonathan. *Harvard Business Review on Brand Management.* Boston: Harvard Business School Press, 1999.

Johnson, Michael. *Branding: In Five and a Half Steps.* New York: Thames & Hudson Inc., 2016.

Kawasaki, Guy. *Reality Check: The Irreverent Guide to Outsmarting, Outmanaging, and Outmarketing Your Competition.* New York: Portfolio, 2008.

Kerzner, Harold. *Project Management: A Systems Approach to Planning, Scheduling, and Controlling.* New York: Van Nostrand Reinhold, 1989.

Klein, Naomi. *No Logo.* New York: Picador, 2002.

Kotler, Philip, and Kevin Lane Keller. *Marketing Management.* Upper Saddle River, NJ. Prentice Hall, 2009.

Kuhlmann, Arkadi, and Bruce Philp. *The Orange Code: How ING Direct Succeeded by Being a Rebel with a Cause.* Hoboken, NJ: John Wiley & Sons, Inc., 2009.

Kumar, Vijay. *101 Design Methods: A Structured Approach for Driving Innovation in Your Organization.* Hoboken, NJ: John Wiley & Sons, Inc., 2013.

Lapetino, Tim, and Jason Adam. *Damn Good: Top Designers Discuss Their All-Time Favorite Projects.* Cincinnati: How Design Books, 2012

Lidwell, William, Kritina Holden, and Jill Butler. *Universal Principles of Design*. Gloucester, MA: Rockport Publishers, 2003.

Liedtka, Jeanne, and Tim Ogilvie. *Designing for Growth: A Design Thinking Toolkit for Managers*. New York: Columbia University Press, 2011. Kindle edition.

Lindstrom, Martin. *Small Data: The Tiny Clues that Uncover Huge Trends*. New York: St. Martin's Press, 2016.

Lippincott Mercer. *Sense: The Art and Science of Creating Lasting Brands*. Gloucester, MA: Rockport, 2004.

Lipton, Ronnie. *Designing Across Cultures*. New York: How Design Books, 2002.

Maeda, John. *The Laws of Simplicity: Design, Technology, Business, Life*. Cambridge, MA: The MIT Press, 2006.

Man, John. *Alpha Beta: How 26 Letters Shaped the Western World*. London: Headline Book Publishing, 2000.

Marcotte, Ethan. *Responsive Web Design*. New York: A Book Apart, 2011.

Martin, Patricia. *Tipping the Culture: How Engaging Millennials Will Change Things*. Chicago: LitLamp Communications, 2010. PDF e-book.

Mau, Bruce. *Massive Change*. London: Phaidon Press Limited, 2004.

Meggs, Philip B. *Meggs' History of Graphic Design*. New York: John Wiley & Sons, Inc., 1998.

Millman, Debbie. *Brand Thinking and Other Noble Pursuits*. New York: Allworth Press, 2011.

Mok, Clement. *Designing Business: Multiple Media, Multiple Disciplines*. San Jose, CA: Macmillan Computer Publishing USA, 1996.

Mollerup, Per. *Marks of Excellence: The History and Taxonomy of Trademarks*. London: Phaidon Press Limited, 1997.

Morgan, Conway Lloyd. *Logo, Identity, Brand, Culture*. Crans-Pres-Celigny, Switzerland: RotoVision SA, 1999.

Müller, Jens, and Julius Weidemann. *Logo Modernism*. Köln, Germany: Taschen, 2015.

Neumeier, Marty. *The Brand Gap: How to Bridge the Distance between Business Strategy and Design*. Berkeley: New Riders, 2003.

Neumeier, Marty. *The Designful Company: How to Build a Culture of Nonstop Innovation*. Berkeley: New Riders, 2008.

Neumeier, Marty. *The Dictionary of Brand*. New York: The AIGA Press, 2004.

Neumeier, Marty. *The 46 Rules of Genius: An Innovator's Guide to Creativity*. San Francisco: New Riders, 2014.

Neumeier, Marty. *ZAG: The Number One Strategy of High-Performance Brands*. Berkeley: New Riders, 2006.

Newark, Quentin. *What Is Graphic Design?* Switzerland: RotoVision, 2002.

Ogilvy, David. *Ogilvy on Advertising*. New York: Crown Publishers, 1983.

Olins, Wally. *Corporate Identity: Making Business Strategy Visible Through Design*. Boston: Harvard Business School Press, 1989.

Olins, Wally. *On Brand*. New York: Thames & Hudson, 2003.

Onaindia, Carlos Martinez, and Brian Resnick. *Designing B2B Brands: Lessons from Deloitte and 195,000 Brand Managers*. Hoboken, NJ: John Wiley & Sons, Inc., 2013.

Osterwalder, Alexander, and Yves Pigneur. *Business Model Generation: A Handbook for Visionaries, Game Changers, and Challengers*. Hoboken, NJ: John Wiley & Sons, Inc., 2010.

Paos, ed. *New Decomas: Design Conscious Management Strategy*. Seoul: Design House Inc., 1994.

Pavitt, Jane, ed. *Brand New*. London: V&A Publications, 2000.

Peters, Tom. *Reinventing Work: The Brand You 50*. New York: Alfred A. Knopf, Inc, 1999.

Phillips, Peter L. *Creating the Perfect Design Brief*. New York: Allworth Press, 2004.

Pine II, B. Joseph, and James H. Gilmore. *The Experience Economy, Updated Edition*. Boston: Harvard Business Review Press, 2011.

Pink, Daniel H. *The Adventures of Johnny Bunko: The Last Career Guide You'll Ever Need*. New York: Riverhead Books, 2008.

Pink, Daniel H. *A Whole New Mind: Why Right-Brainers Will Rule the Future*. New York: Riverhead Books, 2006.

Redish, Janice (Ginny). *Letting Go of the Words: Writing Web Content that Works*. Waltham, MA: Morgan Kaufmann, 2014.

Remington, R. Roger. *Lester Beall: Trailblazer of American Graphic Design*. New York: W. W. Norton & Company, 1996.

Ries, Al, and Jack Trout. *Positioning: The Battle for Your Mind*. New York: Warner Books, Inc., 1986.

Ries, Al, and Laura Ries. *The 22 Immutable Laws of Branding*. London: Harper Collins Business, 2000.

Rogener, Stefan, Albert-Jan Pool, and Ursula Packhauser. *Branding with Type: How Type Sells*. Mountain View, CA: Adobe Press, 1995.

Roush, Wade. "Social Machines." *MIT's Magazine of Innovation*, Technology Review, August 2005.

Rubin, Jeffrey, and Dana Chisnell. *Handbook of Usability Testing: How to Plan, Design, and Conduct Effective Tests*. Indianapolis: Wiley Publishing, Inc., 2008.

Scher, Paula. *Make It Bigger*. New York: Princeton Architectural Press, 2002.

Schmitt, Bernd. *Customer Experience Management*. New York: John Wiley & Sons, Inc., 2003.

Schmitt, Bernd and Alex Simonson. *Marketing Aesthetics: The Strategic Management of Brands, Identity, and Image*. New York: Free Press, 1997.

Sernovitz, Andy. *Word of Mouth Marketing: How Smart Companies Get People Talking*. Austin, TX: Greenleaf Book Group Press, 2012.

Sharp, Harold S. *Advertising Slogans of America*. Metuchen, NJ: The Scarecrow Press, 1984.

Spiekermann, Erik, and E. M. Ginger. *Stop Stealing Sheep & Find Out How Type Works*. Mountain View, CA: Adobe Press, 1993.

Steffen, Alex, ed. *World Changing: A User's Guide for the 21st Century*. New York: Abrams, 2006.

Stengel, Jim. *How Ideals Power Growth and Profit at the World's Greatest Companies*. New York: Crown Business, 2011.

Stone Yamashita Partners. *Chemistry (and the Catalysts for Seismic Change)*. San Francisco: Stone Yamashita Partners, 2001.

Thaler, Linda Kaplan, and Robin Koval. *The Power of Nice: How to Conquer the Business World with Kindness*. New York: Currency Doubleday, 2006.

Thompson, Derek. *Hit Makers: The Science of Popularity in an Age of Distraction*. New York: Penguin Press, 2017.

Traverso, Debra Koontz. *Outsmarting Goliath: How to Achieve Equal Footing with Companies that Are Bigger, Richer, Older, and Better Known*. Princeton, NJ: Bloomberg Press, 2000.

Williams, Gareth. *Branded? Products and Their Personalities*. London: V&A Publications, 2000.

Yamashita, Keith, and Sandra Spataro. *Unstuck: A Tool for Yourself, Your Team, and Your World*. New York: Portfolio, 2004.

Index

Brands

A

AAM. See American Alliance of Museums
AARP, acronym example, 27
Accenture, name, 147
ACHC Family of Companies, case study, 210–211
ACLU (American Civil Liberties Union)
case study, 212–213
redesign, 96
Action Against Hunger
audit readout, 135
case study, 214–215
meaning, 39
Activia, name, 27
Adanu
case study, 216–217
ephemera, 190
Adidas, tagline, 29
AdMob, brand architecture, 22
Aether, letterform mark, 59
Aetna, redesign, 98
AFLAC Insurance
branding sound, 161
character, 69
AIGA Design Conference, 79
Airbnb
app icon, 81
big data analytics, 74
commitment, 47
longevity, 53
name, 27
positioning, 140
redesign, 95
sharing economy, 71
Alaska Airlines
launch, 196
redesign, 96
Alexa, 71
Allstate, tagline, 29
Ally Financial, name, 147
Alphabet, brand architecture, 22
AlphaGo, artificial intelligence, 71
Altria, name, 147
Amazon.com
brand identity, 12
brand symbols, 25
case study, 218–219
clarifying strategy, 137
longevity, 53
name, 27, 146
positioning, 140
Amazon Echo, Internet of things, 71
Amazon Web, cloud storage, 71
American Alliance of Museums (AAM)
employee engagement, 199
redesign, 95
American Civil Liberties Union. See ACLU
American Express, (RED) card, 287
American Girl Place, customer experience, 18

American Red Cross
brandmark, 54
Ancestry.com, name, 27, 147
Andersen Consulting
name, 147
Android
brand architecture, 22
Angie's List
online reviews, 71
Anheuser-Busch InBev, 228
Ansible, case study, 220–221
AOL, branding sound, 161
Apple
apps, 80
brand architecture, 23
brandmark, 55
brand symbols, 24
customer experience, 18
dynamic mark, 66
longevity, 53
name, 147
pictorial mark, 61
tagline, 29
wearable technology, 71
Apple Computer, name, 147
Aramark, employee engagement, 199
Archer Farms, private label, 83
Arctic Slope Regional Corporation (ASRC), 210
Arthritis Foundation
brand brief, 142
redesign, 97
Ashoka, tagline, 28, 29
Ask Jeeves, character, 69
ASRC (Arctic Slope Regional Corporation), 210
ASRC Construction Holding Company (ACHC), 210
Asthmapolis
mobile health, 71
Atlantic Media, 284, 285
AT&T, longevity, 53
Aunt Jemima, character, 69
Australian Open, redesign, 95

B

BackRub, name, 147
Bala, redesign, 98
The Banker's Life Company, name, 147
Barnes, wordmark, 57
Bass Ale, longevity, 53
Bausch + Lomb, tagline, 29
BCG (Boston Consulting Group), case study, 224–225
B Corporation
brandmark, 55
certification, 86
BDG, private label, 83
BEAM by Monigle, 202
Bedrock Manufacturing, 292, 293
Beeline, case study, 222–223
Bel Group, 258, 259
Bell South Mobility, clarifying strategy, 137
Ben & Jerry's, name, 27

Best Buy, private label, 83
Better Together, redesign, 100
Betty Crocker,
character, 68, 69
Bevel
authenticity, 41
brand architecture, 23
brand identity, 4
B&G Foods, character, 69
Birchbox
subscription boxes, 71
Bloomberg Philanthropies, 241
Blue Apron
competitive audit, 131
subscription boxes, 71
BMW, tagline, 29
BNY Mellon
brand center, 206–207
Boomerang, redesign, 94
Boston Consulting Group (BCG), case study, 224–225
Boy Scouts of America (BSA), case study, 226–227
Brad's Drink, name, 147
Braun, wordmark, 57
Brokers Insurance, letterform mark, 59
Brooklyn Brewery, emblem, 65
Bruvelo, product design, 178
BSA (Boy Scouts of America), case study, 226–227
Buddha Bar
branding sound, 160
Buddhify, mindfulness, 71
Budweiser
brand symbols, 25
case study, 228–229
redesign, 101
tagline, 29

C

California Institute of Technology, name, 147
Calm, mindfulness, 71
Caltech, name, 147
Captive Resources, abstract mark, 63
Carl Conrad Co., 228
Carrefour, private label, 83
CBS
brandmark, 55
longevity, 53
pictorial mark, 61
Cerner, case study, 230–231
Charlie the Tuna, character, 69
Chase, brandmark, 55
Chase Design Group, redesign, 101
Chatshopper for Facebook, 71
Chef'd, competitive audit, 131
Chipotle, app icon, 81
Christian Louboutin, name, 27
Chrome, brand architecture, 22
Ciba Geigy + Sandoz, name, 147
Cingular
clarifying strategy, 137

People

Subjects

Infinite gratitude

The greatest gift from writing this book is hearing from colleagues around the world—from CEOs to design and marketing directors to professors to entrepreneurs and people in government agencies. It has been an honor to be part of your passion and process as you build and design the brands of the future.

Alina Wheeler is a branding expert and sought-after speaker whose invigorating presentations are enjoyed by design and business audiences across the US and internationally. Wheeler has led branding and design teams for public and private companies. She's been in the design trenches and in CEO presentations. She's helped brand companies, products, and initiatives, using the proven process outlined in this book.

How to use this book

Use it as a guide for your brand initiative.

Refresh what you already know.

Learn something new.

Educate your client.

Educate your staff.

Educate your students.

Build a better brand.

Write a better contract.

Be inspired by a case study.

Bust through silos.

Get the suits and creative to talk to each other.

Quote an expert or an avatar.

Post-it note your favorite spreads.

Use the diagrams in a presentation.

Get outside your comfort zone.

Recharge your batteries.

Give it as a birthday present.

Use it to beautify your coffee table.

Ten things you never knew about Alina Wheeler

My maiden name is Alina Radziejowska and Polish was my first language. My father was a sea captain—who regaled me with tales of his adventures in the ports of the world.

I have always been fascinated by how people express themselves through their words, actions, values, and environments.

My introduction to brand architecture was color-coding my sins at catechism in second grade.

I have worked with public companies, private enterprises, nonprofits, and visionaries with big dreams.

I have been married to Santa Claus since 7-7-77. Check out santaclassics.com. We have two daughters and two grandchildren.

My soul resides on a mountain. When not traveling or in Philadelphia, we live in a home called Skylight in the Adirondacks.

I saw the Beatles in 1963, met Mick Jagger for a nanosecond in 1966, and am obsessed with David Bowie.

My mantra: Who are you? Who needs to know? How will they find out? Why should they care?

Words I try to live by: It's never too late to be what you could have been.

Writing this book has given me the gift of new friends and like-minded souls on every continent. And this edition is my swan song.

For comments, consulting engagements, and speaking inquiries: alina@alinawheeler.com

@alinawheeler